Bootstrap Site Blueprints Volume II

Maximize the potential of Bootstrap for faster and more responsive web applications

Matt Lambert

BIRMINGHAM - MUMBAI

Bootstrap Site Blueprints Volume II

First published: December 2015

Production reference: 1211215

Published by Packt Publishing Ltd.
Livery Place
35 Livery Street
Birmingham B3 2PB, UK.

ISBN 978-1-78528-109-9

www.packtpub.com

Credits

Author
Matt Lambert

Reviewer
Sherwin Robles

Commissioning Editor
Sarah Crofton

Acquisition Editor
Aaron Lazar

Content Development Editor
Sumeet Sawant

Technical Editor
Utkarsha S. Kadam

Copy Editor
Vikrant Phadke

Project Coordinator
Shweta H Birwatkar

Proofreader
Safis Editing

Indexer
Tejal Daruwale Soni

Production Coordinator
Aparna Bhagat

Cover Work
Aparna Bhagat

About the Author

Matt Lambert is a designer and developer with more than 15 years of experience. He currently works full time as a senior software engineer for CA Technologies in Vancouver, British Columbia, Canada. In his free time, he is an author, artist, and musician. In 2005, Matt founded Cardeo Creative, which is a small web design studio based in Vancouver. He works with a select list of clients on a part-time basis while producing his own products side by side. To date, Matt has self-published three additional development books titled *Mastering Bootstrap, CSS3 Handbook*, and the *Freelance Startup Guide*.

About the Reviewer

Sherwin Robles is a web application developer from the Philippines with a solid 4 years of experience in designing, developing, and implementing automated solutions. Most of his projects have been built with the CakePHP framework with the help of Bootstrap, which makes development even faster. In April 2015, he joined INIGOTECH, a company aimed at making people's ideas into reality.

Sherwin's expertise is rooted in research and development endeavors on how to achieve improved levels of dependability on the Internet and computing systems.

www.PacktPub.com

Support files, eBooks, discount offers, and more

For support files and downloads related to your book, please visit www.PacktPub.com.

Did you know that Packt offers eBook versions of every book published, with PDF and ePub files available? You can upgrade to the eBook version at www.PacktPub.com and as a print book customer, you are entitled to a discount on the eBook copy. Get in touch with us at service@packtpub.com for more details.

At www.PacktPub.com, you can also read a collection of free technical articles, sign up for a range of free newsletters and receive exclusive discounts and offers on Packt books and eBooks.

https://www2.packtpub.com/books/subscription/packtlib

Do you need instant solutions to your IT questions? PacktLib is Packt's online digital book library. Here, you can search, access, and read Packt's entire library of books.

Why subscribe?

- Fully searchable across every book published by Packt
- Copy and paste, print, and bookmark content
- On demand and accessible via a web browser

Free access for Packt account holders

If you have an account with Packt at www.PacktPub.com, you can use this to access PacktLib today and view 9 entirely free books. Simply use your login credentials for immediate access.

Table of Contents

Preface

In 2011, Mark Otto and Jacob Thornton were working at Twitter on a number of projects. The two creators of the Bootstrap framework needed a way to achieve consistency across them all. The solution they developed was the Bootstrap CSS framework. Over time, more developers came on board and the project quickly became the most popular repository on GitHub. As time has passed, the framework has become the backbone of websites and web applications across the Internet. Other companies have tried to emulate their success by creating their own internal frameworks, but Bootstrap still remains the gold standard of open source CSS frameworks.

Bootstrap provides developers with all the CSS tools that they need to quickly develop websites. It has a deep feature set, is easy to learn, is mobile-first, and is cross-browser compatible. Hundreds of additional components and plugins have been developed by programmers, making it the go-to tool for web designers everywhere.

Bootstrap Site Blueprints Volume II provides you with detailed instructions on how to develop some of the most common website and web application types on the Internet. If you have struggled with using Bootstrap in the past or applying a custom look and feel to your projects, this book will give you the foundation that you need to become a Bootstrap master.

What this book covers

Chapter 1, *Advanced Bootstrap Development Tools*, is a quick introduction to Bootstrap. This chapter also covers some advanced development tools that can be used to make Bootstrap site development easier, such as Less, Node.js, EJS, and Harp.js.

Chapter 2, *Building a Restaurant Website*, is where we take our Harp.js development environment and build a restaurant website. This will include building more page templates, introducing Google web fonts, customizing Bootstrap components, and much more.

Chapter 3, Mobile-First Bootstrap, covers how to do the following: create a mobile-first website using Bootstrap, design a mobile-first website, use Google material design colors and styles, do advanced customizations on the Bootstrap modal component, use jQuery to make a search bar hide/show effect, and create a static, single-page app using Bootstrap.

Chapter 4, Bootstrap Wiki, tells us how to create a wiki layout with Bootstrap and how to add multiple templates to a project in Harp. You also get to learn how to customize the navigation modal you made in the previous chapter, how to use Harp partials for more than just the header and footer, and how to code your template in a modular fashion to save time and produce Less code.

Chapter 5, Bootstrap News Magazine, illustrates the creation of a magazine website using Bootstrap, and a new way to lay out a header using inline divs. Here, we see how to construct a complex footer using multiple parts, how to use flexbox with a Bootstrap grid, and how to use a basic jQuery to improve the experience of your article page. We also implement a Disqus-powered comments section.

Chapter 6, Bootstrap Dashboard, teaches you how to code a dashboard using Bootstrap, how to create a project with a dark look and feel, and how to implement and customize the Chartist JavaScript library. In this chapter, we customize the Bootstrap panels component, the Bootstrap table component, and the Boostrap nav and navbar components. We also see how to use a mobile nav outside of the default navbar.

Chapter 7, Bootstrap Social Network, covers the coding of a social network using Bootstrap. We customize the Bootstrap well component, the Bootstrap navbar component, and the Bootstrap alert and button components. Finally, we see how to create a highly modular design for easy reuse of code and components.

What you need for this book

To run the pieces of example code outlined in this book, you'll need a modern browser, such as Google Chrome, Apple Safari, Mozilla Firefox or Microsoft Internet Explorer. To work with the projects outlined in each chapter, you'll also need the following:

- A text editor tool, such as Notepad or Sublime Text 2
- The full code package for each chapter
- You'll need to install Node.js and Harp.js
- A command-line tool such as a terminal or Cygwin

Who this book is for

This book is for developers who are interested in learning how to build common website and web application projects with the Bootstrap CSS framework. Basic knowledge of HTML, CSS, and JavaScript is required to get the most out of this book. It will also be helpful to have some experience with a command-line tool.

By reading this book, you'll learn the syntax and inner workings of Bootstrap (the latest version 3.3.4 at the time of publishing this book), Less, Harp.js, HTML, and CSS. You'll also learn a bit about JavaScript and jQuery.

Conventions

In this book, you will find a number of styles of text that distinguish between different kinds of information. Here are some examples of these styles, and an explanation of their meaning.

Code words in text, folder names, filenames, file extensions, pathnames, and dummy URLs s are shown as follows:

A block of code is set as follows:

```
.red1 {
  color: @red1;
}

.red1-bg {
  background: @red1;
}

.red2 {
  color: @red2;
}

.red2-bg {
  background: @red2;
}
```

Any command-line input or output is written as follows:

```
$ harp server --port 9000
```

New terms and **important words** are shown in bold. Words that you see on the screen, in menus or dialog boxes for example, appear in the text like this: "Choose the **Share** or **Embed Map** option from the menu."

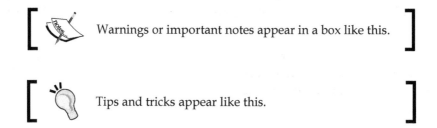

Warnings or important notes appear in a box like this.

Tips and tricks appear like this.

Reader feedback

Feedback from our readers is always welcome. Let us know what you think about this book—what you liked or may have disliked. Reader feedback is important for us to develop titles that you really get the most out of.

To send us general feedback, simply send an e-mail to feedback@packtpub.com, and mention the book title via the subject of your message.

If there is a topic that you have expertise in and you are interested in either writing or contributing to a book, see our author guide on www.packtpub.com/authors.

Customer support

Now that you are the proud owner of a Packt book, we have a number of things to help you to get the most from your purchase.

Downloading the example code

You can download the example code files for all Packt books you have purchased from your account at http://www.packtpub.com. If you purchased this book elsewhere, you can visit http://www.packtpub.com/support and register to have the files e-mailed directly to you.

Downloading the color images of this book

We also provide you a PDF file that has color images of the screenshots/diagrams used in this book. The color images will help you better understand the changes in the output. You can download this file from: `https://www.packtpub.com/sites/default/files/downloads/1099OS_ColorImages.pdf`.

Errata

Although we have taken every care to ensure the accuracy of our content, mistakes do happen. If you find a mistake in one of our books — maybe a mistake in the text or the code — we would be grateful if you would report this to us. By doing so, you can save other readers from frustration and help us improve subsequent versions of this book. If you find any errata, please report them by visiting `http://www.packtpub.com/submit-errata`, selecting your book, clicking on the **errata submission form** link, and entering the details of your errata. Once your errata are verified, your submission will be accepted and the errata will be uploaded on our website, or added to any list of existing errata, under the Errata section of that title. Any existing errata can be viewed by selecting your title from `http://www.packtpub.com/support`.

Piracy

Piracy of copyright material on the Internet is an ongoing problem across all media. At Packt, we take the protection of our copyright and licenses very seriously. If you come across any illegal copies of our works, in any form, on the Internet, please provide us with the location address or website name immediately so that we can pursue a remedy.

Please contact us at `copyright@packtpub.com` with a link to the suspected pirated material.

We appreciate your help in protecting our authors, and our ability to bring you valuable content.

Questions

You can contact us at `questions@packtpub.com` if you are having a problem with any aspect of the book, and we will do our best to address it.

1
Advanced Bootstrap Development Tools

Although Bootstrap is the most popular CSS framework on the block, which polarizes web developers of all skill levels, one of the main complaints against it is that it's too large and hard to use. The primary goal of this book is to give you an advanced set of tools to make building websites with Bootstrap easier and even enjoyable. We'll start out by showing you how to create a development environment and workflow that is easy to set up and reuse in all your Bootstrap projects. From there on, we'll tackle a number of common website designs to get you comfortable with the advanced techniques. Finally, we'll include some JavaScript libraries and really take our Bootstrap projects to the next level. Sit back, fire up your code editor of choice, and get ready to dive into some advanced Bootstrap blueprints.

In this chapter, you'll learn:

- How to create a development environment with `Harp.js`
- How to run a localhost server with `Node.js` to preview your project
- How to write templates with EJS and use variables and partials
- How to set up your theme with Less in the most efficient manner
- How to compile your project for production

Theming is hard!@

I won't lie. Bootstrap theming can be really challenging. There is a large library of components that take some time to understand, and learning the best ways to customize them also takes time. But what if there was an easier way? I'm happy to say that I've designed a workflow using some modern frontend development tools that make it much easier to work with Bootstrap. The problem with frontend languages such as HTML and CSS is that they lack some core programming features, such as variables and includes. Thanks to tools such as Less for CSS and `Harp.js` for templating, these missing features are now available for building static websites.

Harp.js – the static web server with built-in preprocessing

The title says it all, and it is taken from the official `http://harpjs.com/` website. Harp is an open source project from some of the same people who brought us PhoneGap, and it is my tool of choice for any static website project I work on. Why is Harp so great? Here are just a few reasons:

- It includes automatic preprocessing of languages such as EJS, Jade, Markdown, CoffeeScript, Less, Sass, and Stylus
- Harp converts the aforementioned languages into vanilla HTML, CSS, and JavaScript and feeds it to the browser
- It allows powerful templating through the use of common layouts and partials or includes for PHP people
- It includes a lightweight web server that compiles your code in the background for quick and easy testing
- It passes in custom metadata through JSON to save your time
- It compiles all of your code into production-friendly files that you can deploy on your server.

>
> **Downloading the example code**
> You can download the example code files for all Packt books you have purchased from your account at `http://www.packtpub.com`. If you purchased this book elsewhere, you can visit `http://www.packtpub.com/support` and register to have the files e-mailed directly to you.

Creating a development environment

Everything that I outlined earlier basically creates a development environment for your Bootstrap websites. The advantage of using a development environment is that you can use tools such as Harp to make your website development faster and easier. It provides you with a working copy on your local computer, and you can use that copy to develop your projects. When you're done, you can compile it into the production version and deploy it on the Internet. It's a good idea to get into the habit of creating a development environment because it's a better coding practice and makes it easier to maintain your project in the future. This is because the production code is totally separate from the source development files. Running a localhost server for testing also allows you to build new features without having to worry about negatively affecting your live production website.

Installing Node.js

The web server that is built into Harp runs on Node.js. Therefore, you will need to install Node on your computer before you can set up Harp. If you don't have Node already installed, head over to the following link to download the version you need:

```
http://nodejs.org/download/
```

Once you've downloaded and installed Node, you'll have to open and use the command line to test the installation. If you're on a Mac, I'd recommend that you use the terminal or an app such as iTerm to access the command line. If you're working on Windows, you can use Cygwin. Once you've opened up your command-line app, type in the following line:

```
$ node -v
```

If you have installed Node correctly, the number of the version you have installed should be printed on the terminal. You should see something like this:

```
$ v0.10.33
```

Great! Now we can move on to installing Harp.

Installing Harp.js

Actually, setting up Harp.js is really easy. If you have closed your terminal, open it again. Insert this command if you're on a Mac:

```
$ sudo npm install -g harp
```

If you're on Windows, use the following command:

```
$ npm install -g harp
```

After you execute this command, you should see a bunch of packages being installed in the terminal window. Once everything stops loading, Harp is installed. To verify that it has worked, enter the following in the terminal and hit *Enter*:

```
$ harp version
```

This should give you the version number, which means that Harp was successfully installed.

Since Less preprocessing is included with Harp, we don't need to install anything special to use Less. This is great news, because we don't need to rely on less.js or a standalone compiler app. Once we compile our Harp project and run the web server, any changes to Less files will be picked up automatically. For now, just celebrate, and we'll cover compiling Less in more detail a little later.

Setting up a boilerplate project

For the rest of this chapter, I'm going to teach you how to set up a Bootstrap boilerplate project in Harp. Moving forward, this boilerplate will be the basis for all the projects in the book. One of the great things about Harp is that you can simply copy and paste a project to create a new instance of it on your local machine. There are also some other commands that you can run to generate project scaffolding, and I welcome you to check them out at http://harpjs.com/docs/. However, for this book, we aren't going to take any shortcuts, and I'm going to show you how to manually set up a project. The best practice is to do it the hard way first so that you learn how it works. This will save you a headache down the road if you are troubleshooting a problem. The first thing you should do is navigate to a directory on your computer where you want to store your project. In the directory you created the following files and sub directories. For the time being, just leave the .json and .ejs files blank. We'll fill them in a little later. Take a look at the following image to see how your project directory should look.

Note that there is a project boilerplate available for download or forking from GitHub at https://github.com/cardeo/booterator.

This is the root of our project, and here we'll find everything at a high level:

- /css: This directory will contain all our custom CSS and the Bootstrap framework CSS files.

- /fonts: This directory will be for holding any web fonts or icon web fonts. The directory isn't totally necessary, but I always include Font Awesome with all my projects so that I have an icon library to pull from.

- /img: This directory will hold all the images for the project. For the boilerplate, we won't actually need any images, but we're setting this up for future projects too.

- /js: This directory will hold any custom libraries and the Bootstrap framework's JavaScript file.

- /partial: This directory will hold the pieces of code that we want to reuse in our templates, such as our header and footer.

- _data.json: This is the file in which we will define any metadata that we want to use in our template. An example of this could be the page title for each web page.

- _harp.json: This is a file for setting global properties, such as the title of the website, which is used on all pages.

- _layout.ejs: This file is the scaffolding for our page. It includes the <head> and <body> sections of our document. At the very least, you need one layout in every Harp project. It is possible to have multiple layouts if you want to load in JavaScript libraries to only some pages.

- `index.ejs`: This file holds the actual code for our boilerplate home page. This is the body or content of the page minus the wrapping template pieces that are held in `_layout.ejs`.

> The **Embedded JavaScript** (**EJS**) template language is very similar to HTML and is therefore really easy to grasp. The advantage of using EJS is that it allows the use of elements such as variables.

Setting up the CSS

Now that the root of our project is set up, let's set up the subdirectories. We'll start with the CSS directory by adding the following files. Now would be a good time to download the latest version of Bootstrap from `http://getbootstrap.com` if you haven't done so already. Again, just leave `theme.less` blank for now.

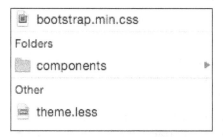

Within the components directory, create a Less file and name it `_variables.less`. Leave this file blank for the time being.

> Starting a file with an underscore in Harp will mark it as a template file that should not be a straight copy to the production directory. It is file that should be compiled into another to create a full HTML page or CSS style sheet.

Let's quickly walk through the files in the `/css` directory:

- `bootstrap.min.css`: This is the Bootstrap CSS framework. When you download the Bootstrap package, there are a number of other CSS files. We don't need any of those files; we only need the minified version of the framework.

- `/components`: This is a directory for storing the Bootstrap component's Less files. If you are customizing a Bootstrap component, you should create a Less file for it and enter the custom CSS.

- `theme.less`: This is the master file for our CSS. All our components should be imported into this file so that upon compilation, it will be a single `theme.css` file for our project.

Setting up the fonts

Bootstrap comes with Glyphicons out of the box, which is fine. I, however, prefer to use font awesome because their license is more flexible. To add font awesome to your project, head to `http://fontawesome.io` and download the package. Unzip it into your computer after downloading and copy the contents of the `/fonts` directory to your project's `/fonts` directory. Next, go to the `/css` folder and copy `font-awesome.min.css` to your project's `/css` directory. For now, that's all you need to do; we'll hook up everything else a little later. The `/fonts` directory should now look like this:

Setting up the JavaScript

For our boilerplate, all that we need to do is copy `bootstrap.min.js` to our `/js` directory. Like the Bootstrap CSS, there are a few JavaScript files included in the download package. You can ignore the other files as we won't need them.

Setting up the partials

The last directory that we need to set up is our partials. If you come from the PHP world, note that partials are includes. They are little snippets of code that are reused across all or many of your pages, such as your header, footer, and navigation. Partials are one of the best features of Harp because you can update these template pieces in one place when changes occur, instead of updating on every page! For now, create two files in your `/partial` directory, called `_header.ejs` and `_footer.ejs`.

Now that we've finished setting up the basic structure of our project, we can move on to actually filling in some code for our `.json` and `.ejs` files.

Setting up _harp.json

I'm going to start with _harp.json before _data.json. This is because the first file deals with the global settings for our project. In this case, we're going to use _harp.json to set up a global variable that will map to the website name for our project. Later on, we'll insert this variable into our layout so that it appears on every page of our website. Enter the following code and save it:

```
{
  "globals": {
    "siteTitle": "My Bootstrap Boilerplate"
  }
}
```

What we've done here is set up a global variable named siteTitle and set its value to My Bootstrap Boilerplate. Once we insert this variable into our layout, the title will be shown on every page of our project.

 This is only a fraction of what you can do here. Check out http://harpjs.com/docs/development/globals to learn more about globals.

Configuring _data.json

If _harp.json applies to all the pages in our website, _data.json contains page-specific data for our project. In this case, I'm going to set up a variable that can be used to insert the page name for each page of my project:

```
{
  "index": {
    "pageTitle": "Home"
  }
}
```

Here's how this data works:

- The index refers to the name of my ejs template that I want to target. Currently, we have only one, called index.ejs.
- The pageTitle is a variable I created for the title of each of my pages. We'll need to insert this variable into the layout later on.
- Finally, I entered a value of Home for my variable.

Again, there is more that you can do with metadata in Harp, but at this point, this is all that we need. To learn more about Harp metadata, visit http://harpjs.com/docs/development/metadata.

Setting up the layout

As I mentioned previously, `_layout.ejs` is the wrapper file for my `index.ejs` page template. Layouts can be reused, and pages will always default to using `_layout.ejs` unless you tell them otherwise. If you want to create a second layout for use on a specific page, you simply have to create a new file called something like `_layout-two.ejs`. Then, in your `_data.json` file, you have to add a second line to your template declaration that points to the new layout:

```
{
  "index": {
    "pageTitle": "Home",
    "layout": "_layout-two"
  }
}
```

 When you're working with your `.json` file, file extensions are not required.

Now, that's an example of how to use multiple layouts. For our boilerplate, we'll need only one layout. A layout file can be written in mostly normal HTML, but we need to insert a yield property to tell Harp where to insert the content from the page file (`index.ejs`). We also need to insert the variables that we defined in `_harp.json` and `_data.json`. Open up your `_layout.ejs` file in the root of the project and insert the following `<head>` code:

```html
<!DOCTYPE html>
<html lang="en">
<head>
  <meta charset="utf-8">
  <meta http-equiv="X-UA-Compatible" content="IE=edge">
  <meta name="viewport" content="width=device-width, initial-
    scale=1">
  <title><%- pageTitle %> | <%- siteTitle %></title>

  <link rel="stylesheet" type="text/css"
    href="css/bootstrap.min.css">
  <link rel="stylesheet" type="text/css" href="css/font-
    awesome.min.css">
  <link rel="stylesheet" type="text/css" href="css/theme.css">

  <!-- HTML5 shim and Respond.js for IE8 support of HTML5 elements
  and media queries -->
```

```
    <!-- WARNING: Respond.js doesn't work if you view the page via
      file:// -->
    <!--[if lt IE 9]>
      <script
      src="https://oss.maxcdn.com/html5shiv/3.7.2/html5shiv.min.js">
      </script>
      <script
      src="https://oss.maxcdn.com/respond/1.4.2/respond.min.js">
      </script>
    <![endif]-->
  </head>
```

The preceding code is the standard Bootstrap header with some small changes:

- Always load the Bootstrap CSS first, as you may want to overwrite something in your theme

- Include the font awesome CSS file so that you can use the icons in your projects

- Insert your theme CSS file, which will contain all your custom CSS

 Make sure you use the CSS extension here for all your files. Once `theme.less` is compiled, it will turn into `theme.css`. Therefore, we need to name it correctly so that it's picked up by the browser.

Inserting the variables

If you look at the `<title>` tag in `<head>`, you'll notice a couple of variables. These are the two variables that we set up in `_harp.json` and `_data.json`. On compiling, `pageTitle` and `siteTitle` will be inserted into the page layout. Depending on the page, the proper `pageTitle` variable will be inserted.

Now that we have the `<head>` element of our layout set up, let's enter the code for `<body>`:

```
<body>
  <%- partial("partial/_header") %>

  <%- yield %>

  <%- partial("partial/_footer") %>

  <!-- javascript //-->
```

```
<script
  src="//ajax.googleapis.com/ajax/libs/jquery/1.11.1/jquery.min.
js"></script>
  <script src="js/bootstrap.min.js"
    type="text/javascript"></script>
</body>
</html>
```

Now, the `<body>` code is going to look a little different from what we are used to with Bootstrap and HTML. Let me go through each part of the layout:

- The `header` partial will include our header code, which we haven't set up yet.

- The yield tag is the marker for loading in the contents of our pages. In this case, it will load `index.ejs`.

- Like the header, the footer partial will be included wherever the tag is inserted.

- At the bottom, I've included jQuery and a link to the Bootstrap JavaScript framework that is in our project.

Setting up the header

To set up the header, we need to edit the `_header.ejs` file that we created earlier in this chapter. Head to the `/partial` directory and open up `_header.ejs`. Then paste the following in the Bootstrap `navbar` code:

```
<nav class="navbar navbar-default" role="navigation">
  <div class="container-fluid">
    <div class="navbar-header">
      <button type="button" class="navbar-toggle collapsed" data-
        toggle="collapse" data-target="#navbar1">
        <span class="sr-only">Toggle navigation</span>
        <span class="icon-bar"></span>
        <span class="icon-bar"></span>
        <span class="icon-bar"></span>
      </button>
     <a href="index.html" class="navbar-brand"><%- siteTitle
       %></a>
    </div>

    <div class="collapse navbar-collapse" id="navbar1">
      <ul class="nav navbar-nav">
```

```
      <li><a href="index.html">Home</a></li>
    </ul>
  </div>
  </div>
</nav>
```

The code for the header is pretty straightforward, except for one thing; it's your standard Bootstrap `navbar`. One more thing that is different is that I've used the `siteTitle` global variable again so that `siteTitle` will automatically be inserted into the `navbar` brand for each page upon compilation. This is a simple example of how you can reuse variables in your templates.

Setting up the footer

Next, open up the `_footer.ejs` file, which is in the same `/partial` directory. Here, we'll just want to insert some super simple footer code that can be used as a placeholder. Notice how I'm wrapping my footer in a `container-fluid` class. It's a good idea to componentize the pieces of your theme so that they are easily interchangeable and don't rely on markup in other components or partials:

```
<div class="container-fluid">
  <div class="row">
    <div class="col-lg-12">
      &copy; 2015 Matt Lambert
    </div>
  </div>
</div>
```

As you can see, it is super simple! The last template or HTML/EJS work that we need to do is set up the body of our page, which lives inside of `index.ejs`. For our boilerplate, let's create a super simple piece of page content:

```
<div class="container-fluid">
  <div class="row">
    <div class="col-lg-12">
      <h1>Bootstrap Boilerplate</h1>
      <p>This is a Bootstrap starter template built with Harp,
        Less, CSS, EJS, and HTML</p>
      <p>Made in Vancouver by <a
        href="http://twitter.com/cardeo">@cardeo</a></p>
    </div>
  </div>
</div>
```

This chunk of code should be self-explanatory. I've purposely kept it simple so that you can easily see where the lines between page templates and partials are. Now that the base of our project is set up, let's compile and preview it!

Compiling for the first time

Now that our initial project is set up, it's time to compile it and test it out to make sure that everything works. When we compile our project for the first time, Harp creates a directory in the root of our project, called /www. Within this directory, it will dump all the compiled HTML, CSS, and JavaScript files. When you are ready to publish your project, simply upload the contents of this directory to your server. See how simple and clean it is? Your development and production files live in the same project directory but are totally separate.

 You should never manually edit any of the files in your /www directory. If you do, on the next compilation, any changes you make will be overwritten.

The compilation of your project is done from the command line or terminal app. If you have closed it, open it again and navigate to your project directory. Once you get there, run the following command:

```
$ harp compile
```

If all goes well, a new line should appear in the terminal. If there is an error, Harp will give you an error message with a clue to the problem. Let's assume that all has gone well and everything has worked fine. Go to your project directory and look for the /www directory. If it's there, it means that the compile worked fine.

Running the local server

The next thing you'll want to do is actually test your project in a browser. To do this, we can use Harp's built-in web server to test the website locally. This is a great feature because you can test drive your project locally without having to upload it to the Internet. To fire up the server, enter the following command in the terminal from your project directory:

```
$ harp server --port 9000
```

This will deploy your project locally on port 9000. Open up a web browser and go to http://localhost:9000 to view the website.

Your page should look like this:

Bootstrap Blueprints 2   Home

Bootstrap Boilerplate

This is a Bootstrap starter template built with Harp, Less, CSS, EJS, and HTML

Made in Vancouver by @cardeo

© 2015 Matt Lambert

Now that you have the server running, you can take advantage of one of Harp's other awesome features. Every time you make a change to a template file, CSS file, and so on, you don't have to recompile your project. You can simply save the file and refresh the browser, and you'll see the updated version. This will save you so much time! One thing to remember, however, is to make sure you compile when you're done so that the changes are applied to the /www directory.

I encourage you to memorize the preceding commands, but if you want something easier to remember, you can use $ `harp server` www to run the local server. The only problem with this command, however, is that I've found it to be a bit buggy. It will start the server but updates to templates in the background won't always be picked up. A more reliable method is to manually declare which port to use when you fire up the server. Now that our project is all set up and running, it's time to set up our Less configuration to theme our project.

Configuring Less

A great advantage of using Harp is that it has a built-in Less compiler. When you run the $ `harp compile` command, it compiles both your `.ejs` templates and your `.less` files into regular HTML and CSS. This is much easier than using something like `less.js`, which you would have to remove from production. When you're compiling your project for the first time, ensure that you include some code inside your `theme.less` file. Otherwise, `theme.css` will not be written.

Defining your Less variables

Head back to the `css/components` directory that you created earlier and open up the `_variables.less` file. Within this file, we'll configure what I call global CSS variables. Moreover, within this file, we'll define only those variables that apply across our entire website. Component-specific variables have no place in this file. I know that some developers like to have one big file for variables, but I prefer to keep the component-specific ones out in their own Less files. We will see more on that later, when we dive into custom components. For now, let's start pasting the following code in `_variables.less`.

Colors

Let's start by inserting some color variables that can be used throughout all our Bootstrap projects:

```
@black: #000;
@dark-grey: #333;
@grey: #ccc;
@light-grey: #ebebeb;
@off-white: #f5f5f5;
@white: #ffffff;
@blue1: #3498db;
@blue2: #2980b9;
@red1: #e74c3c;
@red2: #c0392b;
@yellow1: #f1c40f;
@yellow2: #f39c12;
@green1: #2ecc71;
@green2: #27ae60;
@orange1: #e67e22;
@orange2: #d35400;
@aqua1: #1abc9c;
@aqua2: #16a085;
@purple1: #9b59b6;
@purple2: #8e44ad;
@navy1: #34495e;
@navy2: #2c3e50;
```

As you'll see, I like to define a fairly large color palette. But this doesn't mean that all my projects will use all of these colors. However, like a good typography, it's a good idea over time to develop a library of colors that work well together. We can then easily include them in all our projects so that we have colors that work well together right at our fingertips. When you are diving deep into theming, this is really valuable because you don't have to go and look for a new color palette with every new theme. You already have a collection of colors that you can pull from, which will speed up your theming process.

Backgrounds

Lets add the background variables:

```
@primary-background: @white;
@secondary-background: @off-white;
@third-background: @light-grey;
@fourth-background: @grey;
@inverse-background: @dark-grey;
```

The preceding code is my boilerplate for backgrounds. Note how these colors use a variable name for their value and not a hexadecimal value. The reason that this is done is to speed up theming. Instead of having to change a color in two places, we only have to change it in one, and then it inherits throughout our other variables. Here are a few more key points about backgrounds.

The variable naming convention here is similar to that of Bootstrap, for consistency. This also makes it easier to remember a variable name, such as primary, as against something like white-background.

At the very least, you should have a primary, a secondary, and an inverse background. I like to include a couple more, but feel free to scale this back a bit if it makes it easier for you.

Text

As with our backgrounds, we are following the Bootstrap naming conventions for our text colors:

```
@primary-text: @dark-grey;
@light-text: @light-grey;
@loud-text: @black;
@inverse-text: @white;
@heading-text: @dark-grey;
```

Consistency is the key as it makes it easier to remember variable names. It is critical when you're dealing with a large framework that you make things as easy as possible to remember. Again, make sure you use color variables for the values here and not actual hexadecimal numbers.

Links

Defining the link colors is pretty straightforward:

```
@primary-link-color: @blue1;
@primary-link-color-hover: @blue2;
```

One thing that I'll point out here is that this is the first example where you'll see why you should have at least two versions of every color that you use in your palette. Things such as hover states usually require a base color and a darker or lighter version of the same color to indicate a change in hovering. You may want to expand this section to include a second or even third-link color variation.

Borders

The border variable is the first place where you'll see some values that aren't only color-based:

```
@border-color: @light-grey;
@border-size: 1px;
@border-type: solid;
@border-focus: @grey;
@secondary-border-color: @blue1;
```

In this case, you should always set your size to 1px. The reason for this is that you can use a Less operation like the following to increase the size of your border. Starting from 1px makes your operations simple and easy to follow for other developers who may be maintaining or editing your code:

```
.good-class {
  border-size: (@border-size + 1);
}

.bad-class {
  border-size: 2px;
}
```

Never use pixel values in any of your custom CSS! You would want to use variables so that you can make any units relative and, therefore, controlled by a variable. This will allow you to quickly spin up a new theme by only editing the variable's Less file.

Typography

Next we need to setup the global settings for our typography variables. We'll set our body and heading font stacks, a base font size and line height.

```
@body-copy: "Helvetica Neue", helvetica, arial, verdana, sans-serif;
@heading-copy: "Helvetica Neue", helvetica, arial, verdana, sans-
serif;
@base-font-size: 14px;
@font-size: 1em;
@base-line-height: 1.5;
```

When I set up typography for a theme, I like to follow a few simple rules:

- Make sure you define at least a body and a heading copy variable.
- Set the base font size as a pixel value.
- Set the actual font size to `1em` and use this variable throughout your custom CSS. In this way, you will be using a relative value that is easier with operations. This is exactly the same as the preceding border example.
- I personally prefer to reset Bootstrap's line-height to 1.5 for easier math.

Layout

The only layout variables that you should be setting in your globals are `margin` and `padding`:

```
@margin: 1em;
@padding: 1em;
```

Both should be set to `1em` for easy relative operations. This follows the same unit of measurement patterns set with borders and typography.

Mixins

The other element that I recommend including in your global Less file is mixins. In my opinion, there are only two of them (and maybe only one) that you definitely need to include to speed up your Bootstrap theming.

Border radius

The border radius is by far the most important as it is used a ton through Bootstrap components:

```
.round-corners (@radius: 2px) {
  -moz-border-radius: @radius;
  -ms-border-radius: @radius;
  border-radius: @radius;
}
```

Make sure you set this up and use it for everything. If you are thorough, you can change the border radius of all elements in one place. An example of this would look like the following:

```
.btn {
  /* fill in the rest of the styles here */
```

```
  .round-corners;
}
```

Now, if I change my `@radius` value to a different pixel amount, it will inherit down to my button corners. Do this for all your Bootstrap components!

Animations and transitions

Another property that I use heavily in my themes is the animations or transitions property:

```
.transition (@transition: background .1s linear) {
  -moz-transition: @transition;
  -webkit-transition: @transition;
  transition: background @transition;
}
```

I find that a little transition, when added, can add a lot to a UI. Instead of defining this from the ground up on every component, use this simple mixin. It will speed up your theming time and also ensure that transitions are consistent across your entire theme. That's just good design and coding. Here's an example that shows you how to apply the round corners and transition mixins to a button:

```
.btn {
  /* fill in the rest of the styles here */
  .round-corners;
  .transition;
}
```

This completes your `_variables.less` file. Save the file and close it. Next, we'll cover the setup of the master theme file for our project.

Setting up your theme

Now that we've set up our variables file, we need to set up the master theme that we'll import it into. The master theme file, or `theme.less`, is the primary file that we will link in the `<head>` section of our pages. I've organized the theme using the **Scalable and Modular CSS (SMACSS)** system. Using a modular approach while coding the CSS will make the job easier and the code more maintainable over time.

SMACSS overview

The scalable and modular CSS system was created by Jonathan Snook, who is currently a product manager at Shopify. It divides your style sheet into five sections in order to make it easier to categorize your CSS. Let's review each SMACSS category to see how it applies to our Bootstrap theme structure.

Base rules

A base rule applies to any element that is an element selector, descendent selector, child selector, or pseudo-class. It doesn't apply to CSS classes or IDs. These are basically all your core HTML tags.

Layout rules

The layout section is dedicated to any custom classes that you've written for the layout of your project. This could be something simple, such as a header, or something more complex, such as a widget. If you're following best practices, your layout should only use classes. However, if you have used some IDs, you should include them here as well.

Module rules

This is the big one for Bootstrap, because this is where you should import all your component Less files. Later on, I'll explain how you should break down each Bootstrap component into its own Less file and then import it into the master theme. The code for this will look a little something like the following:

```
@import "components/_badges.less";
@import "components/_typography.less";
@import "components/_tables.less";
```

State rules

These styles refer to anything that applies to a state change, such as form validation or alert bars.

Theme rules

This part of your style sheet is optional. You may cover it in the preceding sections. However, if you find yourself needing a section for styles specific to your theme, this is where you should insert them.

Now that I've explained how we'll organize our master theme, let's actually start putting it together. The first thing we need to do is import the _variables.less file that we created. We want this to be the first thing that we load into the theme, so we place the following line of code at the top:

```
@import "components/_variables";
```

 With the variables file in Harp, you shouldn't include the file extension. The reason behind this is that multiple preprocessor types are supported and variables is a keyword.

Setting up the base

The next section that we want to set up in our theme is the base. Insert the following boilerplate CSS. We want to keep this really basic so that we have a starting point for our future projects:

```
body {
    background: @primary-background;
    font-family: @body-copy;
    font-size: @base-font-size;
    line-height: @base-line-height;
    color: @primary-text;
}

ul,
ol {
}

li {
}

a, a:link, a:visited {
}

a:hover {
}

p {
}

hr {
}
```

I'm not even going to fill in any of the tags at this point, as they will be defined in the actual project. The only tag I will fill in is `<body>`. Let's review the properties that we have added to the body tag at the top of the preceding section of code:

- We'll set our background to the `@primary-background` variable. The `@primary-background` variable should be set to the color you want for the background of your project.

- We set the `font-family` property to our `@body-copy` variable.

- Set the `font-size` property to the `@base-font-size` variable. Remember that this is the one that has the pixel value, and it should be a value of this type on the body tag. In any future use of the `font-size` property, you should use the `@font-size` variable.

- The line-height is set using the `@base-line-height` variable.

- Finally, we'll set the font color to our `@primary-text` variable.

As I mentioned earlier, we'll leave the rest of this section blank as it will be filled in to match the actual project that we will be designing in the future.

Setting up the layout

Since this is a boilerplate project, we don't really have a layout. We can fall back on the Bootstrap's grid and we don't need anything custom. Therefore, just leave this section blank for now, but you might want to insert a comment to show where the layout code should be inserted for future projects:

```
/*
02. LAYOUT
Styles specific to your layout or website
*/
```

Setting up the modules

This section should be a list of `@import` keywords that load into our Less component files. As I mentioned earlier, you should break down any custom Bootstrap component CSS into its own Less file and save it in the `/components` directory. This is the way to keep your CSS neat and tidy in the development version of your theme. On compile, all of these Less files will be combined into a single CSS file called `theme.css`. However, for development purposes, it makes a ton of sense to break down the CSS for easier maintenance and writing.

As you create a project, you may not need to overwrite code in every Bootstrap component. Personally, I think it's good practice to customize everything, but it's not always practical to do this. The following is a list of potential Less component files that you can make with Bootstrap:

- badges
- breadcrumbs
- buttons
- button groups
- button dropdowns
- carousel
- code
- collapse
- dropdown
- forms
- icons
- input groups
- images
- helpers
- jumbotron
- labels
- The list group
- The media object
- modal
- navs
- navbar
- pager
- The page header
- pagination
- panels
- pills

- popover
- progress bars
- scrollspy
- tables
- tabs
- thumbnails
- tooltip
- typography
- well

When you're creating a component Less file, first save it at `css/components`, and then use the `@import` keyword to import it into `theme.less`. You need a different `@import` statement for each file to load it in:

```
@import "components/_badges.less";
@import "components/_typography.less";
@import "components/_tables.less";
```

Setting up the states

With Bootstrap, the States section works much like modules, but I like to divide the following two components into the states section:

```
@import "components/_alerts.less";
@import "components/_form-validation.less";
```

These two make sense from a Bootstrap component standpoint. If you are using a different JavaScript library to perform your form validation, you should include the corresponding styles here. This should also apply for any component that has a state change.

Setting up the theme

The final section is the theme, and it is totally optional. One thing that would be theme-specific is your color palette. I break my color palette into another Less file and import it under the modules section.

You may be wondering what goes into this `colors.less` file, since we have defined our colors in the `_variables.less` file. In the variables file, we only assign hexadecimal numbers to variables. In the `colors.less` file, I assign these variable names to actual CSS classes so that we can use them in our layouts. In this way, we stay more modular because we can assign a color class to a widget instead of putting the color in the widget's CSS layout code. I usually define a text and background color class for each color in my palette:

```
.red1 {
  color: @red1;
}

.red1-bg {
  background: @red1;
}

.red2 {
  color: @red2;
}

.red2-bg {
  background: @red2;
}
```

Now, those class names are way easier to remember than hexadecimal numbers, and this allows you to apply them to a widget, as follows:

```
<div class="custom-box red1-bg">this is a custom box with a red background</div>
```

Using this method, I can leave out any color styles in my `custom-box` class and only worry about layout styles. I can then apply the color using a CSS class, which is much more modular and reusable.

Finishing up theme.less

Now that we've finished the last section of `theme.less`, our style sheet is ready to roll. Go back to the terminal and compile your project again. Once that's done, go to `www/css` and you should see `theme.css`. Our boilerplate CSS development environment is ready to roll for an actual project.

Summary

In this chapter, you learned how to — and why it's important to — build a development environment with `Harp.js`. You also learned how to write templates in EJS using variables and partials. Lastly, you got to know how to set up your theme with Less and compile your project for production.

In the next chapter, we'll begin our first project, where we'll build a full-fledged restaurant website. Eager to get started? Flip those pages and dive right in!

2

Building a Restaurant Website

In the previous chapter, we laid down the foundation that will be used in all our blueprints moving forward. In the second chapter, we'll use our `Harp.js` development environment and build an actual restaurant website. This will include building more page templates, introducing Google Web Fonts, customizing Bootstrap components, and much more. But before we jump right into it by expanding on the files we set up in the first chapter, let's preview the home page for our new restaurant website:

Building our development environment

In the first chapter, we kept our Harp.js development environment pretty basic. We did this because we want to be able to use it as a boilerplate for all our projects. The first thing that we need to do in this chapter is expand on our original work to customize and extend it for our restaurant website.

Adding more pages

Now, the first thing we should do is update _data.json with all the new pages that we'll be building for our restaurant website. Along with our home page, let's add three new pages: **Home Menu**, **About**, and **Contact**. Our file should look like this:

```
{
  "index": {
    "pageTitle": "Home"
  },
  "menu": {
    "pageTitle": "Menu"
  },
  "about": {
    "pageTitle": "About"
  },
  "contact": {
    "pageTitle": "Contact"
  }
}
```

As you can see, I've added three new sections to our JSON file. Make sure you name your files to match the first part. Then, I've defined a pageTitle value for each page. Save the file and close it.

 The _harp.json doesn't require any updates for this project.

Expanding the layout

We need to make a couple of additions to _layout.ejs for our restaurant website. We're going to load a secondary web icon font library and some Google Web Fonts.

Adding Google Web Fonts

I don't want our restaurant website to look like every other Bootstrap website, so I'm going to import some Google Web Fonts to give it a more original look. If you're unfamiliar with this service, remember that it's an open source library of web fonts provided for free from Google. You can even download the actual font files on your computer for use in programs such as Photoshop or Illustrator. For this project, I've selected the Raleway font and I'll need four weights: light (300), normal (400), bold (700), and ultra-bold (900). To import the fonts, simply add this line of code to the `<head>` tag of `_layout.ejs`:

```
<link
href='//fonts.googleapis.com/css?family=Raleway:400,300,700,900'
rel='stylesheet' type='text/css'>
```

Now that we've imported the fonts from Google's CDN, we need to hook them up in our Less theme. Pop open the `_variables.less` component located at `css/components`. Locate the `Typography` section of the file and add `Raleway` as the first option in your font stack:

```
@body-copy: "Raleway", "Helvetica Neue", helvetica, arial,
verdana, sans-serif;
@heading-copy: "Raleway", "Helvetica Neue", helvetica, arial,
verdana, sans-serif;
```

Now our fonts are all set to use `Raleway`. In the current configuration, Raleway will be the only font used across the entire website. In some cases, you might want to use something like `Helvetica Neue` for the body copy and `Raleway` for the heading copy. If that's the case, just remove `Raleway` from the `@body-copy` variable. However, for my design, I'm going to use `Raleway` for both copy types.

Our updates to `_layout.ejs` are now complete. The entire file should look like this:

```
<!DOCTYPE html>
<html lang="en">
<head>
  <meta charset="utf-8">
  <meta http-equiv="X-UA-Compatible" content="IE=edge">
  <meta name="viewport" content="width=device-width, initial-
    scale=1">
  <title><%- pageTitle %> | <%- siteTitle %></title>

  <link type="text/css" href="css/bootstrap.min.css"
    rel="stylesheet">
  <link type="text/css" href="css/font-awesome.min.css"
    rel="stylesheet">
```

```
<link type="text/css" href="css/theme.css" rel="stylesheet">
<link
href='//fonts.googleapis.com/css?family=Raleway:400,300,700,900'
    rel='stylesheet' type='text/css'>

<!-- HTML5 shim and Respond.js for IE8 support of HTML5 elements
    and media queries -->
<!-- WARNING: Respond.js doesn't work if you view the page via
    file:// -->
<!--[if lt IE 9]>
    <script
src="https://oss.maxcdn.com/html5shiv/3.7.2/html5shiv.min.js"></
script>
    <script
src="https://oss.maxcdn.com/respond/1.4.2/respond.min.js"></script>
  <![endif]-->
</head>
<body>

  <%- partial("partial/_header") %>

  <%- yield %>

  <%- partial("partial/_footer") %>

  <!-- javascript //-->
  <script
    src="//ajax.googleapis.com/ajax/libs/jquery/1.11.1/jquery.min.
js"></script>
  <script src="js/bootstrap.min.js"
    type="text/javascript"></script>
</body>
</html>
```

Updating the Less variables

Before we go any further with this project, we should update a few of the global variables to match the look and feel of our restaurant website.

Backgrounds

I'm going to change the primary background to be light gray and the secondary background to be white. The main background of the website will be light gray. It will have a centered section that holds the majority of the content, which will be white for easy readability:

```
// background colors
@primary-background: @off-white;
@secondary-background: @white;
```

Links

I'm also going to move away from the default Bootstrap link colors by setting them to red. The basic color palette for our website will be white, light grey, dark grey, and red:

```
// link colors
@primary-link-color: @red1;
@primary-link-color-hover: @red2;
```

That's all the updates that our global variables will need. Let's move on to editing our header, which will require us to write some new CSS in our theme.

Updating the header

The next thing that we need to update is the header partial. Open up _header.ejs, located in the /partial directory. Select the contents of the file and delete them all. For this project, it's going to be easier to create custom header navigation instead of using Bootstraps. When creating Bootstrap websites or themes, it's important to remember that you don't have to use all the native components. This is actually a good way to avoid a generic-looking Bootstrap website. This is also a technique that you will start to see throughout this book, for creating a unique look and feel. Here's the code for our new header:

```
<div class="header">
  <div class="container">
    <div class="row">
      <div class="col-lg-3">
        <h1>Public</h1>
      </div>
      <div class="col-lg-9 right">
        <div class="main-nav pull-right">
          <ul class="list-inline">
            <li><a href="index.html">Home</a></li>
```

```
               <li class="divider">/</li>
               <li><a href="menu.html">Menu</a></li>
               <li class="divider">/</li>
               <li><a href="about.html">About</a></li>
               <li class="divider">/</li>
               <li><a href="contact.html">Contact</a></li>
               <li><button type="button" class="btn btn-default"
                 data-toggle="modal" data-target="#reservation-
                   modal">Reservations</button></li>
            </ul>
          </div>
        </div>
      </div>
    </div>
  </div>
```

As you can see, I may not be using the default Bootstrap `navbar` component, but I'm still using the basic grid classes to build a new custom header. Let's go through each part and talk about the custom CSS that goes with it.

The first thing that I've done is added a wrapping class around a container so that I can apply some styles to this specific chunk of layout. Let's update `theme.less` by adding the following styles:

```
.header .container {
  background: @primary-background;
  padding-left: 0;
  padding-right: 0;
}
```

In a future step, we're going to set our default container to use our `secondary-background` variable, which is white. However, for this header, we want the background to be light gray, so we'll set it to the `@primary-background` variable. We also want the text in our header to line up vertically with our layout box, so we've removed the left and right padding.

I'm a big supporter of minimal layouts with lots of white space, so let's add some vertical padding to our header to give it some breathing room:

```
.header {
  padding: (@padding * 4) 0;
}
```

I've used a Less operation here to render the padding value. Instead of writing something like 4em, I've used (@padding * 4). This is very powerful because we can control the overall global padding values from our global Less variables. In our actual theme, we are simply creating a relative measurement. This will save you a ton of time. You don't need to go through your entire theme while making edits; you can simply update the variables file. I hope it's clearer now why we set the margin and padding to 1em. It makes doing the math in your head super easy when you are multiplying, adding, dividing, or subtracting from a base value of 1.

Setting up the page title

The next thing that I'll do is set up the page title with an <h1> to optimize it for SEO. For this tag, we're going to write some custom CSS to change the font size and use our Google web font. I'll also use this as an example to create a new Less component.

Open a new file and save it to the css/components folder with the filename as _typography.less. We're going to break all of our custom type out into its own Less component file, which we will then import back into theme.less. This keeps our Less files small and easier to read. Once you've created the file, paste the following code in it:

```
h1 {
    font-weight: 900;
    height: 36px;
    margin: 0;
    line-height: 1;
}
```

Remember that we're using the Raleway web font, so I'm setting font-weight to a value of 900 to apply the **ultra-bold** font option. I've also changed the font size to 36px, removed the margin and set line-height to 1. The reason I've normalized these values is that this will make it easier to line up the page title with the nav links unordered list, which we haven't added yet.

Before we can apply these styles, we need to import _typography.less back into theme.less. Head back to that file and scroll down to the modules section of the file. Once you're there, insert the following line of code to import the type component file.

```
@import "components/_typography.less";
```

That's all we need to do for the page title. For the purposes of the project, I've named the restaurant public. Feel free to keep this name or rename it to something else. The next step is to set up the navigation component.

Setting up the navigation

You'll notice that I've set up a custom div to wrap an inline list named `main-nav`. What I'm doing here is using Bootstrap's built-in inline list component and then building on it a bit more to get the look that I want. This is the power of using a framework. I don't have to write the whole unordered list component; I can use what is provided and customize it. The `main-nav` component has a few CSS customizations, so let's jump into them all:

```
.main-nav {
  line-height: 36px; // vertical center with logo
}
```

The first thing that we'll do is set `line-height` to `36px`, which matches the height of the public page title. This will vertically center the page title and the navigation. It's basically a quick and easy way to apply vertical centering in CSS:

```
.main-nav ul {
  margin-bottom: 0;
}
```

Next, we'll remove the bottom margin from the `<ul>` tag to maintain the same vertical alignment. If we were to leave that in, then it would push the next container down and ruin our nice equal space above and below our header, which we set to 4ems:

```
.main-nav li.divider {
  color: @grey;
}
```

You'll notice that in our unordered list, every other `<li>` tag has a class of `.divider`. This is a quick and easy way to add a little design element to your `nav` to make it look different. I've styled the color of these dividers to be a bit lighter so that they're an accent and don't clash with the page links, which are the main thing that we want your user to notice:

```
.main-nav a {
  text-decoration: none;
}
```

The last thing we need to cover is the appearance of the links in our navigation. For our static state, I've simply removed the underline. On hover, things get a little more interesting:

```
.main-nav a:hover {
  border-bottom: (@border-size * 5) @border-type @grey;
  transition: border-color 0.2s ease;
}
```

I've used a CSS3 transition to fade in the border bottom color of each link. I've also increased the border size to five pixels, using a Less operation, to make it stand out more. This is purely a design element, so feel free to play around with it to get the effect you want.

Setting up the reservations modal

The last part of the header and navigation is the **Reservations** button. Clicking on this button will launch a modal popup where the user can fill in and submit a form to request a reservation at the restaurant. We'll need to insert our button into our header. Then, the corresponding modal code will have to be inserted into every page template. Here's what the modal will look like:

Next, let's start with the code for the button:

```
<button type="button" class="btn btn-default" data-toggle="modal"
data-target="#reservation-modal">
```

There's nothing out of the ordinary here. Just be sure to note the data-target value, or ID, as we'll need it when we set up our modal code in the page template.

Once we've inserted our button, we need to open up index.ejs and insert the modal code, which will be executed once the button is clicked on. Paste the following snippet of code in your index file. I prefer to insert my modal code at the bottom of the file so that it doesn't confuse other developers.

Make sure that you also comment what the modal is for:

```
<!-- reservation modal //-->
<div class="modal fade" id="reservation-modal">
  <div class="modal-dialog">
    <div class="modal-content">
      <div class="modal-header">
        <button type="button" class="close" data-dismiss="modal"
          aria-label="Close"><span aria-
            hidden="true">&times;</span></button>
        <h4 class="modal-title">Book Reservation</h4>
      </div>
      <div class="modal-body">
        <form>
          <div class="form-group">
            <label>Name</label>
            <input type="text" class="form-control"
              placeholder="Enter your name">
          </div>
          <div class="form-group">
            <label>Date</label>
            <input type="text" class="form-control"
              placeholder="Enter your date">
          </div>
          <div class="form-group">
            <label>Guests</label>
            <input type="text" class="form-control"
              placeholder="Enter the number of guests">
          </div>
        </form>
      </div>
      <div class="modal-footer">
        <button type="button" class="btn btn-default" data-
          dismiss="modal">Close</button>
        <button type="button" class="btn btn-
          primary">Submit</button>
      </div>
    </div><!-- /.modal-content -->
  </div><!-- /.modal-dialog -->
</div><!-- /.modal -->
```

Let's review the key parts of this modal for reservations:

- In the first line of the modal code, make sure that the CSS ID matches the `data-target` that was entered on the button code in the previous step. In this case, it should be `reservation-modal`. If you change the name, make sure that it is something descriptive, as we'll be adding more modals on the menu page.
- Insert the code for a basic form in the `modal-body`, and you're done. If you save the file and fire up the `Harp.js` server, you can test out the header and the modal. On a click of the button, the modal should launch over the top of your page.

This concludes the setup of the header for this project. Before we jump into page templates, let's set up the global footer.

Setting up the footer

The last part of our base template that we need to update is the footer. We're going to give the footer a unique new look, use some Font Awesome social media icons, and define our first utility CSS classes.

The footer layout

First, open up `_footer.ejs`, which is located in the `/partial` directory. Delete the existing code in there and replace it with the following snippet:

```
<div class="footer">
  <div class="container">
    <div class="col-lg-12">
      <h1>Public</h1>
      <p>1234 Street Name / Vancouver, BC / 604.123.1234</p>
      <p>Hours: Open 12pm to 9pm 7 days a week</p>
      <div class="social-media">
        <a href="#"><i class="fa fa-facebook"></i></a>
        <a href="#"><i class="fa fa-twitter"></i></a>
        <a href="#"><i class="fa fa-pinterest"></i></a>
        <a href="#"><i class="fa fa-instagram"></i></a>
      </div>
      <p>&copy; 2015 Public Restaurant</p>
    </div>
  </div>
</div>
```

Like our header, I've wrapped the footer section in a `.footer` class so that I can target all of the code within it. The first thing that we'll do is set up the following styles on the wrapping class:

```
.footer {
  text-align: center;
  color: @inverse-text;
  padding-bottom: (@padding * 4);
}
```

I'm using the `@inverse-text` variable here to set the text to white. In the next step, I'm going to reverse the background color, so that's why we are also reversing the text. I've also added some bottom padding to the footer and centered the contents of the section.

 If you prefer, you can choose to use the `<footer>` HTML5 tag here instead of a `.footer` class.

Next, we need to make some customizations to the `.container` class, which is nested inside of `.footer`. As with our header, we'll want to customize this container without affecting the primary container used in the body of the page:

```
.footer .container {
  background: @inverse-background;
  padding: (@padding * 4) 0;
}
```

Here, I've used the `@inverse-background` variable to reverse the background footer color. I've also applied some top and bottom padding to the section.

Now that we've set up our wrapping styles, we can go through the actual HTML code for our footer. First off, we've reused our `<h1>` tag and added in the name of the restaurant. Following that, we add in the address and hours of operation for the restaurant. All that is straightforward. The next section is the social media icons, which will require some special styles. First of all, we'll add some vertical padding around the icons to give them some breathing space:

```
// add padding around social media links
.social-media {
  padding: @padding 0;
}
```

Next, we'll set up some custom link states for the icons. The default red links would be a bit loud here, so we'll go with a more subtle light gray treatment. I've also added some horizontal padding to each icon link for additional breathing room:

```
// space out social media icons and change link color
.social-media a {
  padding: 0 (@padding - 0.5);
  color: @white;
}

// hover link color for social media icons
.social-media a:hover {
  color: @grey;
}
```

You may have noticed that the HTML for the icons is using some new classes. These are the Font Awesome icons that we set up in our header. As I mentioned, the Glyphicon library that comes with Bootstrap doesn't provide social media icons, so we've also added them in Font Awesome:

```
<a href="#"><i class="fa fa-facebook"></i></a>
<a href="#"><i class="fa fa-twitter"></i></a>
<a href="#"><i class="fa fa-pinterest"></i></a>
<a href="#"><i class="fa fa-instagram"></i></a>
```

That's it for our footer. We've now finished expanding all the template files that we created in *Chapter 1, Advanced Bootstrap Development Tools*. In the next step, we'll work on customizing `index.ejs` and build the home page of our restaurant website.

Home page

The home page for the restaurant website will be split into four main parts: a primary image banner, an "about the restaurant" statement, a few food thumbnails that will link to our menu page, and a Bootstrap reviews carousel. Here's what the page that we'll be creating will look like:

Adding the primary header image

We're going to set up some reusable styles for this image banner, which will be present across multiple pages of the website. Here's the code for the home page banner:

```
<div class="public-banner">
    <div class="row">
      <div class="col-lg-12">
        <img src="img/banner.jpg" width="1170" height="500"
          alt="Public Restaurant Banner">
      </div>
    </div>
  </div>
```

Our design has the image going all the way to the left and right of the container. The problem is that Bootstrap provides some padding here by default. Using the `.public-banner` class, we'll remove that default padding:

```
// here - allows image to go right to the edge
.public-banner .col-lg-12 {
  padding-left: 0;
  padding-right: 0;
}
```

We also need to add a couple of styles to our banner image to make it bulletproof for mobile. The actual image is larger than the default container size, but `width` is set to `100%`, so it fills the width of the container. The `height` property is set to `auto`, so the image will automatically resize at smaller screen resolutions:

```
.public-banner img {
  width: 100%;
  height: auto;
}
```

Now we'll insert the actual image into our layout with the following line of code:

```
<img src="img/banner.jpg" width="1170" height="500" alt="Public
Restaurant Banner">
```

We provide some set dimensions here so that our HTML code will validate. However, this is just a starting point. The image will automatically resize depending on the viewport size. The first part of our home page is done; the next thing that we'll cover is the About text section.

Adding the about text to the home page

Let's add the About text section. This is a place to add a tagline or a quick description about the restaurant. Here's what the code looks like:

```html
<div class="home-about">
    <div class="row">
      <div class="col-lg-12">
        <div class="text-center">
          <h2>About</h2>
          <div class="row">
            <div class="col-lg-6 col-lg-offset-3">
              <h4>Pellentesque habitant morbi tristique senectus
                  et netus et malesuada fames ac turpis
                  egestas.</h4>
            </div>
          </div>
        </div>
      </div>
    </div>
</div>
```

You'll notice that this section has a wrapping class called .home-about. This is similar to the approach we took with the header and footer. I'm reusing this pattern because I want to apply some padding to the section of the text:

```less
// add some padding around the about headline
.home-about {
  padding: (@padding * 4) 0 (@padding * 6) 0;
}
```

For the actual text in this section, I don't want it to stretch the width of the layout, so I'll get a little creative with the Bootstrap grid. Consider the following code:

```html
<div class="col-lg-6 col-lg-offset-3">
  <h4>Pellentesque habitant morbi tristique senectus et netus et
    malesuada fames ac turpis egestas.</h4>
</div>
```

I'd be happy if the total width of the paragraph was about half the width of the container, so I'll use the .col-lg-6 grid class. That leaves me with another six spans of grid, so I'll divide that into two. Using the offset class, I can now center my paragraph in the layout.

Setting up the food tiles

The next part of this page is the four food tiles that show some featured restaurant items. Each of these images will be a link that leads to our menu page. Here's what the code for the section looks like:

```
<div class="home-food">
    <div class="row">
      <div class="col-lg-3">
        <a href="menu.html">
          <img src="img/food-feature1.jpg" width="250"
            height="250" alt="Food Feature 1">
        </a>
        <h4>Sandwich</h4>
      </div>
      <div class="col-lg-3">
        <a href="menu.html">
          <img src="img/food-feature2.jpg" width="250"
            height="250" alt="Food Feature 2">
        </a>
        <h4>Dessert</h4>
      </div>
      <div class="col-lg-3">
        <a href="menu.html">
          <img src="img/food-feature3.jpg" width="250"
            height="250" alt="Food Feature 3">
        </a>
        <h4>Salad</h4>
      </div>
      <div class="col-lg-3">
        <a href="menu.html">
          <img src="img/food-feature4.jpg" width="250"
            height="250" alt="Food Feature 4">
        </a>
        <h4>Coffee</h4>
      </div>
    </div>
  </div>
```

Again I've wrapped the section in its own class; this time, it is called .home-food. You're likely seeing a pattern emerge here of wrapping sections in their own classes. This is a good practice to follow as it allows you to componentize sections of a page. This will make it easier to apply specific styles to these sections if needed. You should strive to avoid being too specific in your CSS, but sometimes it will be necessary to get the look and feel you are going for.

In this case, we're going to use the wrapping class to center everything within it:

```
// center all items
.home-food {
  text-align: center;
}
```

The second customization that we want to add to this section is the application of some bottom padding to each of the images. Since we have the wrapping class, it's easy to target the contained images without worrying about negatively affecting other images on our page:

```
// add a little extra padding under images
.home-food img {
  padding-bottom: @padding;
}
```

The rest of the code here is basic Bootstrap grid code, and it should be easy to decipher. If you need a refresher, check out the complete code for the preceding section.

Adding the review carousel

The final piece for this page will be a review carousel. Using this component here allows you to add multiple social proof examples for the website in a slick-looking execution. Here's the code for the carousel:

```
<div class="reviews">
  <div class="row">
    <div class="col-lg-12">
      <div class="text-center">
        <h2>Reviews</h2>
        <div id="carousel-reviews" class="carousel slide" data-
          ride="carousel">
          <!-- Indicators -->
          <ol class="carousel-indicators">
            <li data-target="#carousel-reviews" data-slide-
              to="0" class="active"></li>
            <li data-target="#carousel-reviews" data-slide-
              to="1"></li>
            <li data-target="#carousel-reviews" data-slide-
              to="2"></li>
          </ol>
```

```
<!-- Wrapper for slides -->
<div class="carousel-inner" role="listbox">
  <div class="item active">
    <p>This is the best sandwich I've ever had! I
      Highly recommend trying the chicken sandwich
        for lunch.</p>
  </div>
  <div class="item">
    <p>The desserts are to die for. Make sure you
      save enough room after you eat your dinner.</p>
  </div>
  <div class="item">
    <p>They have some of the best locally brewed
      coffee I have ever tasted. So fresh and eye
        opening early in the morning.</p>
  </div>
</div>

<!-- Controls -->
<a class="left carousel-control" href="#carousel-
  reviews" role="button" data-slide="prev">
  <span class="glyphicon glyphicon-chevron-left"
    aria-hidden="true"></span>
  <span class="sr-only">Previous</span>
</a>
<a class="right carousel-control" href="#carousel-
  reviews" role="button" data-slide="next">
  <span class="glyphicon glyphicon-chevron-right"
    aria-hidden="true"></span>
  <span class="sr-only">Next</span>
</a>
          </div>
        </div>
      </div>
    </div>
```

Like all our previous sections, I've wrapped this one in a class called `.reviews`. I'll simply use this class to add some vertical padding around the review carousel:

```
// add review padding consistent with about
.reviews {
  padding: (@padding * 4) 0 (@padding * 6) 0;
}
```

From here on, the rest of the HTML is stock Bootstrap markup. I've added in some of my own made-up reviews to give you an idea. What we need to do, however, is customize the look and feel of this component so that it matches our website's design. In this case, we are going to customize a Bootstrap component, so we'll create another component Less file to hold the styles. First things first, create a new Less file called `_carousel.less` and save it in the `css/components` directory. Next, import that file into `theme.less` with the following line of code:

```
@import "components/_carousel.less";
```

Now that we've imported our file, we need to add in some custom styles. Let's go through each declaration, explaining what it does:

```
.carousel .item {
  padding: @padding (@padding * 12) (@padding * 4) (@padding * 12);
  font-size: (@font-size * 1.5);
}
```

The first thing that we'll do is add some padding to the carousel. I don't want the text to stretch the width of the layout, so I'll add some generous horizontal padding to condense the paragraph size. Next, I want to increase `font-size` 1.5 times so that the reviews are nice and easy to read:

```
.carousel-control.right,
.carousel-control.left {
  background-image: none;
}
```

The default Bootstrap carousel has a gradient behind the left and right sides of the carousel on hover. I personally don't like this treatment as I'm more of a minimalist. The preceding snippet of CSS will remove the default gradient:

```
a.carousel-control {
  color: @light-grey;
}
```

Now that we've removed the background gradient, the CSS that you just saw will change the color of the carousel arrows to match the new color scheme. Little things like this might seem tedious, but they are the small details that will make your website look unique and not like a generic Bootstrap website:

```
.carousel-indicators li {
  border: @border-size @border-color @border-type;
}
```

This declaration is about consistency. Let's simply reset the borders on the carousel indicators to use our border variables' names and values. We do this so that if we change the global variable's value, it will automatically be picked up through the component. This saves us the effort of coming to the actual component CSS to make an edit:

```
.carousel-indicators .active {
  background: @light-grey;
}
```

The last step is to change the color of the indicators to match the left/right arrow colors. Consistency is the name of the game, and paying attention to these little details will take your website from good to great. But your home page is not complete! Recompile your files using the $ harp compile command, then launch the local server, and inspect your work. Just in case something doesn't look quite right, here's the entire page template for reference:

```
<div class="container">
  <!-- img banner //-->
  <div class="public-banner">
    <div class="row">
      <div class="col-lg-12">
        <img src="img/banner.jpg" width="1170" height="500"
          alt="Public Restaurant Banner">
      </div>
    </div>
  </div>
  <!-- about //-->
  <div class="home-about">
    <div class="row">
      <div class="col-lg-12">
        <div class="text-center">
          <h2>About</h2>
          <div class="row">
            <div class="col-lg-6 col-lg-offset-3">
              <h4>Pellentesque habitant morbi tristique senectus
                et netus et malesuada fames ac turpis
                  egestas.</h4>
            </div>
          </div>
        </div>
      </div>
    </div>
  </div>
  <!-- food thumbs //-->
```

```
<div class="home-food">
  <div class="row">
    <div class="col-lg-3">
      <a href="menu.html">
        <img src="img/food-feature1.jpg" width="250"
          height="250" alt="Food Feature 1">
      </a>
      <h4>Sandwich</h4>
    </div>
    <div class="col-lg-3">
      <a href="menu.html">
        <img src="img/food-feature2.jpg" width="250"
          height="250" alt="Food Feature 2">
      </a>
      <h4>Dessert</h4>
    </div>
    <div class="col-lg-3">
      <a href="menu.html">
        <img src="img/food-feature3.jpg" width="250"
          height="250" alt="Food Feature 3">
      </a>
      <h4>Salad</h4>
    </div>
    <div class="col-lg-3">
      <a href="menu.html">
        <img src="img/food-feature4.jpg" width="250"
          height="250" alt="Food Feature 4">
      </a>
      <h4>Coffee</h4>
    </div>
  </div>
</div>
<!-- reviews slider //-->
<div class="reviews">
  <div class="row">
    <div class="col-lg-12">
      <div class="center">
        <h2>Reviews</h2>
        <div id="carousel-reviews" class="carousel slide" data-
          ride="carousel">
          <!-- Indicators -->
          <ol class="carousel-indicators">
            <li data-target="#carousel-reviews" data-slide-
              to="0" class="active"></li>
```

```
      <li data-target="#carousel-reviews" data-slide-
        to="1"></li>
      <li data-target="#carousel-reviews" data-slide-
        to="2"></li>
    </ol>

    <!-- Wrapper for slides -->
    <div class="carousel-inner" role="listbox">
      <div class="item active">
        <p>This is the best sandwich I've ever had! I
          Highly recommend trying the chicken sandwich
            for lunch.</p>
      </div>
      <div class="item">
        <p>The desserts are to die for. Make sure you
          save enough room after you eat your dinner.</p>
      </div>
      <div class="item">
        <p>They have some of the best locally brewed
          coffee I have ever tasted. So fresh and eye
            opening early in the morning.</p>
      </div>
    </div>

    <!-- Controls -->
    <a class="left carousel-control" href="#carousel-
      reviews" role="button" data-slide="prev">
      <span class="glyphicon glyphicon-chevron-left"
        aria-hidden="true"></span>
      <span class="sr-only">Previous</span>
    </a>
    <a class="right carousel-control" href="#carousel-
      reviews" role="button" data-slide="next">
      <span class="glyphicon glyphicon-chevron-right"
        aria-hidden="true"></span>
      <span class="sr-only">Next</span>
    </a>
  </div>
</div>
</div>
</div>
</div>
```

```
<!-- reservation modal //-->
<div class="modal fade" id="reservation-modal">
  <div class="modal-dialog">
    <div class="modal-content">
      <div class="modal-header">
        <button type="button" class="close" data-dismiss="modal"
          aria-label="Close"><span aria-
            hidden="true">&times;</span></button>
        <h4 class="modal-title">Book Reservation</h4>
      </div>
      <div class="modal-body">
        <form>
          <div class="form-group">
            <label>Name</label>
            <input type="text" class="form-control"
              placeholder="Enter your name">
          </div>
          <div class="form-group">
            <label>Date</label>
            <input type="text" class="form-control"
              placeholder="Enter your date">
          </div>
          <div class="form-group">
            <label>Guests</label>
            <input type="text" class="form-control"
              placeholder="Enter the number of guests">
          </div>
        </form>
      </div>
      <div class="modal-footer">
        <button type="button" class="btn btn-default" data-
          dismiss="modal">Close</button>
        <button type="button" class="btn btn-
          primary">Submit</button>
      </div>
    </div><!-- /.modal-content -->
  </div><!-- /.modal-dialog -->
</div><!-- /.modal -->
```

The About page

The next page for our restaurant website is the **About** page. This page will feature a two-column layout and some custom text styles to give it a unique look. Here's a screenshot of what we'll be building:

Changing the feature image

The first thing that we need to do is create a new file called about.ejs. Next, we'll change the feature image as displayed in the preceding screenshot. To do this, we'll simply update this image line of code:

```
<img src="img/banner-about.jpg" width="1170" height="500"
alt="Public Restaurant About Banner">
```

Make sure you update the alt text to optimize your image for search results. The next thing we need to do is set up our two-column layout. I'm going to wrap a <div> with a class of .page-body around the row, as we've done in the past:

```
<div class="page-body">
```

This will allow us to apply some padding around our main page body:

```
.page-body {
  padding: (@padding * 4);
}
```

I do this to add some whitespace and give the layout room to breathe.

Setting up the large subtitle

Let's start with the column on the left first, and we'll set up the oversized subtitle with the following line of code:

```
<h2 class="large">Great food, great people, good times.</h2>
```

We're using the <h2> tag here; I've applied a class of .large to it. This class is a reusable utility that you can add to any text tag to increase its size four times. Open up the type component named _typography.less in css/components and add in the following styles:

```
h2 {
  font-weight: 900;
}

.large {
  font-size: (@font-size * 4);
}
```

Now you can see how I've set up the .large class to multiply font-size by 4. I've also changed the font weight of the <h2> tag to 900, which will trigger the heaviest weight of our Google web font that we previously imported.

Adding the social media icons

For the About page, I think it's important to move the links to the restaurant's social media profiles more to the forefront. We can also combine them with our large headline to create a nice visual element without the use of any images, thus creating a nice, lightweight effect. Let's reuse the social media icon code that we set up in our footer, as follows:

```
<div class="about-social-media">
  <a href="#"><i class="fa fa-facebook"></i></a>
  <a href="#"><i class="fa fa-twitter"></i></a>
  <a href="#"><i class="fa fa-pinterest"></i></a>
  <a href="#"><i class="fa fa-instagram"></i></a>
</div>
```

Note that there is one small but critical difference in this code compared to the footer, which is the class name on the wrapping <div>. In this case, I've applied a class called .about-social-media. It's a great practice to reuse our HTML code and then simply apply some different styling to it with a new class name:

```
.about-social-media {
  margin: (@margin * 2) 0;
  font-size: (@font-size * 2);
}
```

For these icons, I'm going to apply top and bottom margins to give them some vertical space. I'm also going to increase the font size a bit so that they stand out more.

Adding the address

The last part of the left-hand-side column is a repetition of the restaurant's address. No special classes here, but I'm using the <small> tag to give this section a unique look, like this:

```
<p>
  <small>
    Public Restaurant<br/>
    1234 Street Name<br/>
    Vancouver, BC<br/>
    604.123.1234
  </small>
</p>
```

I'm using a simple `<p>` tag here with a number of line breaks to create the text layout. You may want to use an unordered list with the `list-unstyled` class, but that is a little more code heavy.

This completes the left column. Let's move on to the right column in the next step.

Reviewing the layout

Before we jump to the next column, we should review the layout code. Here's the code for the two columns:

```
<div class="row">
  <div class="col-lg-5">left col</div>
  <div class="col-lg-6 col-lg-offset-1">right col</div>
</div>
```

You'll notice that I haven't divided the columns into two equal widths. I've followed this layout for two reasons:

- I want to use an asymmetric layout. Uneven layouts are more pleasing to the eye and will give your design some personality. Wherever possible, you should always shoot to create asymmetric layouts. This is a rule taken from the print design world that, when used properly in web design, can create a very nice-looking layout.

- I want to provide some extra horizontal space between my two columns. As we've done with the vertical space, it can be nice to give our text some horizontal breathing space. This makes the text easier to read and breathes some life into your layout. Following some simple design tips like this will also prevent your website from looking like a generic Bootstrap site.

Inserting the About text

Now that we've set up our layout, it's a simple exercise to insert our text. Here's my code for this:

```
<h3>Our Story</h3>
<h4>Pellentesque habitant morbi tristique senectus et netus et
malesuada fames ac turpis egestas. Vestibulum tortor quam,
feugiat vitae, ultricies eget, tempor sit amet, ante. Donec eu
libero sit amet quam egestas semper. Aenean ultricies mi vitae
est. Mauris placerat eleifend leo.</h4>
<p>Pellentesque habitant morbi tristique senectus et netus et
malesuada fames ac turpis egestas. Vestibulum tortor quam,
feugiat vitae, ultricies eget, tempor sit amet, ante. Donec eu
libero sit amet quam egestas semper. Aenean ultricies mi vitae
```

```
est. Mauris placerat eleifend leo. Quisque sit amet est et sapien
ullamcorper pharetra. Vestibulum erat wisi, condimentum sed,
commodo vitae, ornare sit amet, wisi. Aenean fermentum, elit eget
tincidunt condimentum, eros ipsum rutrum orci, sagittis tempus
lacus enim ac dui. Donec non enim in turpis pulvinar facilisis.
Ut felis. Praesent dapibus, neque id cursus faucibus, tortor
neque egestas augue, eu vulputate magna eros eu erat. Aliquam
erat volutpat. Nam dui mi, tincidunt quis, accumsan porttitor,
facilisis luctus, metus</p>
```

You'll notice that I'm using some header tags here, specifically `<h3>` and `<h4>`. Again, taking the time to use some other text tags will give your design some life and differentiate it from regular Bootstrap sites. I've also customized the `<h3>` tag a bit to give it a different look:

```
h3 {
   font-weight: 700;
   color: @red1;
}
```

I've upped `font-weight` to `700`, or bold, and I've applied one of our Less color variables (`@red1` in this case) to change the `color` of the header tag. I've also made a small change to the `<h4>` tag:

```
h4 {
   line-height: 1.5
}
```

By default, header tags in Bootstrap are set to `1.1` for the `line-height` property. The reason for this is that headers are usually on one line only, so you don't necessarily want to add a ton of extra vertical spacing. However, in this case, I'm using an `<h4>` across multiple lines, so I want to increase `line-height` to match the default for my regular paragraphs of text. Otherwise, the `<h4>` text will be cramped and too hard to read.

Don't forget the modal

The last thing that we need to do for this page is copy and paste the reservation modal code at the bottom. If we leave this out, our reservation modal won't work on the **About** page. If I were smart, I would actually drop this modal code into a new partial and then just import it into the page. In that way, we only have to manage one reservation modal component. Why don't we do that right now? Take the following code and create a new file at `/partial` called `_reservation-modal.ejs`:

```
<!-- reservation modal //-->
<div class="modal fade" id="reservation-modal">
```

```
<div class="modal-dialog">
  <div class="modal-content">
    <div class="modal-header">
      <button type="button" class="close" data-dismiss="modal"
        aria-label="Close"><span aria-
          hidden="true">&times;</span></button>
      <h4 class="modal-title">Book Reservation</h4>
    </div>
    <div class="modal-body">
      <form>
        <div class="form-group">
          <label>Name</label>
          <input type="text" class="form-control"
            placeholder="Enter your name">
        </div>
        <div class="form-group">
          <label>Date</label>
          <input type="text" class="form-control"
            placeholder="Enter your date">
        </div>
        <div class="form-group">
          <label>Guests</label>
          <input type="text" class="form-control"
            placeholder="Enter the number of guests">
        </div>
      </form>
    </div>
    <div class="modal-footer">
      <button type="button" class="btn btn-default" data-
        dismiss="modal">Close</button>
      <button type="button" class="btn btn-
        primary">Submit</button>
    </div>
  </div><!-- /.modal-content -->
</div><!-- /.modal-dialog -->
</div><!-- /.modal -->
```

Once you've saved the file, go back to about.ejs and paste this line of code at the very bottom of your file:

```
<%- partial("partial/_reservation-modal") %>
```

Recompiling your project

Now is a great time to talk about recompiling your project. One of the great things about Harp is that it will pick up changes as you make them and display them in the browser. However, if you make a significant change, such as adding a new partial, it's a good idea to recompile your code. The best practice would be to recompile after each new page that you create. You'll want to make sure that you test each page as you go. If you have a typo in your filename, it will throw an error in the terminal until you correct it. It's easier to do this one page at a time compared to trying to figure out which page is wrong once you've created ten of them. Anyhow, head back to your command-line tool and stop the web server by hitting *Ctrl + C*. Next enter the Harp compile command again:

```
$ harp compile
```

If all is good, you shouldn't see any errors. If you do see an error, make sure you check the page filename against what you entered in the _data.json file. Most of the time, it will be a simple typo here that needs to be corrected to get your production site to compile properly again. After you've completed your compile, fire up the server again, as follows:

```
$ harp server -port 9000
```

Then head back to your browser and refresh the **About** page. Click on the **Reservations** button in the header and the modal should launch. You're now using a partial to import a chunk of code that is reused across multiple pages. This is one of the awesome parts of Harp!

This concludes the design and coding of the **About** page. Next, let's tackle one of the most important pages of our restaurant website—the menu! However, before we do that, here's the complete code for the **About** page:

```html
<div class="container">
  <!-- img banner //-->
  <div class="public-banner">
    <div class="row">
      <div class="col-lg-12">
        <img src="img/banner-about.jpg" width="1170" height="500"
          alt="Public Restaurant About Banner">
      </div>
    </div>
  </div>
  <!-- about //-->
  <div class="page-body">
    <div class="row">
      <div class="col-lg-5">
```

```
        <h2 class="large">Great food, great people, good
          times.</h2>
        <div class="about-social-media">
          <a href="#"><i class="fa fa-facebook"></i></a>
          <a href="#"><i class="fa fa-twitter"></i></a>
          <a href="#"><i class="fa fa-pinterest"></i></a>
          <a href="#"><i class="fa fa-instagram"></i></a>
        </div>
        <p>
          <small>
            Public Restaurant<br />
            1234 Street Name<br />
            Vancouver, BC<br />
            604.123.1234
          </small>
        </p>
      </div>
      <div class="col-lg-6 col-lg-offset-1">
        <h3>Our Story</h3>
        <h4>Pellentesque habitant morbi tristique senectus et
netus et malesuada fames ac turpis egestas. Vestibulum tortor
quam, feugiat vitae, ultricies eget, tempor sit amet, ante. Donec
eu libero sit amet quam egestas semper. Aenean ultricies mi vitae
est. Mauris placerat eleifend leo.</h4>
        <p>Pellentesque habitant morbi tristique senectus et
netus et malesuada fames ac turpis egestas. Vestibulum tortor
quam, feugiat vitae, ultricies eget, tempor sit amet, ante. Donec
eu libero sit amet quam egestas semper. Aenean ultricies mi vitae
est. Mauris placerat eleifend leo. Quisque sit amet est et sapien
ullamcorper pharetra. Vestibulum erat wisi, condimentum sed,
commodo vitae, ornare sit amet, wisi. Aenean fermentum, elit eget
tincidunt condimentum, eros ipsum rutrum orci, sagittis tempus
lacus enim ac dui. Donec non enim in turpis pulvinar facilisis.
Ut felis. Praesent dapibus, neque id cursus faucibus, tortor
neque egestas augue, eu vulputate magna eros eu erat. Aliquam
erat volutpat. Nam dui mi, tincidunt quis, accumsan porttitor,
facilisis luctus, metus</p>
      </div>
    </div>
  </div>
</div>

<%- partial("partial/_reservation-modal") %>
```

The Menu page

It's time to code the tastiest part of our restaurant website (sorry, that was a terrible pun). For our menu page, we'll use a three-column layout combined with some additional modal popups for our featured dishes. The following is a preview of what the page will look like:

As you can see, I've kept the layout pretty minimal, which is my style and will transfer well to the mobile view. Let's start by going over the page header style that is used for each section of the menu.

Customizing the .page-header class

For each section of the menu, I'm using a `<h2>` tag with the Bootstrap `.page-header` class to make it stand out. Here's what the code looks like:

```
<h2 class="page-header">Appetizers</h2>
```

Since we don't want our site to look like a generic Bootstrap project, I'm going to customize the look and feel of the `page-header` component:

```
.page-header {
  padding-bottom: (@padding * 1.5);
  margin: @margin 0;
  border-bottom: (@border-size * 5) @border-type @border-color;
}
```

As you can see, I've inserted some additional bottom padding, increased the vertical margin around the title, and beefed up the bottom border to give it a unique look. The fatter border also fits in better with the overall look and feel of the restaurant site.

Setting up the layout

Before we jump into the menu items, let's quickly talk about the page layout. Make sure you wrap the page in the `page-body` class that you created for the **About** page. Each section of the menu has a `col-lg-12` for the section title, and after that is a three-column layout that uses the `col-lg-4` grid classes. In this case, I'm choosing a symmetrical layout as it makes sense for a menu. Here's some sample layout code:

```
<div class="row">
  <div class="col-lg-12">
    <h2 class="page-header">Appetizers</h2>
  </div>
</div>
<div class="row">
  <div class="col-lg-4">
    <h3>Item Name</h3>
    <p>Item description goes here.</p>
    <p class="price">$5</p>
```

```
    </div>
    <div class="col-lg-4">
      <h3>Item Name</h3>
      <p>Item description goes here.</p>
      <p class="price">$5</p>
    </div>
    <div class="col-lg-4">
      <h3>Item Name</h3>
      <p>Item description goes here.</p>
      <p class="price">$5</p>
    </div>
  </div>
</div>
```

The grid here should be pretty straightforward. Let's talk a bit more about the menu items. I'm using an `<h3>` tag for the title of each menu item. This allows them to stand out and will help optimize our food titles for searching. You'll notice a new class named `.price` that is attached to a `<p>` tag and wrapped around a dollar price. I've created it because I want the price to stand out but don't want to use a header tag here. This is purely for readability of the menu and has nothing to do with searching, so a class is a better call:

```
.price {
  color: @red1;
  font-weight: 700;
}
```

As you can see, I'm using the `@red1` color variable again and I've upped `font-weight` to bold, or `700`. This will allow the price to stand out easily when read.

Adding the featured modal

Near a few of the menu items, you'll notice a **View** link. This link will launch a modal to show an image of the food item. You could also add more information about the food item here if you like. For the purposes of this demo, I've added this modal to only a couple of the items, but you might want to add it for all food items on your restaurant website. Here's what our modal will look like once launched:

Now let's take a look at the code that is required to launch our food modal:

```
<div class="col-lg-4">
  <h3>Green Salad</h3>
  <p>A great healthy start to your meal. <a href="#" data-
    toggle="modal" data-target="#salad-modal">View</a></p>
  <p class="price">$9</p>
</div>
```

The code here is exactly the same, with only an addition of the **View** link that will trigger the modal:

```
<a href="#" data-toggle="modal" data-target="#salad-
modal">View</a>
```

Now that we've set up the trigger, let's create the actual modal code. Here it is for review:

```
<!-- salad modal //-->
<div class="modal fade" id="salad-modal">
  <div class="modal-dialog">
    <div class="modal-content">
      <div class="modal-header">
        <button type="button" class="close" data-dismiss="modal"
          aria-label="Close"><span aria-
            hidden="true">&times;</span></button>
        <h4 class="modal-title">Appetizer</h4>
      </div>
      <div class="modal-body">
        <div class="text-center">
          <p><img src="img/salad.jpg" width="400" height="267"
            alt="Salad"></p>
          <h2>Green Salad</h2>
          <p>A great healthy start to your meal.</p>
          <p class="price">$9</p>
        </div>
      </div>
    </div><!-- /.modal-content -->
  </div><!-- /.modal-dialog -->
</div><!-- /.modal -->
```

You'll notice that this modal code is a bit simpler than the reservations one. That's for a couple of reasons. Firstly, we could be reusing this code on a number of items, so we should try and keep it simple if we can. Secondly, I don't want this to look like a generic Bootstrap modal. I want it to look like a nicer popup geared for a restaurant. So, by removing some of the default parts that aren't needed, we can provide a more customized look and feel. Let's go over what has changed:

```
<div class="modal-body">
  <div class="text-center">
    <p><img src="img/salad.jpg" width="400" height="267"
      alt="Salad"></p>
    <h2>Green Salad</h2>
    <p>A great healthy start to your meal.</p>
    <p class="price">$9</p>
  </div>
</div>
```

First, you'll notice that I've inserted an image. The width is set to 400 pixels, which is a bit smaller than the overall width of our modal. Make sure you keep your image size within that limit. If you'd like to use a larger image, increase the size of your modal. You may even want to experiment with making your modal full screen.

The other big difference with this modal is that I have deleted the `.modal-footer` section. Remember that with Bootstrap, some of these parts are optional. Just because they are in the core code doesn't mean you can't experiment with them. In the case of the footer, the default content is a **submit** or **cancel** button. This doesn't make a ton of sense in the context of how we are using the modal, so just delete that part. We still have the **Close** button in the header of the modal, or the user can click outside the modal window to close it. Again, this is another example of customizing a Bootstrap component to make it your own. I encourage you to push the design of your modals even further.

You'll notice that on the menu, I've added a second modal under the Sandwich heading. Here's the code for that modal:

```
<!-- sandwich modal //-->
<div class="modal fade" id="sandwich-modal">
  <div class="modal-dialog">
    <div class="modal-content">
      <div class="modal-header">
        <button type="button" class="close" data-dismiss="modal"
          aria-label="Close"><span aria-
            hidden="true">&times;</span></button>
        <h4 class="modal-title">Sandwiches</h4>
      </div>
      <div class="modal-body">
        <div class="center">
          <p><img src="img/sandwich.jpg" width="400" height="274"
            alt="Sandwich"></p>
          <h2>Veggie Sandwich</h2>
          <p>tomatoes, lettuce, cheese, salsa.</p>
          <p class="price">$12</p>
        </div>
      </div>
    </div><!-- /.modal-content -->
  </div><!-- /.modal-dialog -->
</div><!-- /.modal -->
```

Multiple modals

In your own restaurant website, if you do go by the route of the popup for every menu item, you may want to consider a cleaner approach for all your modal code. Currently, you need to create a new instance of the modal HTML for each food item. This could become quite long if you have a big menu. A better technique would be to create a template for the modal into which you can load your values. One way you can do this is with a JavaScript MVC library, such as Backbone or Angular. They will allow you to create a view for that page, with a template (such as a Handlebar template) that you can then load in the different values. This book isn't about JavaScript MVCs, so I won't go further into that subject, but this is just something to keep in mind as you build your production-ready restaurant website. The way that I've shown you will work for a large menu, but using an MVC may be a cleaner solution.

This concludes the **Menu** section. Before we move on to our last page, the **Contact** page, here's all the code for the menu:

```
<div class="container">
  <!-- page body //-->
  <div class="page-body">
    <!-- appetizers //-->
    <div class="row">
      <div class="col-lg-12">
        <h2 class="page-header">Appetizers</h2>
      </div>
    </div>
    <div class="row">
      <div class="col-lg-4">
        <h3>Garlic Bread</h3>
        <p>Delicious pan fried bread with olive oil.</p>
        <p class="price">$7</p>
      </div>
      <div class="col-lg-4">
        <h3>Chicken Wings</h3>
        <p>One dozen wings, come in hot or bbq flavour.</p>
        <p class="price">$12</p>
      </div>
      <div class="col-lg-4">
        <h3>Nachos</h3>
        <p>Great for sharing with friends. Tons of cheese and all
          the toppings.</p>
        <p class="price">$14</p>
      </div>
    </div>
```

```
<div class="row">
  <div class="col-lg-4">
    <h3>Yam Fries</h3>
    <p>Servied with garlic mayo for dipping.</p>
    <p class="price">$8</p>
  </div>
  <div class="col-lg-4">
    <h3>Green Salad</h3>
    <p>A great healthy start to your meal. <a href="#" data-
      toggle="modal" data-target="#salad-modal">View</a></p>
    <p class="price">$9</p>
  </div>
  <div class="col-lg-4">
    <h3>Chips &amp; Salsa</h3>
    <p>Crisp tortilla chips and dip.</p>
    <p class="price">$6</p>
  </div>
</div>
<!-- sandwiches //-->
<div class="row">
  <div class="col-lg-12">
    <h2 class="page-header">Sandwiches <small>All sandwiches
      are served with yam fries or salad.</small></h2>
  </div>
</div>
<div class="row">
  <div class="col-lg-4">
    <h3>Veggie</h3>
    <p>tomatoes, lettuce, cheese, salsa. <a href="#" data-
      toggle="modal" data-target="#sandwich-
        modal">View</a></p>
    <p class="price">$12</p>
  </div>
  <div class="col-lg-4">
    <h3>Turkey</h3>
    <p>turkey, lettuce, cranberry, cheese, tomato.</p>
    <p class="price">$14</p>
  </div>
  <div class="col-lg-4">
    <h3>Roast Beef</h3>
    <p>roast beef, mustard, pickles.</p>
    <p class="price">$14</p>
  </div>
</div>
```

```
    <!-- burgers //-->
    <div class="row">
      <div class="col-lg-12">
        <h2 class="page-header">Burgers <small>All burgers are
          served with yam fries or salad.</small></h2>
      </div>
      <div class="row">
      <div class="col-lg-4">
        <h3>Beef</h3>
        <p>tomatoes, lettuce, cheese, pickles.</p>
        <p class="price">$16</p>
      </div>
      <div class="col-lg-4">
        <h3>Chicken</h3>
        <p>lettuce, cucumber, pickles.</p>
        <p class="price">$16</p>
      </div>
      <div class="col-lg-4">
        <h3>Veggie</h3>
        <p>lettuce, mushrooms, salsa.</p>
        <p class="price">$14</p>
      </div>
    </div>
    </div>
  </div>
</div>

<%- partial("partial/_reservation-modal") %>

<!-- salad modal //-->
<div class="modal fade" id="salad-modal">
  <div class="modal-dialog">
    <div class="modal-content">
      <div class="modal-header">
        <button type="button" class="close" data-dismiss="modal"
          aria-label="Close"><span aria-
            hidden="true">&times;</span></button>
        <h4 class="modal-title">Appetizer</h4>
      </div>
      <div class="modal-body">
        <div class="text-center">
          <p><img src="img/salad.jpg" width="400" height="267"
            alt="Salad"></p>
          <h2>Green Salad</h2>
```

```
      <p>A great healthy start to your meal.</p>
      <p class="price">$9</p>
    </div>
  </div>
</div><!-- /.modal-content -->
  </div><!-- /.modal-dialog -->
</div><!-- /.modal -->

<!-- sandwich modal //-->
<div class="modal fade" id="sandwich-modal">
  <div class="modal-dialog">
    <div class="modal-content">
      <div class="modal-header">
        <button type="button" class="close" data-dismiss="modal"
          aria-label="Close"><span aria-
            hidden="true">&times;</span></button>
        <h4 class="modal-title">Sandwiches</h4>
      </div>
      <div class="modal-body">
        <div class="text-center">
          <p><img src="img/sandwich.jpg" width="400" height="274"
            alt="Sandwich"></p>
          <h2>Veggie Sandwich</h2>
          <p>tomatoes, lettuce, cheese, salsa.</p>
          <p class="price">$12</p>
        </div>
      </div>
    </div><!-- /.modal-content -->
  </div><!-- /.modal-dialog -->
</div><!-- /.modal -->
```

The Contact page

We're down to the final page of our restaurant website. The last thing do is set up our Contact page, which will include an actual Google map along with some required content that all restaurants should ideally list on their website. Here's what the Contact page will look like once we're done:

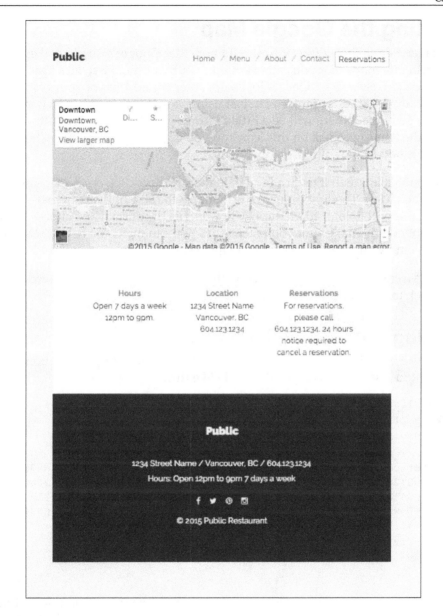

Inserting the Google Map

If you haven't done this before, you should note that Google actually makes it quite easy to generate maps that you can insert into your website. First, let's head over to `http://google.com/maps`. Once it loads up, enter the address of your restaurant. I don't have an actual restaurant, so I'm just using `Vancouver` as my search term. After the map is generated, there will be a little **Settings** gear icon near the bottom-right corner of the window. Click on this icon and you'll see a pop-up menu. Choose the **Share** or **Embed Map** option from the menu.

Clicking on this link will launch a modal. Make sure you click on the second tab, called **Embed Map**. The first thing in the modal is the size of the map that you want to embed; this will default to Medium. Click on this dropdown and choose **Custom size**. For the width, make sure you enter `1170`. You can make the height whatever you want, but I've decided to make my map 500 pixels high.

After you've entered the size values, copy the iframe code given in the next section and go back to the `contact.ejs` file.

Inserting the Google Map code

Under the `<div>` with the `.public-banner` class that you set up on the home page, you'll want to insert your Google Map code like this:

```
<div class="public-banner">
  <div class="row">
    <div class="col-lg-12">
      <iframe
src="https://www.google.com/maps/embed?pb=!1m18!1m12!1m3!1d20822.3905
3484898!2d-123.11777955000004!3d49.28020924999999!2m3!1f0!2f0!3f0!3m
2!1i1024!2i768!4f13.1!3m3!1m2!1s0x5486717f41ba2fb1%3A0xc6952794560a4
4aa!2sDowntown%2C+Vancouver%2C+BC!5e0!3m2!1sen!2sca!4v1434608605144"
width="1170" height="500" frameborder="0" style="border:0"></iframe>
    </div>
  </div>
</div>
```

Save the file and your map code is complete. You may want to recompile it at this point and test it out before moving on to the rest of the **Contact** page. Note that in the iframe code, you can see the width and height values. Feel free to tweak them in the file if you want to perhaps change the height. You don't need to go back to Google Maps to do that.

Setting up the body of the page

After we finish setting up the map in the header of the page, we need to set up some content in the body. As in our other pages, we use the .page-body class to wrap the entire section. For the remainder of the page, we're going to use the same three-column layout that we had in our menu page.

I'm also going to reuse the .text-center utility class here to center all of the content in the child <div> of this section. Let's take a look at all of the code and then we'll review it:

```
<div class="page-body">
  <div class="row text-center">
      <div class="col-lg-4">
        <h3>Hours</h3>
        <p>Open 7 days a week 12pm to 9pm.</p>
      </div>
      <div class="col-lg-4">
        <h3>Location</h3>
        <p>
          1234 Street Name<br />
          Vancouver, BC<br />
          604.123.1234
        </p>
      </div>
      <div class="col-lg-4">
        <h3>Reservations</h3>
        <p>For reservations, please call 604.123.1234. 24 hours
          notice required to cancel a reservation.</p>
      </div>
    </div>
  </div>
```

As you can see, I've wrapped the entire section in the page-body class. I've also added the .center class to the .row <div> so that everything is centered:

- The first column should display the hours for the restaurant. As with the menu page, I'm using an <h3> tag here for the heading. It's good to try and keep your headings consistent from a design standpoint.

- For the center column, you should insert the address of your restaurant.

- The last column has some additional information about how a person can book a reservation. Not everyone may want to book online, so it's a good idea to also provide a phone number for the Internet illiterate.

The reservation modal

Like all your other pages, don't forget to add the partial to load in the reservation modal at the bottom of the page:

```
<%- partial("partial/_reservation-modal") %>
```

That brings the final page of our restaurant website to a close. Let's review all of the code for the Contact page before we move onto the chapter summary.

```
<div class="container">
  <!-- img banner //-->
  <div class="public-banner">
    <div class="row">
      <div class="col-lg-12">
        <iframe src="https://www.google.com/maps/embed?pb=!1m18!1m12!
1m3!1d20822.39053484898!2d-123.11777955000004!3d49.28020924999999!2m
3!1f0!2f0!3f0!3m2!1i1024!2i768!4f13.1!3m3!1m2!1s0x5486717f41ba2fb1%3
A0xc6952794560a44aa!2sDowntown%2C+Vancouver%2C+BC!5e0!3m2!1sen!2sca!
4v1434608605144"
width="1170" height="500" frameborder="0"
style="border:0"></iframe>
      </div>
    </div>
  </div>
  <!-- about //-->
  <div class="page-body">
    <div class="row text-center">
      <div class="col-lg-4">
        <h3>Hours</h3>
        <p>Open 7 days a week 12pm to 9pm.</p>
      </div>
      <div class="col-lg-4">
        <h3>Location</h3>
        <p>
          1234 Street Name<br />
          Vancouver, BC<br />
          604.123.1234
        </p>
      </div>
      <div class="col-lg-4">
        <h3>Reservations</h3>
```

```
      <p>For reservations, please call 604.123.1234. 24 hours
         notice required to cancel a reservation.</p>
    </div>
   </div>
  </div>
</div>

<%- partial("partial/_reservation-modal") %>
```

Summary

That brings the second chapter to a close. We built on what you learned in *Chapter 1, Advanced Bootstrap Development Tools*, and used it to create a restaurant website. Let's review what we learned. We learned how to build out actual pages with our Harp development environment; import and use the Font Awesome web icon library; import and use open source Google Web Fonts; use and customize Bootstrap components such as the modal, page header, and carousel; create a Harp partial that is used within a page template; use design principles when laying out grids and type to create a unique look with Bootstrap; and create and insert a custom Google map into our website.

3
Mobile First Bootstrap

Being the seasoned developer you are, you probably know that Bootstrap is actually a mobile first CSS framework. Up until now, we haven't focused that much on the mobile first philosophy. However, that will change in this chapter, as I teach you how to build a mobile first aggregator website template. Along with taking the mobile first approach for the first time, I'll cover using some custom JavaScript to improve the UI and use a flat Google material inspired design.

First of all, let's take a look at what the mobile website will look like when completed:

Let's also take a look at what the desktop version of this project will look like:

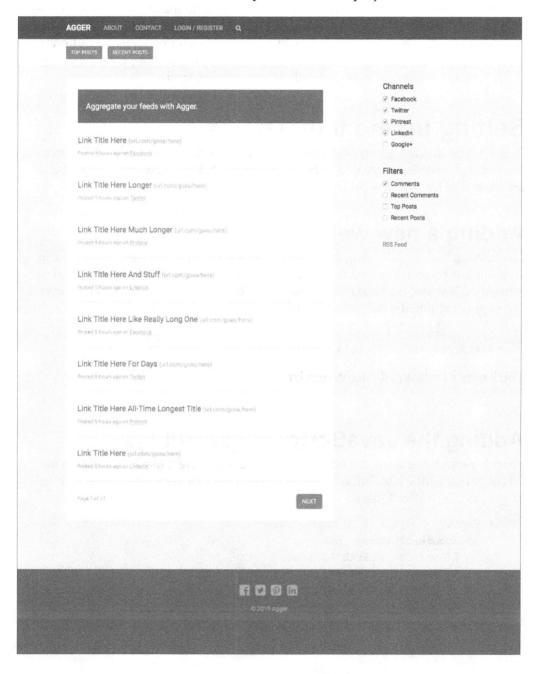

As you can see in the preceding screenshot, the layout is going to change depending on our viewport size. I've optimized the mobile layout to make sure it's easy to use on a phone or tablet. This is done through the use of buttons and text links that are easy to touch. We also aren't relying on any hover states for our links or buttons since you cannot hover on mobile devices. Finally, I've kept the layout pretty minimal to allow for easy reading no matter which device is being used.

Setting up the template

Before we get too far, let's create a new project called `Chapter 3` by copying over our boilerplate code we created in the first chapter. Let's update some of the basic template files for this new project.

Adding a new web font

I mentioned that we are going to use some Google material design principals and styles in this project. The first thing I'd like you to do is to use the material design font called **Roboto**. It's available for free from the Google web fonts website or you can simply include the following line of code in the `_layout.ejs` file:

```
<link href='http://fonts.googleapis.com/css?family=Robo
to:400,300,700,900' rel='stylesheet' type='text/css'>
```

You'll notice I'm using the light, regular, bold, and super bold weights of the web font.

Adding the JavaScript to _layout.ejs

For this project, I've written a little custom jQuery that we'll use in our search bar. I'll cover that a little later but for now, just insert the following code at the bottom of `_layout.ejs` after jQuery:

```
<script>
    $(document).ready(function() {
      $("#header-search").hide();
      $("#search-trigger").on("click", function() {
        $("#header-search").toggle();
      });
    });
  </script>
```

After pasting that snippet in, the `_layout.ejs` file is ready to go. Here's what the full file should now look like:

```html
<!DOCTYPE html>
<html lang="en">
<head>
  <meta charset="utf-8">
  <meta http-equiv="X-UA-Compatible" content="IE=edge">
  <meta name="viewport" content="width=device-width, initial-
    scale=1">
  <title><%- pageTitle %> | <%- siteTitle %></title>

  <link rel="stylesheet" type="text/css"
    href="css/bootstrap.min.css">
  <link rel="stylesheet" type="text/css" href="css/font-
    awesome.min.css">
  <link rel="stylesheet" type="text/css" href="css/theme.css">
  <link
    href='http://fonts.googleapis.com/css?family=Robo
to:400,300,700,900' rel='stylesheet' type='text/css'>

  <!-- HTML5 shim and Respond.js for IE8 support of HTML5 elements
    and media queries -->
  <!-- WARNING: Respond.js doesn't work if you view the page via
    file:// -->
  <!--[if lt IE 9]>
    <script src="https://oss.maxcdn.com/html5shiv/3.7.2/html5shiv.min.
js"></script>
    <script src="https://oss.maxcdn.com/respond/1.4.2/respond.min.
js"></script>
  <![endif]-->
</head>
<body>

  <%- partial("partial/_header") %>

  <%- yield %>

  <%- partial("partial/_footer") %>

  <!-- javascript //-->
  <script src="//ajax.googleapis.com/ajax/libs/jquery/1.11.1/jquery.
min.js"></script>
  <script src="js/bootstrap.min.js"
    type="text/javascript"></script>
```

```
<!-- show and hide search bar //-->
<script>
  $(document).ready(function() {
    $("#header-search").hide();
    $("#search-trigger").on("click", function() {
      $("#header-search").toggle();
    });
  });
</script>
</body>
</html>
```

Updating the Less variables

The next template file we need to make some changes to is our Less variables file. If you've forgotten, you can find that file at:

```
/css/components/_variables.less
```

Open the file and paste in the following color variables. We're not going to replace our existing colors, we're going to simply add more for this project. It's not a good idea to replace the base colors as that won't make your theme interchangeable:

```
@md-black: #212121;
@md-dark-blue: #303f9f;
@md-blue: #3f51b5;
@md-light-blue: #c5cae9;
@md-pink: #ff4081;
@md-grey: #727272;
@md-light-grey: #b6b6b6;
```

I've name spaced each of the colors with md- so it's easy to tell the difference between our base color palette and our new material design colors. By the way, if you're looking for a great tool to generate material design color palettes, check out http://www.materialpalette.com/.

Updating the text colors

Next, let's update our text color variables to use the new material design colors:

```
@primary-text: @md-black;
@light-text: @md-grey;
@loud-text: @md-black;
@inverse-text: @white;
@heading-text: @md-dark-blue;
```

I'll also update the link colors to use or you can use new colors:

```
@primary-link-color: @md-blue;
@primary-link-color-hover: @md-grey;
```

The last colors we need to update are the border colors:

```
@border-focus: @md-blue;
@secondary-border-color: @md-blue;
```

That's it for color updates. The last thing we need to change in this file is our typeface properties. Let's update our text variables to use Roboto:

```
@body-copy: "Roboto", helvetica, arial, verdana, sans-serif;
@heading-copy: "Roboto", helvetica, arial, verdana, sans-serif;
@heading-copy-bold: "Roboto", helvetica, arial, verdana, sans-serif;
```

That's it, that's all. Let's take a look at the entire `_variables.less` file to make sure we haven't missed anything:

```
// color palette
@black: #000;
@dark-grey: #333;
@grey: #ccc;
@light-grey: #ebebeb;
@off-white: #f5f5f5;
@white: #ffffff;

@blue1: #3498db;
@blue2: #2980b9;
@red1: #e74c3c;
@red2: #c0392b;
@yellow1: #f1c40f;
@yellow2: #f39c12;
@green1: #2ecc71;
@green2: #27ae60;
@orange1: #e67e22;
@orange2: #d35400;
@aqua1: #1abc9c;
@aqua2: #16a085;
@purple1: #9b59b6;
@purple2: #8e44ad;
@navy1: #34495e;
@navy2: #2c3e50;
```

```less
// material design colors materialpalette.com
@md-black: #212121;
@md-dark-blue: #303f9f;
@md-blue: #3f51b5;
@md-light-blue: #c5cae9;
@md-pink: #ff4081;
@md-grey: #727272;
@md-light-grey: #b6b6b6;

// background colors
@primary-background: @white;
@secondary-background: @off-white;
@third-background: @md-light-grey;
@fourth-background: @md-grey;
@inverse-background: @md-dark-blue;

// text colors
@primary-text: @md-black;
@light-text: @md-grey;
@loud-text: @md-black;
@inverse-text: @white;
@heading-text: @md-dark-blue;

// link colors
@primary-link-color: @md-blue;
@primary-link-color-hover: @md-grey;

// primary border properties
@border-color: @md-light-grey;
@border-size: 1px;
@border-type: solid;
@border-focus: @md-blue;
@secondary-border-color: @md-blue;

// typography
@body-copy: "Roboto", helvetica, arial, verdana, sans-serif;
@heading-copy: "Roboto", helvetica, arial, verdana, sans-serif;
@heading-copy-bold: "Roboto", helvetica, arial, verdana, sans-serif;
@base-font-size: 14px;
@font-size: 1em;
@base-line-height: 1.5;

// layout
@margin: 1em;
```

```
@padding: 1em;

// MIXINS

// round corners or Border radius
.round-corners (@radius: 2px) {
  -moz-border-radius: @radius;
  -ms-border-radius: @radius;
  border-radius: @radius;
}

// animation transitions
.transition (@transition: background .1s linear) {
  -moz-transition: @transition;
  -webkit-transition: @transition;
  transition: background @transition;
}
```

Our project's look and feel is now updated. By the way, isn't it great that we can create a new visual design so easily? That's why it's really important to have a base theme, as in *Chapter 1, Advanced Bootstrap Development Tools*, which you can use as a boilerplate for all your projects. Why reinvent the wheel each time? We'll be adding a bunch of additional CSS as we work through this chapter. For now, let's finish up the header and the footer. We'll jump back to the CSS as it comes up.

Setting up the header

For the projects header, we are going to use the default Bootstrap navbar and style it to match our look and feel. We are also going to expand are header to use a couple of custom sections. The first will be a collapsible search bar section and the second will be some feed filters. We'll start off by wrapping the entire header in a <div> with the class of .header:

```
<div class="header">
```

We are wrapping the entire header so we can apply some bottom-margin to the entire section:

```
.header {
  margin-bottom: (@margin * 2);
}
```

We'll also wrap the default Bootstrap `navbar` in another `<div>` with a class of `.header-nav`:

```
<div class="header-nav">
```

This additional `<div>` will allow us to set the background color for the entire width of the section. Otherwise, there would be a few pixels on either side that aren't covered by styling the `.navbar` class:

```
.header-nav {
  background: @md-blue;
}
```

The next section I'll setup is the collapsible search bar. I'm going to wrap this section in a `<div>` tag with an ID of `#header-search`. In this case, I'm going to use an ID because I want to target this section with jQuery a little later:

```
<div id="header-search">
```

I'll go into full detail on the search bar a little later. For now, just set up the section. The last section of our header that we need to set up is the filters. For this part, insert a third `<div>` tag with the class name `.header-filters`:

```
<div class="header-filters">
```

Close that section off and the skeleton for our header is complete. You should enter all this code into our `_header.ejs` partial if you're wondering. Let's jump back to the Bootstrap `navbar` section and go over the HTML and CSS.

Navbar

The actual markup for this is pretty straightforward. If you've coded a Bootstrap header before, then this will look very familiar. Here's the entire section of code:

```
<nav class="navbar navbar-default">
    <div class="container">
      <!-- Brand and toggle get grouped for better mobile
        display -->
      <div class="navbar-header">
        <button type="button" class="navbar-toggle collapsed"
          data-toggle="collapse" data-target="#bs-example-
            navbar-collapse-1" aria-expanded="false">
          <span class="sr-only">Toggle navigation</span>
          <span class="icon-bar"></span>
          <span class="icon-bar"></span>
          <span class="icon-bar"></span>
        </button>
```

```
        <a class="navbar-brand" href="#">Agger</a>
    </div>

    <!-- Collect the nav links, forms, and other content for
        toggling -->
    <div class="collapse navbar-collapse" id="bs-example-
        navbar-collapse-1">
        <ul class="nav navbar-nav">
            <li><a href="#" data-toggle="modal" data-
                target="#about-modal">About</a></li>
            <li><a href="#" data-toggle="modal" data-
                target="#contact-modal">Contact</a></li>
            <li><a href="#" data-toggle="modal" data-
                target="#login-modal">Login / Register</a></li>
            <li><a href="#" id="search-trigger"><i class="fa fa-
                search"></i></a></li>
        </ul>
    </div>
    </div>
</nav>
```

As I mentioned, this should be pretty straightforward. However, let's go over the parts that aren't right out of the Bootstrap box. I've added a name for our `.navbar-brand`, which is Agger. This is the name of the fictional aggregator product.

Modal triggers

In the navigation list of links, you'll notice I'm using modals for **About**, **Contact**, and **Login/Register**. I'm doing this because we are going to make this a one page app. The homepage or feed will be the primary view where the user can see their aggregated feeds. When they click on, say, **About** in the nav tag, a full page modal will appear over the top of the main page and contain the content for the **About** page. This way we can keep everything on one page instead of having to navigate away. For now, simply add in the link code and we'll go over the modals more in detail later:

```
<ul class="nav navbar-nav">
        <li><a href="#" data-toggle="modal" data-
            target="#about-modal">About</a></li>
        <li><a href="#" data-toggle="modal" data-
            target="#contact-modal">Contact</a></li>
        <li><a href="#" data-toggle="modal" data-
            target="#login-modal">Login / Register</a></li>
        <li><a href="#" id="search-trigger"><i class="fa fa-
            search"></i></a></li>
    </ul>
```

That concludes the setup of the primary navigation HTML for the project. To get the look and feel we want, we're going to need to do some customization to the navbar styles in our theme. Let's go over each part as follows:

```
.navbar {
  margin-bottom: 0;
}
```

First of all, I've removed the bottom margin from the navbar. This is done because once we reveal the hidden search field, we don't want a space between the two sections:

```
.navbar-default,
.navbar-default .navbar-collapse,
.navbar-default .navbar-form {
  background: @md-blue;
  text-transform: uppercase;
}
```

Next, I've changed the default navbar tag to use our material design blue. I've also converted the links to uppercase to match the material design style:

```
.navbar-default .navbar-brand {
  color: @inverse-text;
  font-weight: 700;
}
```

For the navbar brand, I want it to stick out a bit from the actual navigation links. To do that, I've set the color to c, which is set to @white. I've also bumped up the font-weight tag to bold or 700 to give it some extra emphasis:

```
.navbar-default .navbar-brand:focus,
.navbar-default .navbar-brand:hover {
  color: @md-light-blue;
}
```

I've also changed the focus and hover states for the navbar brand to use a material design color:

```
.navbar-default {
  border-color: @md-blue;
}
```

We need to set the border-color for the default `navbar` to the same color as the background. I don't want a different border color here, so just set it to this to match the flat design style:

```
.navbar-default .navbar-nav > li > a {
  color: @md-light-blue;
  text-transform: uppercase;
}
```

For our navigation links, I've set them to the material design light blue color. This is slightly subdued compared to our brand color, creating some typographic hierarchy. I've also converted the text to uppercase to match the material design style:

```
.navbar-default .navbar-nav > li > a:focus,
.navbar-default .navbar-nav > li > a:hover {
  color: @inverse-text;
}
```

For the hover state of the `navbar` links, I've gone with something a little more bold, which is the `@inverse-text` color again. Remember that is set to `@white`:

```
.navbar-default .navbar-toggle,
.navbar-default .navbar-toggle .icon-bar {
  border-color: @md-blue;
}
```

The preceding styles are the first ones that are mobile specific to our `navbar` tag. If the viewport is small enough, the `nav` will be rolled into a menu automatically that has a toggle button to open or close it. To make our design look a little less Bootstrap-y, I've actually set the border color of the toggle to the same color as the background. That way, you won't see the border and it will help to give you a more unique look. This is also more inline with the material design style:

```
.navbar-default .navbar-toggle .icon-bar {
  background-color: @md-light-blue;
}
```

The bars within the mobile toggle switch are actually drawn with code. Therefore, I'm changing their default color to use our color palette:

```
.navbar-default .navbar-toggle:focus,
.navbar-default .navbar-toggle:hover {
  background-color: @md-dark-blue;
}
```

The last part of this mobile toggle button is the hover state. I've set the background to our dark blue but I've left the lines the same. This way only the background of the button changes, which creates a nice subtle effect:

```
.navbar-default .navbar-collapse,
.navbar-default .navbar-form {
  border-color: @md-dark-blue;
}
```

These last styles control the bottom border of the mobile navbar once it's opened. I've set this to dark blue to add a simple visual treatment to divide the header from the list of links. That's it for our header styles, let's move onto the next section of the header, which is the search bar.

Search bar

One thing I didn't cover previously is the **Search** icon in the primary navigation. I'm using the Font Awesome, which we covered in the previous chapter, to insert a magnifying glass icon. This icon is wrapped in a link with the #search-trigger ID. As it's named, clicking on this link will be the trigger that reveals the search field:

```
<li><a href="#" id="search-trigger"><i class="fa fa-search"></i></a></li>
```

Go back to the <div> tag we setup earlier with the #header-search ID, and insert the following section of code:

```
<div class="container">
    <div class="row">
      <div class="col-lg-12">
        <div class="input-group">
          <input type="text" class="form-control"
            placeholder="Search for...">
          <span class="input-group-btn">
            <button class="btn btn-default"
              type="button">Go!</button>
          </span>
        </div>
      </div>
    </div>
  </div>
```

Before I jump into this code, let's actually review the styles for the `#header-search` ID:

```
#header-search {
    height: 60px;
    background: @secondary-background;
    padding: 0 (@padding * 1.5);
}
```

I want the height of the search section to match the `navbar` tag so I've manually set it to `60px`. I'd like the background color to be different, though, so I'm using the `@secondary-background` color variable. Finally, I've added some additional padding to the section.

Back to the code within our main section. First of all, I'm wrapping the whole thing in a `container` class so we can componentize this section. Next, I'll insert a full width column using the largest view port. In this case, we only need that one class because we want this column to stretch the width of our layout.

Before I jump further into the **Search** bar, I should mention that I've added `100px` of horizontal padding to the `container` class to add some breathing space in the layout:

```
.container {
    padding: 0 100px;
}
```

Within the column, you'll see I'm using a Bootstrap `.input-group` component. This component combines a form input with a button. They butt up right next to each other and give the feeling that they are actually one component. There is only one custom style that is needed on this input-group:

```
#header-search .input-group {
    margin-top: 13px;
}
```

I want the search field to be centered vertically in the section, so I've had to add `13px` of top margin to achieve this layout. That's it for the search section styles. Let's go over the jQuery that will trigger the toggle.

Search bar jQuery

Open up `_layout.ejs` and head to the bottom of the file. There you'll find the script we inserted when we setup this file a little while ago:

```
<script>
    $(document).ready(function() {
        $("#header-search").hide();
        $("#search-trigger").on("click", function() {
            $("#header-search").toggle();
        });
    });
</script>
```

I'll assume that you have a basic understanding of jQuery and not cover `document.ready`. Here's a breakdown of what this script is doing:

- Once the DOM is ready on page load, `#header-search <div>` is being hidden.
- If the `#search-trigger` link in the navigation is clicked, the click function is called and the `#header-search` section is shown using the `.toggle()` method.
- This method will also hide the section if the trigger button is clicked on again.

I'm not a jQuery master so you should be able to follow along pretty easily here. Save your file, fire up the Harp server and give this a try. Make sure you get this working before you go any further because you don't want to be troubleshooting JavaScript issues once the project is done. It's much easier to do it now before we add a bunch of additional code.

That completes the search bar section of the header. Click on the **Search** icon in the main `nav` bar a few times to ensure you are happy with the effect. You could consider adding a `.fadeIn()` jQuery method if you want to polish the transition further. If not, then move onto the final section of the header, which is our filters.

Filters

The filters section of the header is also pretty simple to setup. Let's start by looking at the CSS for wrapping the `.header-filters` class:

```
.header-filters {
  background: @primary-background;
  height: 60px;
  line-height: 60px;
}
```

I'm using a third color here for this section. If the search bar is visible, we want a different color for each section so you can see where the division is. I've also set the height of this section to 60px to match the previous two. Finally, the line-height property is also set to 60px as this will center anything in this area vertically. Let's take a look at the HTML for this section:

```html
<div class="container">
    <div class="row">
      <div class="col-lg-12">
        <ul class="list-inline">
          <li><a href="#" class="btn btn-primary btn-sm">Top
            Posts</a></li>
          <li><a href="#" class="btn btn-primary btn-sm">Recent
            Posts</a></li>
        </ul>
      </div>
    </div>
  </div>
```

You'll notice the structure of this section is very similar to the previous one. The exception here is that I'm using an unordered list to display the content instead of the input group. It's worth mentioning that you should strive to be as consistent as possible when planning the structure of sections like this. It makes your code much more modular and easier to scale and understand for other developers.

At this point, I'm using the default Bootstrap inline list component. Within each list item, we have a small button that will be used as a filter. You'll notice that the buttons are pink so I have definitely customized the primary button class. Let's take a look at the CSS:

```css
.btn-primary {
  background: @md-pink;
  border-color: @md-pink;
  text-transform: uppercase;
}
```

The background color and border color have both been set to the Material Design pink from our palette. I've also converted the text to uppercase:

```css
.btn-primary:hover {
  background: (@md-pink - #111);
  border-color: (@md-pink - #111);
}
```

Our button hover state is using a Less operator to change our background and border colors. You could insert a different color value here if you like. However, with buttons, you generally want a subtle change on hover. Using an operator like this will adjust the hex color slightly and give you a different shade of your primary color, which is a nice trick to have in your bag.

With this, we have completed the markup and styles for our header. Let's take a look at the complete HTML for the header partial before we move onto the footer:

```html
<div class="header">
  <!-- main nav //-->
  <div class="header-nav">
    <nav class="navbar navbar-default">
      <div class="container">
        <!-- Brand and toggle get grouped for better mobile
          display -->
        <div class="navbar-header">
          <button type="button" class="navbar-toggle collapsed"
            data-toggle="collapse" data-target="#bs-example-
              navbar-collapse-1" aria-expanded="false">
            <span class="sr-only">Toggle navigation</span>
            <span class="icon-bar"></span>
            <span class="icon-bar"></span>
            <span class="icon-bar"></span>
          </button>
          <a class="navbar-brand" href="#">Agger</a>
        </div>

        <!-- Collect the nav links, forms, and other content for
          toggling -->
        <div class="collapse navbar-collapse" id="bs-example-
          navbar-collapse-1">
          <ul class="nav navbar-nav">
            <li><a href="#" data-toggle="modal" data-
              target="#about-modal">About</a></li>
            <li><a href="#" data-toggle="modal" data-
              target="#contact-modal">Contact</a></li>
            <li><a href="#" data-toggle="modal" data-
              target="#login-modal">Login / Register</a></li>
            <li><a href="#" id="search-trigger"><i class="fa fa-
              search"></i></a></li>
          </ul>
        </div>
      </div>
    </nav>
```

```
      </div>
      <!-- search field //-->
      <div id="header-search">
        <div class="container">
          <div class="row">
            <div class="col-lg-12">
              <div class="input-group">
                <input type="text" class="form-control"
                    placeholder="Search for...">
                <span class="input-group-btn">
                  <button class="btn btn-default"
                      type="button">Go!</button>
                </span>
              </div>
            </div>
          </div>
        </div>
      </div>
      <!-- top filters //-->
      <div class="header-filters">
        <div class="container">
          <div class="row">
            <div class="col-lg-12">
              <ul class="list-inline">
                <li><a href="#" class="btn btn-primary btn-sm">Top
                    Posts</a></li>
                <li><a href="#" class="btn btn-primary btn-sm">Recent
                    Posts</a></li>
              </ul>
            </div>
          </div>
        </div>
      </div>
    </div>
```

 Remember to make sure you are breaking the Less code for each
component into its own `.less` file. Those component files should be
living in a subdirectory of /css called /components. You should then
be importing the component files into your master theme file.

Setting up the footer

For the project footer, we're going to keep things pretty simple. I'll be inserting some social media icon links using the Font Awesome and a simple copyright statement. Open up the `_footer.ejs` partial and paste in the following HTML:

```
<footer>
  <div class="container-fluid">
    <div class="row">
      <div class="col-lg-12">
        <ul class="list-inline">
          <li><a href="#"><i class="fa fa-facebook-
            official"></i></a></li>
          <li><a href="#"><i class="fa fa-twitter-
            square"></i></a></li>
          <li><a href="#"><i class="fa fa-pinterest-
            square"></i></a></li>
          <li><a href="#"><i class="fa fa-linkedin-
            square"></i></a></li>
        </ul>
        <p>&copy; 2015 Agger</p>
      </div>
    </div>
  </div>
</footer>
```

The layout here is pretty basic. We only need to set the large viewport grid class as this section will always span the width of the layout. I'm using the Bootstrap inline list component to display the social media icons. You'll notice I'm using the Font Awesome icon classes for the social media links. Finally, I've wrapped the entire section in the `<footer>` tag and am using it to apply some global footer styles:

```
footer {
  margin-top: (@margin * 6);
  padding-bottom: (@padding * 6);
  padding-top: (@padding * 2);
  background: @md-grey;
  color: @md-light-grey;
  text-align: center;
}
```

Here's a breakdown of the styles for the header section of the project:

- I've added a healthy top margin of 6 ems to allow for some breathing room from the body of the page.

- I've also added a good amount of bottom padding so the text is not butted up right against the bottom of the browser window.

- I've also added a little bit of top padding so that our icons will have some space above them.
- I've set the background color to use the material design dark grey from our palette.
- To create a nice subtle effect, I've set the text color to the light grey from our palette. This will also be the color for our social media icons.
- Finally, I've set the alignment to center for the entire section.

The other styles we need to apply to the footer are for the links:

```
footer a {
  font-size: (@font-size * 2);
  color: @md-light-grey;
}

footer a:hover {
  color: @inverse-text;
}
```

I've bumped up the font size of the links to double the normal size so that the social media icons are more noticeable. I also set the link color to the same as the text color. Finally, the hover color is set to `@inverse-text` or `@white`. That concludes the footer section and our template is now ready to go. Next, we'll focus on the body of our page and the modals that will be used for the **About, Contact,** and **Login** sections.

Single page apps

A popular trend in web development today is the single page app. From a static website design standpoint, that might sound a little scary. How do I approach an app that is only one page when I'm used to dealing in multiple pages? It's actually not that tough if you are strategic in how you design your project.

For this chapter, our project has the following pages or sections: **Home, About, Contact,** and **Login/Registration**. Normally, you would treat those as four different pages. With my design, home is the only actual page. The other elements will be built off the home page. A little later, we'll do some heavy customization to the Bootstrap modal component for the other sections we need.

For now, don't worry about this. I'm bringing it up because this project will only have one actual page template, which is `index.ejs`.

Setting up the index page

The layout for the body of the page is the first place where we will use some different grid classes. When the project is viewed on the desktop, there will be a main feed on the left and a sidebar on the right. If we switch to viewing this on a mobile device, there will be only one column with the sidebar sliding in below the main feed. Here's the grid code we'll use to set this up:

```
<div class="col-xs-12 col-lg-8">
...
</div>
<div class="col-xs-12 col-lg-3 col-lg-offset-1">
...
</div>
```

The first column uses the `col-lg-8` class for the desktop, which will set the feed to roughly three-fourth of the width of the layout. However, for mobile devices, I'm using the `col-xs-12` class because I want it to span the width of the layout. The second column is the sidebar and for the desktop I'm offsetting it by one column with the `col-lg-offset-1` class, then I'm using the `col-lg-3` class to fill in the rest of the row. This will set the sidebar to be roughly the remaining one-fourth of the layout. For mobile devices, I'm using the `col-xs-12` class again. This will cause the sidebar to slide in below the feed on mobile viewport.

Feed

Let's now look at the HTML for the feed section of the page. Within the feed section, I'm going to create a new reusable class called `.post` that we'll use for each aggregator entry:

```
<div class="feed">
    <div class="well">
      <h4>Aggregate your feeds with Agger.</h4>
    </div>
    <div class="row">
      <div class="col-lg-12">
        <div class="post">
          <h4><a href="#">Link Title Here</a>
            <small>(url.com/goes/here)</small></h4>
          <p><small>Posted 5 hours ago on <a
            href="#">Facebook</a></small></p>
        </div>
        <div class="post">
```

```
      <h4><a href="#">Link Title Here Longer</a>
        <small>(url.com/goes/here)</small></h4>
      <p><small>Posted 5 hours ago on <a
        href="#">Twitter</a></small></p>
    </div>
    <div class="post">
      <h4><a href="#">Link Title Here Much Longer</a>
        <small>(url.com/goes/here)</small></h4>
      <p><small>Posted 5 hours ago on <a
        href="#">Pintrest</a></small></p>
    </div>
    <div class="post">
      <h4><a href="#">Link Title Here And Stuff</a>
        <small>(url.com/goes/here)</small></h4>
      <p><small>Posted 5 hours ago on <a
        href="#">Linkedin</a></small></p>
    </div>
    <div class="post">
      <h4><a href="#">Link Title Here Like Really Long
        One</a> <small>(url.com/goes/here)</small></h4>
      <p><small>Posted 5 hours ago on <a
        href="#">Facebook</a></small></p>
    </div>
    <div class="post">
      <h4><a href="#">Link Title Here For Days</a>
        <small>(url.com/goes/here)</small></h4>
      <p><small>Posted 5 hours ago on <a
        href="#">Twitter</a></small></p>
    </div>
    <div class="post">
      <h4><a href="#">Link Title Here All-Time Longest
        Title</a> <small>(url.com/goes/here)</small></h4>
      <p><small>Posted 5 hours ago on <a
        href="#">Pintrest</a></small></p>
    </div>
    <div class="post">
      <h4><a href="#">Link Title Here</a>
        <small>(url.com/goes/here)</small></h4>
      <p><small>Posted 5 hours ago on <a
        href="#">Linkedin</a></small></p>
    </div>
  </div>
</div>
<!-- nav //-->
<div class="row">
```

```
            <div class="col-lg-6 col-xs-6">
              <div class="feed-pages">
                <small>Page 1 of 21</small>
              </div>
            </div>
            <div class="col-lg-6 col-xs-6q">
              <div class="feed-nav pull-right">
                <button class="btn btn-primary">Next</button>
              </div>
            </div>
          </div>
        </div>
```

This section is pretty long so let me break down each part for you. We'll start with the wrapping feed class. The entire feed is contained in a `<div>` tag with a class of `.feed` on it. We'll use this section to hold all of our aggregator entries. Here are the styles for this wrapping section:

```
.feed {
  background: @primary-background;
  padding: (@padding * 2);
  margin-bottom: (@margin * 2);
  .round-corners;
}
```

The background color of the entire page is light-grey. I want the feed section to pop so I'm going to set it to white using the `@primary-background` color variable. Since we're using a different background color here, let's add some padding to the section to apply some whitespace. I'll also add a little bit of a bottom margin so if you were to add another section, it will be spaced out properly. Finally, I've added the border-radius mixin to give the whole white section round corners.

Adding the feed header

Primarily, for visual design reasons, I've decided to add a subheader inside the feed that you can use to enter a little marketing message. In this case, I've entered a basic description of what the web app would do: "Aggregate your feeds with Agger". To make this stick out, I've stuck it inside a Bootstrap well component:

```
<div class="well">
  <h4>Aggregate your feeds with Agger.</h4>
</div>
```

I've also added some custom `well` styles so that it matches our look and feel. Create a new component Less file in `css/components` called `_well.less`. Then, update your master theme to import this new file. Within the less file, add the following styles:

```
.well {
  border: 0;
  box-shadow: none;
  .round-corners;
}

.feed .well {
  background-color: @md-grey;
  color: @white;
}
```

First of all, I've removed the well border and box-shadow so that it matches the material design style. I've also applied the border-radius mixin so that the value of the round corners is consistent throughout the project.

The second section creates some styles specific to the well that appears inside the feed section. The reason I've done so that incase you want to use a well outside of the feed. You might not want to apply the same colors, so it's good to make these colors specific to this section. I've set the background-color to the Material Design grey and the text color to white.

Filling in the posts section

The following section is the actual feed of social media posts. Within this section, I've created a reusable class called `.post` for each entry. I've also wrapped the entire section in a new row that has another column class on it:

```
<div class="col-lg-12">
```

You'll notice that I've only applied a desktop specific column class here and it's set to span the width of the layout. Remember, this is a nested row within the three-fourth layout, so in this case we always want it to span the width of the section. Therefore, it doesn't matter if you're viewing this on a desktop or mobile, you want the feed to fill in the entire parent column.

Within this new row and column, we have a collection of `<div>` with the new `.post` class on them. Let's take a look at a single post and breakdown the markup and styles:

```
<div class="post">
            <h4><a href="#">Link Title Here</a> <small>(url.com/
goes/here)</small></h4>
            <p><small>Posted 5 hours ago on <a href="#">Facebook</
a></small></p>
        </div>
```

First off, I've wrapped the entire section in a `<div>` tag with the class of `.post`:

```
.post {
  padding-bottom: @padding;
  border-bottom: @border-size @light-grey @border-type;
  margin-top: (@margin * 2);
}
```

For each post, we want to space them out a bit so I've added some bottom padding. I also want a bottom border to help divide each post so I've added that in. Finally, I've added a top margin so the contained text doesn't bump up right against the bottom border. One problem with this layout is that the first feed post doesn't need the top margin. The well component has already provided the necessary spacing. So, what we need to do is apply a pseudo selector to the first post and remove that top margin:

```
.post:first-child {
  margin-top: 0;
}
```

We can do that easily enough by targeting the first post child with the first-child pseudo selector. Then, we can remove the margin for that post only.

Now, let's cover the contents of each post section. We'll start off by wrapping the post title in a `<h4>` tag and making it a link to the actual post or story on the appropriate social network. Nesting the `<small>` tag within the `<h4>` tag, we can take advantage of some default Bootstrap typography styles. Within the `<small>` tag, I've inserted the URL to the page for the user's reference. Following the post title, I've used a `<p>` tag with a nested `<small>` tag for the post meta.

I've used the `<small>` tag a few times in this section and I've also applied some custom CSS for the tag:

```
.post small {
  color: @md-light-grey;
}

.post small a {
  color: @md-light-grey;
  text-decoration: underline;
}

.post small a:hover {
  color: @md-grey;
}
```

Let's take a closer look at what's happening with the CSS in this section.

- I've changed the text color of the `<small>` tag to use the light grey from our Material Design palette.
- I've also changed the link color within a `<small>` tag to use the same light grey.
- The link underline has also been removed from any `hrefs` inside a `<small>` tag.
- The hover color for links nested in a `<small>` tag has also been updated to use a Material Design color.
- Also note that I'm only targeting `<small>` tags nested inside `.post`. Therefore, if you use the tag outside of a post, it will fall back to the default Bootstrap styling.

That concludes the markup and styles for the posts in the feed. The last thing we need to add to the feed is some pagination.

Adding pagination to the feed

Once you've closed off the post's row, we need to add another row that will hold the pagination for the feed. Pagination will consist of a post count and a next button to load the next ten posts:

```
<div class="row">
        <div class="col-lg-6 col-xs-6">
          <div class="feed-pages">
            <small>Page 1 of 21</small>
          </div>
        </div>
```

```
<div class="col-lg-6 col-xs-6q">
  <div class="feed-nav pull-right">
    <button class="btn btn-primary">Next</button>
  </div>
</div>
</div>
```

For pagination, we're going to use some mobile column classes again. The reason for this is that we want the post count and the next button to stay on their respective sides of the layout. I don't want the button to slide in under the post count on mobile devices. To do this, we simply have to split the columns into two equals halves:

```
<div class="col-lg-6 col-xs-6">
...
</div>
<div class="col-lg-6 col-xs-6">
...
</div>
```

The code here should be pretty straightforward based on the previous explanation of the feed. One thing to keep in mind is that if your count gets really large, like several thousand posts, you might need to rebalance this a bit to make the first column wider to allow for the large numbers. Otherwise, the count might break onto two lines. However, I think it would be pretty hard to get it that wide.

Adding the feed count and the next button

For the feed count part of the pagination, I've wrapped the count in a `<div>` tag with a class of `.feed-pages`. This will allow me to style this a bit. The styling for this section is actually the same as the next button, which has a `<div>` tag with a class of `.feed-nav`:

```
.feed-nav,
.feed-pages {
  margin-top: (@margin * 2);
}
```

All I've done here is add the same top margin to the pagination that the post entries had. This will keep the flow of the layout consistent. Within the `.feed-pages` section, I'm using the `<small>` tag again to make this text subtle. In the `.feed-nav` section, I've added a primary button and the wrapping class takes advantage of the Bootstrap `.pull-right` utility class to align the button on the right side of the column. That concludes the feed section of the layout. The last part of the homepage we need to go over is the sidebar.

Sidebar

The sidebar of the web app is designed to be a deeper filters section for controlling what content shows up. This is all static so you need to use your imagination a bit. The idea is that you would check or uncheck boxes and the feed would automatically update to show the changes. Here's the full markup for the section:

```
<div class="col-xs-12 col-lg-3 col-lg-offset-1">
    <h4>Channels</h4>
    <div class="checkbox">
      <label>
        <input type="checkbox" checked> Facebook
      </label>
    </div>
    <div class="checkbox">
      <label>
        <input type="checkbox" checked> Twitter
      </label>
    </div>
    <div class="checkbox">
      <label>
        <input type="checkbox" checked> Pintrest
      </label>
    </div>
    <div class="checkbox">
      <label>
        <input type="checkbox" checked> Linkedin
      </label>
    </div>
    <div class="checkbox">
      <label>
        <input type="checkbox"> Google+
      </label>
    </div>
    <hr />
    <h4>Filters</h4>
    <div class="checkbox">
      <label>
        <input type="checkbox" checked> Comments
      </label>
    </div>
    <div class="checkbox">
      <label>
```

```
          <input type="checkbox"> Recent Comments
        </label>
      </div>
      <div class="checkbox">
        <label>
          <input type="checkbox"> Top Posts
        </label>
      </div>
      <div class="checkbox">
        <label>
          <input type="checkbox"> Recent Posts
        </label>
      </div>
      <hr />
      <p><a href="#">RSS Feed</a></p>
    </div>
```

This section is actually pretty easy to breakdown. I'm using all default Bootstrap styling and components here. Each filter section has a title wrapped in a `<h4>` tag. Below that is a collection of checkbox form components that would be used to toggle posts on and off. Finally, at the bottom, there is a simple text link to an RSS Feed of the master feed. The RSS Feed link should be a standard feature with any aggregator app incase the user wants to subscribe to your feed.

That concludes the sidebar design and the markup for the homepage view of the project. The last sections we need to review are all the modals. To make this a one-page app, we're going to include the markup for the modals at the bottom of `index.ejs`. This contains all of our views to one file, which is really handy. If you wanted to get a bit more fancy, you could break each modal into its own partial and simply import them into the bottom of `index.ejs`. However, for this exercise, I'm going to keep it simple and add the markup right into the file.

About modal

The first modal we're going to tackle is the **About** section. What I'm doing here is wrangling the modal component to make it fill the entire screen, giving it the appearance of a page floating over the top of the homepage. The actual HTML structure of the modal doesn't change very much, but we will be doing some advanced styling. Here's the markup for the modal:

```
<div class="modal fade" id="about-modal">
  <div class="modal-dialog">
    <div class="modal-content">
      <div class="modal-header">
```

```
    <button type="button" class="close" data-dismiss="modal"
      aria-label="Close"><span aria-
        hidden="true">&times;</span></button>
    <h4 class="modal-title">About</h4>
  </div>
  <div class="modal-body">
    <div class="row">
      <div class="col-lg-8">
        <p><img src="http://fillmurray.com/400/300"></p>
        <p>Pellentesque habitant morbi...</p>
        <p>Pellentesque habitant morbi...</p>
      <p>Pellentesque habitant morbi...</p>
      </div>
    </div>
  </div>
</div><!-- /.modal-content -->
</div><!-- /.modal-dialog -->
</div><!-- /.modal -->
```

The first thing you should do is give the modal a unique ID on the first `<div>`. In this case, I've given it an ID of #about-modal. Each modal needs a unique ID so that the browser knows which one to trigger on the button press. From there, the modal markup is out-of-the-box Bootstrap with one exception. The only difference is that we are going to remove the .modal-footer section. This section contains the **Close** and **Submit** buttons, which don't really fit our design. We want to give the appearance that this is a page floating over the homepage, not a modal. We keep the closing X in the .modal-header tag, which is how we will dismiss the modal.

Now that we've laid out the markup for the modal, let's go over all the styles that need customization. Create a new Less component file in css/components called _modal.less. Make sure you import this file into your master theme:

```
.modal-dialog {
  margin: 0;
  width: auto;
}
```

The first thing we're going to do is edit the .modal-dialog class. We'll remove the margin and set the width to auto, which will make the modal span the width of the browser:

```
.modal-backdrop {
  background: @md-pink;
  opacity: 0.9!important;
}
```

Next, we need to edit the .modal-backdrop class. This class controls the semi-transparent black background that shows in the default modal. I've made a couple of changes here that are important. First, I've changed the background to @md-pink to fit in with our color palette. Second, I've set the opacity function of the backdrop to 0.9. By default, the opacity is much lower and that makes text on top of it harder to read. We want to darken this for readability. You'll also notice, I'm using the !important helper here. Normally, this should be avoided at all costs. The reason it's acceptable here is because this property is applied in Bootstrap.min,js. I don't really want to start editing the library JavaScript so we're going to overwrite this property once the DOM loads using !important:

```
.modal-content {
  background: none;
  color: @inverse-text;
  box-shadow: none;
  border: 0;

  -moz-border-radius: 0px;
  border-radius: 0px;
}
```

The next part we need to customize is the .modal-content class. We're going to remove the background here so that the pink we set in the backdrop shows through. This will make the overlay look more like a page and Less like a modal. Since the background is pink, I've changed the text color to @inverse-text or white. I've also removed the box-shadow, borders, and border-radius from the modal to make it look like a page. These changes are more about resetting the default component to wrestle it into something new. This is a great example of how you can make websites unique using Bootstrap. I constantly hear the complaint that all Bootstrap sites look the same. That couldn't be more false if you put a little effort and creativity in:

```
.modal-content p {
  margin-bottom: (@margin * 1.5);
}
```

The default modal isn't really designed to hold paragraphs of content. Therefore, the spacing between <p> tags is really tight. This customization is adding in spacing more consistent to what you'd see on a regular text page. It's all about making the content more readable:

```
.modal-header {
  border-bottom: 0;
}
```

For the `.modal-header` class, I've removed the bottom border to, once again, make this look more like a page, not a modal:

```
.close {
  color: @inverse-text;
  text-shadow: none;
  opacity: 1;
}
```

The last part of the header we need to change is the `.close` class. This is the X button in the top-right corner of the modal. I've changed the color to `@inverse-text` so that it matches our body copy color. I've removed the text-shadow to make it fit into the material design style. Finally, I bumped up the opacity of the button. We want it to be really noticeable as this is the only way to close the modal:

```
.modal a {
  color: @inverse-text;
  text-decoration: underline;
}

.modal a:hover {
  color: @md-black;
}
```

I've also updated the link styles for the modal to better match the overall new look and feel. I've set the link color to `@inverse-text` and added the link underline back in so they stand out from the regular text. I've also added a really contrasting hover color so that it's really clear when you hover over a link.

That's the final CSS we need to customize for the first modal. There are a few other form styles we'll need to update for the **Contact** and **Login** modals. I'll cover those next.

The Contact modal

The `Contact` modal is setup exactly like the `About` modal, with the exception that we are going to include a form in this section. Insert the following modal code below the `About` modal in `index.ejs`:

```
<div class="modal fade" id="contact-modal">
  <div class="modal-dialog">
    <div class="modal-content">
      <div class="modal-header">
        <button type="button" class="close" data-dismiss="modal"
          aria-label="Close"><span aria-
            hidden="true">&times;</span></button>
```

```
        <h4 class="modal-title">Contact</h4>
      </div>
      <div class="modal-body">
        <div class="row">
          <div class="col-lg-6">
            <p>Pellentesque habitant morbi tristique senectus et
              netus et malesuada fames ac turpis egestas.
                Vestibulum tortor quam, feugiat vitae, ultricies
                  eget, tempor sit amet, ante. Donec eu libero sit
                    amet quam egestas semper. Aenean ultricies mi
                      vitae est. Mauris placerat eleifend leo.</p>
            <form>
              <div class="form-group">
                <label>Name</label>
                <input type="text" class="form-control">
              </div>
              <div class="form-group">
                <label>Email</label>
                <input type="text" class="form-control">
              </div>
              <div class="form-group">
                <label>Message</label>
                <textarea class="form-control"
                  rows="10"></textarea>
              </div>
              <button type="submit" class="btn btn-
                default">Send</button>
            </form>
          </div>
        </div>
      </div>
    </div><!-- /.modal-content -->
  </div><!-- /.modal-dialog -->
</div><!-- /.modal -->
```

The first thing you should do with this second modal is give it a unique ID. For the example, I've called the modal #contact-modal. For the body of this modal, I've included a new row with a column class of col-lg-6. The reason I've done that is because I don't want the form inputs to stretch the width of the layout. That would look a bit weird so I'm going to limit their width.

At the top of the body section, I've included a `<p>` tag where you can enter a message or description for the **Contact** form. Below that, I've inserted a basic Bootstrap form. There are a few styles for the form that we need to customize, which are outlined as follows:

```
.modal form {
  margin-bottom: (@margin * 2);
}
```

I've added a bottom margin to our form so that it doesn't bump up against the bottom of the browser window. This will insert a little bit of whitespace for readability:

```
.modal .form-control {
  border: 0;
  box-shadow: none;

  .round-corners;
}
```

For the form control or input, I've reset a few styles to make the form fit our look and feel. First off, I've removed the border around the inputs. Since the background is pink, we don't really need these borders to make the fields stand out. I've also removed the box-shadow because that doesn't jive with our flat design style. Finally, I've reset the border-radius of the inputs to match our other components for consistency:

```
.modal .btn-default {
  border: 0;
}
```

Similar to the input borders, we don't really need the button border here since it's sitting on a pink background. I'm also using the `default` button here, which is white, instead of using the pink primary button. That button type wouldn't work very well on a pink background. That concludes the customizations we need to make to the form styles inside of a modal. Let's move onto the following modal, which is for the Login and Registration section.

Login modal

The last modal or section we need to cover is the **Login** and **Registration** modal. This one is going to be very similar to the Contact modal because it's a form. Let's jump in and look at the HTML markup:

```html
<div class="modal fade" id="login-modal">
  <div class="modal-dialog">
    <div class="modal-content">
      <div class="modal-header">
        <button type="button" class="close" data-dismiss="modal"
          aria-label="Close"><span aria-
            hidden="true">&times;</span></button>
        <h4 class="modal-title">Login</h4>
      </div>
      <div class="modal-body">
        <div class="row">
          <div class="col-lg-6">
            <p>Pellentesque habitant morbi tristique senectus et
              netus et malesuada fames ac turpis egestas.
                Vestibulum tortor quam, feugiat vitae, ultricies
                  eget, tempor sit amet, ante. Donec eu libero sit
                    amet quam egestas semper. Aenean ultricies mi
                      vitae est. Mauris placerat eleifend leo.</p>
            <form>
              <div class="form-group">
                <label>Email</label>
                <input type="text" class="form-control">
              </div>
              <div class="form-group">
                <label>Password</label>
                <input type="password" class="form-control">
              </div>
              <p><small><a href="#">Forgot
                Password?</a></small></p>
              <button type="submit" class="btn btn-default">Sign
                Up</button>
            </form>
            <p>If you don't have an account, you can <a
              href="#">Register Here</a>.</p>
          </div>
        </div>
      </div>
    </div><!-- /.modal-content -->
  </div><!-- /.modal-dialog -->
</div><!-- /.modal -->
```

Like we did with the previous modals, make sure you give this one a unique ID. I've named the Login modal #login-modal. Like with the Contact modal, I've made the form span only half of the page with the col-lg-6 column class. I've inserted a new form that uses the same inputs as the previous modal. We're not using any new components here, so we don't actually need to add anymore CSS. That brings our single page app layout to its completion. Let's take a look at all of the markup together for reference purposes:

```
<div class="container">
  <div class="row">
    <div class="col-xs-12 col-lg-8">
      <div class="feed">
        <div class="well">
          <h4>Aggregate your feeds with Agger.</h4>
        </div>
        <div class="row">
          <div class="col-lg-12">
            <div class="post">
              <h4><a href="#">Link Title Here</a>
                <small>(url.com/goes/here)</small></h4>
              <p><small>Posted 5 hours ago on <a
                href="#">Facebook</a></small></p>
            </div>
            <div class="post">
              <h4><a href="#">Link Title Here Longer</a>
                <small>(url.com/goes/here)</small></h4>
              <p><small>Posted 5 hours ago on <a
                href="#">Twitter</a></small></p>
            </div>
            <div class="post">
              <h4><a href="#">Link Title Here Much Longer</a>
                <small>(url.com/goes/here)</small></h4>
              <p><small>Posted 5 hours ago on <a
                href="#">Pintrest</a></small></p>
            </div>
            <div class="post">
              <h4><a href="#">Link Title Here And Stuff</a>
                <small>(url.com/goes/here)</small></h4>
              <p><small>Posted 5 hours ago on <a
                href="#">Linkedin</a></small></p>
            </div>
            <div class="post">
              <h4><a href="#">Link Title Here Like Really Long
                One</a> <small>(url.com/goes/here)</small></h4>
```

```
        <p><small>Posted 5 hours ago on <a
          href="#">Facebook</a></small></p>
      </div>
      <div class="post">
        <h4><a href="#">Link Title Here For Days</a>
          <small>(url.com/goes/here)</small></h4>
        <p><small>Posted 5 hours ago on <a
          href="#">Twitter</a></small></p>
      </div>
      <div class="post">
        <h4><a href="#">Link Title Here All-Time Longest
          Title</a> <small>(url.com/goes/here)</small></h4>
        <p><small>Posted 5 hours ago on <a
          href="#">Pintrest</a></small></p>
      </div>
      <div class="post">
        <h4><a href="#">Link Title Here</a>
          <small>(url.com/goes/here)</small></h4>
        <p><small>Posted 5 hours ago on <a
          href="#">Linkedin</a></small></p>
      </div>
    </div>
  </div>
  <!-- nav //-->
  <div class="row">
    <div class="col-lg-6 col-xs-6">
      <div class="feed-pages">
        <small>Page 1 of 21</small>
      </div>
    </div>
    <div class="col-lg-6 col-xs-6q">
      <div class="feed-nav pull-right">
        <button class="btn btn-primary">Next</button>
      </div>
    </div>
  </div>
</div>
</div>
<!-- right //-->
<div class="col-xs-12 col-lg-3 col-lg-offset-1">
  <h4>Channels</h4>
  <div class="checkbox">
    <label>
      <input type="checkbox" checked> Facebook
    </label>
```

```
    </div>
    <div class="checkbox">
      <label>
        <input type="checkbox" checked> Twitter
      </label>
    </div>
    <div class="checkbox">
      <label>
        <input type="checkbox" checked> Pintrest
      </label>
    </div>
    <div class="checkbox">
      <label>
        <input type="checkbox" checked> Linkedin
      </label>
    </div>
    <div class="checkbox">
      <label>
        <input type="checkbox"> Google+
      </label>
    </div>
    <hr/>
    <h4>Filters</h4>
    <div class="checkbox">
      <label>
        <input type="checkbox" checked> Comments
      </label>
    </div>
    <div class="checkbox">
      <label>
        <input type="checkbox"> Recent Comments
      </label>
    </div>
    <div class="checkbox">
      <label>
        <input type="checkbox"> Top Posts
      </label>
    </div>
    <div class="checkbox">
      <label>
        <input type="checkbox"> Recent Posts
      </label>
    </div>
    <hr />
```

```
            <p><a href="#">RSS Feed</a></p>
        </div>
    </div>
</div>


<!-- modals //-->

<!-- about modal //-->
<div class="modal fade" id="about-modal">
    <div class="modal-dialog">
        <div class="modal-content">
            <div class="modal-header">
                <button type="button" class="close" data-dismiss="modal"
                    aria-label="Close"><span aria-
                        hidden="true">&times;</span></button>
                <h4 class="modal-title">About</h4>
            </div>
            <div class="modal-body">
                <div class="row">
                    <div class="col-lg-8">
                        <p><img src="http://fillmurray.com/400/300"></p>
                        <p>Pellentesque habitant morbi tristique senectus et netus
et malesuada fames ac turpis egestas. Vestibulum tortor quam, feugiat
vitae, ultricies eget, tempor sit amet, ante. Donec eu libero sit amet
quam egestas semper. Aenean ultricies mi vitae est. Mauris placerat
eleifend leo. Quisque sit amet est et sapien ullamcorper pharetra.
Vestibulum erat wisi, condimentum sed, commodo vitae, ornare sit amet,
wisi. Aenean fermentum, elit eget tincidunt condimentum, eros ipsum
rutrum orci, sagittis tempus lacus enim ac dui. Donec non enim in
turpis pulvinar facilisis. Ut felis. Praesent dapibus, neque id cursus
faucibus, tortor neque egestas augue, eu vulputate magna eros eu erat.
Aliquam erat volutpat. Nam dui mi, tincidunt quis, accumsan porttitor,
facilisis luctus, metus</p>
                        <p>Pellentesque habitant morbi tristique senectus et netus
et malesuada fames ac turpis egestas. Vestibulum tortor quam, feugiat
vitae, ultricies eget, tempor sit amet, ante. Donec eu libero sit amet
quam egestas semper. Aenean ultricies mi vitae est. Mauris placerat
eleifend leo. Quisque sit amet est et sapien ullamcorper pharetra.
Vestibulum erat wisi, condimentum sed, commodo vitae, ornare sit amet,
wisi. Aenean fermentum, elit eget tincidunt condimentum, eros ipsum
rutrum orci, sagittis tempus lacus enim ac dui. Donec non enim in
turpis pulvinar facilisis. Ut felis. Praesent dapibus, neque id cursus
faucibus, tortor neque egestas augue, eu vulputate magna eros eu erat.
Aliquam erat volutpat. Nam dui mi, tincidunt quis, accumsan porttitor,
facilisis luctus, metus</p>
```

```
          <p>Pellentesque habitant morbi tristique senectus et netus
et malesuada fames ac turpis egestas. Vestibulum tortor quam, feugiat
vitae, ultricies eget, tempor sit amet, ante. Donec eu libero sit amet
quam egestas semper. Aenean ultricies mi vitae est. Mauris placerat
eleifend leo. Quisque sit amet est et sapien ullamcorper pharetra.
Vestibulum erat wisi, condimentum sed, commodo vitae, ornare sit amet,
wisi. Aenean fermentum, elit eget tincidunt condimentum, eros ipsum
rutrum orci, sagittis tempus lacus enim ac dui. Donec non enim in
turpis pulvinar facilisis. Ut felis. Praesent dapibus, neque id cursus
faucibus, tortor neque egestas augue, eu vulputate magna eros eu erat.
Aliquam erat volutpat. Nam dui mi, tincidunt quis, accumsan porttitor,
facilisis luctus, metus</p>
          </div>
        </div>
      </div>
    </div><!-- /.modal-content -->
  </div><!-- /.modal-dialog -->
</div><!-- /.modal -->

<!-- contact modal //-->
<div class="modal fade" id="contact-modal">
  <div class="modal-dialog">
    <div class="modal-content">
      <div class="modal-header">
        <button type="button" class="close" data-dismiss="modal"
          aria-label="Close"><span aria-
            hidden="true">&times;</span></button>
        <h4 class="modal-title">Contact</h4>
      </div>
      <div class="modal-body">
        <div class="row">
          <div class="col-lg-6">
            <p>Pellentesque habitant morbi tristique senectus et
              netus et malesuada fames ac turpis egestas.
                Vestibulum tortor quam, feugiat vitae, ultricies
                  eget, tempor sit amet, ante. Donec eu libero sit
                    amet quam egestas semper. Aenean ultricies mi
                      vitae est. Mauris placerat eleifend leo.</p>
          <form>
            <div class="form-group">
              <label>Name</label>
              <input type="text" class="form-control">
            </div>
            <div class="form-group">
              <label>Email</label>
```

```
                <input type="text" class="form-control">
              </div>
              <div class="form-group">
                <label>Message</label>
                <textarea class="form-control"
                  rows="10"></textarea>
              </div>
              <button type="submit" class="btn btn-
                default">Send</button>
            </form>
          </div>
        </div>
      </div>
    </div><!-- /.modal-content -->
  </div><!-- /.modal-dialog -->
</div><!-- /.modal -->

<!-- login modal //-->
<div class="modal fade" id="login-modal">
  <div class="modal-dialog">
    <div class="modal-content">
      <div class="modal-header">
        <button type="button" class="close" data-dismiss="modal"
          aria-label="Close"><span aria-
            hidden="true">&times;</span></button>
        <h4 class="modal-title">Login</h4>
      </div>
      <div class="modal-body">
        <div class="row">
          <div class="col-lg-6">
            <p>Pellentesque habitant morbi tristique senectus et
              netus et malesuada fames ac turpis egestas.
                Vestibulum tortor quam, feugiat vitae, ultricies
                  eget, tempor sit amet, ante. Donec eu libero sit
                    amet quam egestas semper. Aenean ultricies mi
                      vitae est. Mauris placerat eleifend leo.</p>
          <form>
            <div class="form-group">
              <label>Email</label>
              <input type="text" class="form-control">
            </div>
            <div class="form-group">
              <label>Password</label>
              <input type="password" class="form-control">
            </div>
```

```
            <p><small><a href="#">Forgot
              Password?</a></small></p>
            <button type="submit" class="btn btn-default">Sign
              Up</button>
          </form>
          <p>If you don't have an account, you can <a
            href="#">Register Here</a>.</p>
        </div>
      </div>
    </div>
  </div><!-- /.modal-content -->
 </div><!-- /.modal-dialog -->
</div><!-- /.modal -->
```

Summary

That brings the third chapter to a close. We've covered how to create mobile first websites using Bootstrap. We covered how to design a mobile first website, how to use Google material design colors and styles, how to make advanced customizations to the Bootstrap modal component, how to use some jQuery to make a search bar hide/show effect, and how to create static single page apps using Bootstrap.

4
Bootstrap Wiki

In this chapter, we're going to use Bootstrap to create a project that you might not usually think would be suited for the framework. I'm a firm believer that you can use the power of Bootstrap to create any type of web application, so we're going to build a wiki. I'll take you through the process of building pages such as the wiki home page, content page, and search results page. We'll also touch on creating some mobile-specific styles using media queries to optimize the layout for phones and tablets.

Before we jump into creating the home page, let's take a look at what we'll be building:

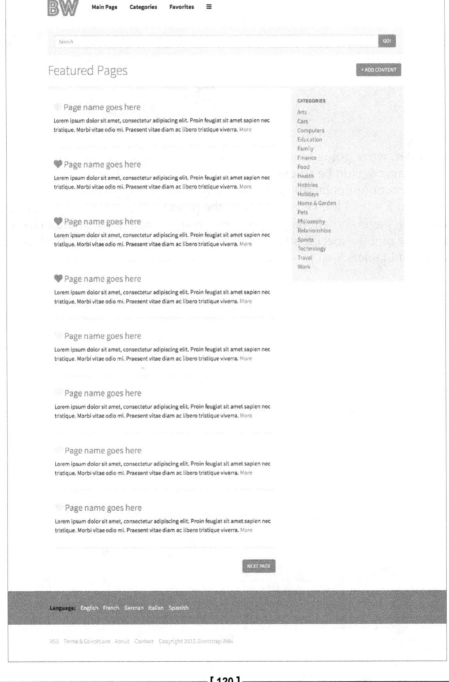

Customizing the template

As in our previous projects, let's update our Harp templates, theme, and Less files before we start with the actual pages. Make a copy of your boilerplate from `chapter 1` and rename it to `chapter 4` or `Bootstrap Wiki`. Open up the `_data.json` file and insert the following code into it:

```
{
  "index": {
    "pageTitle": "Bootstrap Wiki"
  },
  "article": {
    "pageTitle": "Article"
  },
  "search-results": {
    "pageTitle": "Search Results"
  },
  "profile": {
    "pageTitle": "Profile"
  }
}
```

For this project, we'll have four different page templates, so we need to create an entry for each of them. Remember that the first portion is the actual `.ejs` filename and the `pageTitle` variable is what we'll use to set the `<title>` of each page. Go ahead and create these four `.ejs` files in the root of your project directory. You can just leave them blank for now:

- `index.ejs`
- `article.ejs`
- `search-results.ejs`
- `profile.ejs`

Updating _layout.ejs

The next thing that we'll do is update `_layout.ejs`, adding in any new code that is specific to our new wiki project. I'm going to use a different Google web font for this project, called `Source Sans Pro`. Insert the following line of code after `theme.css` in the `<head>` of the file:

```
<link href='http://fonts.googleapis.com/css?family=Source+Sans+P
ro:300,400,700' rel='stylesheet' type='text/css'>
```

This will import three type weights: light (300), regular (400), and bold (700).

Adding a new partial

We're going to add something else new to the layout for this project. Just as we did in the previous project, I'm going to use the modal component for the main navigation menu. The difference here is that this will be a multipage app, compared to the last project, which was a single-page app.

We don't want to insert the same modal code at the bottom of each page template. This is excess of work, and it exposes you to possible errors or inconsistencies. It's a better, more modular practice to create a new partial and put the modal code into it. We'll then include it in the layout so that it is available for all page templates in the wiki. We'll go over the actual modal code a little later; for now, just enter the following line of code below the footer partial:

```
<%- partial("partial/_nav-modal") %>
```

You might as well create the new partial file at this point. Create a new file called `_nav-modal.ejs`. You can leave it blank for now, and save it in the `/partial` directory in the root of the project. This completes the updates that you need to make to the layout file. Here's what the entire file looks like when completed:

```html
<!DOCTYPE html>
<html lang="en">
<head>
  <meta charset="utf-8">
  <meta http-equiv="X-UA-Compatible" content="IE=edge">
  <meta name="viewport" content="width=device-width, initial-
    scale=1">
  <title><%- pageTitle %> | <%- siteTitle %></title>

  <link rel="stylesheet" type="text/css"
    href="css/bootstrap.min.css">
  <link rel="stylesheet" type="text/css" href="css/font-
    awesome.min.css">
  <link rel="stylesheet" type="text/css" href="css/theme.css">
  <link
href='http://fonts.googleapis.com/css?family=Source+Sans+P
ro:300,400,700' rel='stylesheet' type='text/css'>

  <!-- HTML5 shim and Respond.js for IE8 support of HTML5 elements
    and media queries -->
  <!-- WARNING: Respond.js doesn't work if you view the page via
    file:// -->
  <!--[if lt IE 9]>
```

```
    <script
src="https://oss.maxcdn.com/html5shiv/3.7.2/html5shiv.min.js"></
script>
    <script
src="https://oss.maxcdn.com/respond/1.4.2/respond.min.js"></script>
  <![endif]-->
</head>
<body>

  <%- partial("partial/_header") %>

  <%- yield %>

  <%- partial("partial/_footer") %>

  <%- partial("partial/_nav-modal") %>

  <!-- javascript //-->
  <script src="//ajax.googleapis.com/ajax/libs/jquery/1.11.1/jquery.
min.js"></script>
  <script src="js/bootstrap.min.js"
    type="text/javascript"></script>
</body>
</html>
```

Setting up the Less variables

As in our previous projects, the next step is to update our Less variables for our new project. Open _variables.less, which is located in /css/components. Let's go through each new part section by section.

Adding new colors

I've added a few new colors that I want to use in the project. Each of these colors is prepended with bw- so that we can easily identify that they are project-specific; bw- stands for Bootstrap wiki, if it's not obvious. Here are the new colors:

```
@bw-dark-primary: #00796b;
@bw-primary: #009688;
@bw-light-primary: #b2dfdb;
@bw-black: #212121;
@bw-grey: #727272;
@bw-light-grey: #b6b6b6;
```

You might notice a different naming convention here. I've changed it to use `primary` instead of the actual color name for the main color. This is simply to show you that there is more than one way to organize your colors and you don't have to do it the same way each time. For this project, there is one primary color, so it makes sense to use this type of naming convention.

Background colors

As I mentioned earlier, the color palette for this project is pretty simple, so I've eliminated some of the background color options because we won't need them:

```
@primary-background: @white;
@secondary-background: @light-grey;
@inverse-background: @bw-primary;
```

I'm using white and light grey from our base palette, and then the primary color is used for the inverse background. The reason I didn't use the Bootstrap Wiki light grey here is that it has a darker value than I want. It's perfectly fine to combine color palettes in this way. That's why we have a base palette. The base colors should be your regular go-to colors that you feel comfortable using.

Text colors

The updates to the text colors are straight forward. I've simply changed the values to use the new color palette:

```
@primary-text: @bw-black;
@light-text: @bw-grey;
@inverse-text: @white;
@heading-text: @bw-primary;
```

Link and border colors

The same goes for the link and border colors. We're just replacing the values with the new color palette:

```
@primary-link-color: @bw-primary;
@primary-link-color-hover: @bw-dark-primary;

@border-color: @light-grey;
@border-size: 1px;
@border-type: solid;
@border-focus: @bw-primary;
```

Typography

For the typography variables, you'll need to update the copy to use the new typeface, which is called Source Sans Pro. I've also bumped up the base font-size to 16px. This is done to increase the readability of the text; since this is a wiki, we want it to be easy to read!

```
@body-copy: "Source Sans Pro", helvetica, arial, verdana, sans-serif;
@heading-copy: "Source Sans Pro", helvetica, arial, verdana, sans-serif;
@base-font-size: 16px;
```

Rounder corners

The final update needed in this file is bumping up the border-radius value to 5px. I thought I'd mix it up and make the round corners more obvious in this design:

```
.round-corners (@radius: 5px) {
  -moz-border-radius: @radius;
  -ms-border-radius: @radius;
  border-radius: @radius;
}
```

The updates here should be pretty simple for you. Let's check out what the entire file looks like:

```
// color palette
@black: #000;
@dark-grey: #333;
@grey: #ccc;
@light-grey: #ebebeb;
@off-white: #f5f5f5;
@white: #ffffff;

@blue1: #3498db;
@blue2: #2980b9;
@red1: #e74c3c;
@red2: #c0392b;
@yellow1: #f1c40f;
@yellow2: #f39c12;
@green1: #2ecc71;
@green2: #27ae60;
@orange1: #e67e22;
@orange2: #d35400;
@aqua1: #1abc9c;
```

```less
@aqua2: #16a085;
@purple1: #9b59b6;
@purple2: #8e44ad;
@navy1: #34495e;
@navy2: #2c3e50;

// custom colors prepended with bw-
@bw-dark-primary: #00796b;
@bw-primary: #009688;
@bw-light-primary: #b2dfdb;
@bw-black: #212121;
@bw-grey: #727272;
@bw-light-grey: #b6b6b6;

// background colors
@primary-background: @white;
@secondary-background: @light-grey;
@inverse-background: @bw-primary;

// text colors
@primary-text: @bw-black;
@light-text: @bw-grey;
@inverse-text: @white;
@heading-text: @bw-primary;

// link colors
@primary-link-color: @bw-primary;
@primary-link-color-hover: @bw-dark-primary;

// primary border properties
@border-color: @light-grey;
@border-size: 1px;
@border-type: solid;
@border-focus: @bw-primary;

// typography
@body-copy: "Source Sans Pro", helvetica, arial, verdana, sans-serif;
@heading-copy: "Source Sans Pro", helvetica, arial, verdana, sans-serif;
@base-font-size: 16px;
@font-size: 1em;
@base-line-height: 1.5;
```

```less
// layout
@margin: 1em;
@padding: 1em;

// MIXINS

// round corners or Border radius
.round-corners (@radius: 5px) {
  -moz-border-radius: @radius;
  -ms-border-radius: @radius;
  border-radius: @radius;
}

// animation transitions
.transition (@transition: background .1s linear) {
  -moz-transition: @transition;
  -webkit-transition: @transition;
  transition: background @transition;
}
```

Updating the header and footer

Now that our Less variables are ready to go, let's move on to updating our template partials. At this point, we'll set up a new header and footer. We'll also create a couple of more placeholder files for sidebars, which will be added a little later. For now, create the following blank files for later use:

- `_nav-modal.ejs` (if you haven't already)
- `_sidebar.ejs`
- `_sidebar-search.ejs`

As explained earlier, the `nav` modal will be our primary navigation component. The sidebar partial will be used on almost every page, so I've broken it down into a partial. Thus, it can be easily edited. Our search results page will have a different sidebar, so a partial has been created for that as well.

Coding the header

As we've done in a past project, we're not going to use the default Bootstrap header here. We're going to use the basic grid, the inline list component, and some wrapper classes to create a custom header. The header will be divided into two sections. The first will be the logo and actual navigation links. The second will be the full-width search bar.

One thing to keep in mind is that this is a wiki. The links along the top are not the primary navigation. They are simply a collection of useful links that help the user find what they are looking for faster. I wanted to mention this so that you don't get confused when we cover the nav modal. First things first, let's insert the wrapper code for the entire header:

```
<div class="container">
  <div class="header">
    ..
  </div>
</div>
```

We're using the default Bootstrap container here, but I have added some custom styles to it as I want to squish the width a little:

```
.container {
  padding: 0 100px;
}
```

The `.header` class will be our wrapper for the entire header. It has the following basic styles applied to it:

```
.header {
  margin-top: (@margin * 2);
}

.header a {
  color: @bw-black;
  font-weight: bold;
}

.header a:hover {
  color: @bw-grey;

}
```

Let's take a closer look at the CSS for our header and what's going on:

- I've added a top margin to the header to move it off the top edge of the browser.

- I don't want to use the default link colors here, so I've changed them. I've also made the header links bold.

Coding the header nav

Let's code the first portion of the header, which is the logo and header links. Insert the following markup inside `.header` `<div>`:

```
<div class="header-nav">
    <div class="row">
      <div class="col-lg-12">
        <ul class="list-inline">
          <li><a href="index.html"><img src="img/logo.png"
width="90" height="43" alt="Bootstrap Wiki Logo"></a></li>
          <li class="desktop-only"><a href="#">Main Page</a></li>
          <li class="desktop-only"><a href="#">Categories</a></li>
          <li class="desktop-only"><a href="#">Favorites</a></li>
          <li><a href="#" data-toggle="modal" data-target="#nav-
modal"><i class="fa fa-bars"></i></a></li>
        </ul>
      </div>
    </div>
  </div>
```

The `nav` is wrapped in a class called `.header-nav`. Within this `<div>`, I'm using the Bootstrap inline list component to create the layout of the logo and header links. For this project, I thought I'd mix it up and use an image for the logo.

You'll notice that the text link `<li>` tags have a class of `.desktop-only` on them. That is there because we are going to hide them in the mobile view. The reason I'm doing this is to make the header work for phones. You'll also remember that these text links are not our actual `nav`; they are just helpers. The final list item is a hamburger menu icon that triggers the `nav`. This icon/link will not be hidden in the mobile view. Let's review the styles that construct this part of the page:

```
.header-nav {
  margin-bottom: (@margin * 2);
}
```

I've added a little margin at the bottom of the header `nav`; this is equal to the margin I added at the top of the header wrapper:

```
.header ul {
  margin-bottom: 0;
}

.header ul.list-inline li {
  margin-right: (@margin * 1.25);
}
```

We need to tweak the list component a bit so that it works for our layout:

- I've removed the bottom margin from `<ul>` so that it doesn't give me extra spacing. Remember that we set the spacing on `.header-nav`.

- I want more horizontal spacing than what comes out of the box with this component, so I've bumped up the right margin.

Coding the header search bar

Now that the logo and header links are complete, let's insert the full-width search bar. After `.header-nav <div>`, insert the following code:

```
<div class="header-search">
    <div class="row">
      <div class="col-lg-12">
        <div class="well">
          <div class="input-group">
            <input type="text" class="form-control"
              placeholder="Search">
            <span class="input-group-btn">
              <button class="btn btn-primary"
                type="button">Go!</button>
            </span>
          </div>
        </div>
      </div>
    </div>
</div>
```

The section is wrapped in a `<div>` with the class of `.header-search`. Contained within, we're using a `well` component that has an input-group nested inside. But before we can totally finish this, we need to update a couple of Bootstrap components, namely the `button` and `well` components.

Adding custom button styles

Create a new file called `_buttons.less` and save it in the `/css/components` directory. Next, pop open `theme.less` and insert this line of code in the **Modules** section:

```
@import "components/_buttons.less";
```

Go back to the `_buttons.less` file and insert the following code:

```less
.btn {
  text-transform: uppercase;
}

.btn-primary {
  background: @bw-primary;
  border-color: @bw-primary;
  color: @white;
}

.btn-primary:hover {
  background: @bw-dark-primary;
  border-color: @bw-dark-primary;
}
```

Let's review the CSS code for our buttons:

- I want to capitalize the labels of all my buttons, so I've transformed the text to uppercase in the `.btn` class.
- For the primary button, I'll use the primary color from the palette. The hover state will use the dark version of the primary color.

Adding custom well styles

Next, we need to add some custom well styles for the search bar section. Create a new file called `_well.less` in `/css/components`. Open up `theme.less` and insert the following line of code after the button one you just added:

```less
@import "components/_well.less";
```

Head back to `_well.less` and insert this code:

```less
.well {
  border: 0;
  box-shadow: none;
  background-color: @secondary-background;
  .round-corners;
}
```

Let's review the CSS in more detail for the well component:

- I've removed the border and box-shadow from the well

- I've set the background-color to use one of our colors

- I've inserted the round-corners or border-radius mixin so that the `well` uses our `5px` value

Finishing off the header search

Now that we've updated those two components, let's finish off going through the header search section. Here's the code again, for reference:

```html
<div class="header-search">
    <div class="row">
      <div class="col-lg-12">
        <div class="well">
          <div class="input-group">
            <input type="text" class="form-control"
              placeholder="Search">
            <span class="input-group-btn">
              <button class="btn btn-primary"
                type="button">Go!</button>
            </span>
          </div>
        </div>
      </div>
    </div>
</div>
```

The entire section is wrapped in the `.header-search` class, which actually doesn't have any styles applied to it—mostly just for organization at this point. Within the section, insert a well component and then insert an input group. That will finish off this section, and the header will be complete. Here's what the full header partial code should look like:

```html
<div class="container">
  <div class="header">
    <!-- nav //-->
    <div class="header-nav">
      <div class="row">
        <div class="col-lg-12">
          <ul class="list-inline">
```

```
            <li><a href="index.html"><img src="img/logo.png"
              width="90" height="43" alt="Bootstrap Wiki
                Logo"></a></li>
            <li class="desktop-only"><a href="#">Main
              Page</a></li>
            <li class="desktop-only"><a
              href="#">Categories</a></li>
            <li class="desktop-only"><a
              href="#">Favorites</a></li>
            <li><a href="#" data-toggle="modal" data-
              target="#nav-modal"><i class="fa fa-
                bars"></i></a></li>
          </ul>
        </div>
      </div>
    </div>
    <!-- search bar //-->
    <div class="header-search">
      <div class="row">
        <div class="col-lg-12">
          <div class="well">
            <div class="input-group">
              <input type="text" class="form-control"
                placeholder="Search">
              <span class="input-group-btn">
                <button class="btn btn-primary"
                  type="button">Go!</button>
              </span>
            </div>
          </div>
        </div>
      </div>
    </div>
  </div>
</div>
```

Adding the navigation modal

Before we move on to coding the footer, I think this would be a good time to set up the navigation modal. As in the previous chapter, we're going to use a Bootstrap modal component and customize it to look like a full page overlay when you click on the hamburger icon in the header links. Let's start by opening up _nav-modal.ejs, which is in the /partial directory. Once you have it open, insert the following code:

```
<div class="modal fade" id="nav-modal">
  <div class="modal-dialog">
    <div class="modal-content">
      <div class="modal-header">
        <button type="button" class="close" data-dismiss="modal"
          aria-label="Close"><span aria-
            hidden="true">&times;</span></button>
      </div>
      <div class="modal-body">
        <div class="row">
          <div class="col-lg-12">
            <div><a href="#">+ Add Content</a></div>
            <div><a href="#">Profile</a></div>
            <div><a href="#">About</a></div>
            <div><a href="#">Contact</a></div>
            <div><a href="#">Logout</a></div>
          </div>
        </div>
      </div>
    </div><!-- /.modal-content -->
  </div><!-- /.modal-dialog -->
</div><!-- /.modal -->
```

The code here is very similar to what we did in the last chapter, but with one exception; I've removed the modal title section as I don't want to display a title when this opens up. Aside from this, we have a collection of links within the body of the modal, with some custom styles. Let's go over the styles next by popping up modal.less, which is located inside /css/components:

```
.modal-dialog {
  margin: 0;
  width: auto;
}

.modal-backdrop {
  background: @white;
```

```less
  opacity: 0.9!important;
}

.modal-content {
  background: none;
  box-shadow: none;
  border: 0;
  text-align: center;

  -moz-border-radius: 0px;
  border-radius: 0px;
}

.modal-header {
  border-bottom: 0;
}

.close {
  color: @bw-black;
  text-shadow: none;
  opacity: 1;
}

.modal a {
  color: @bw-black;
  text-decoration: none;
  font-weight: 700;
  font-size: (@font-size * 4);
}

.modal a:hover {
  color: @bw-primary;
}
```

Let's go over all the CSS in depth for the modal component:

- The .modal-dialog is unchanged from the previous chapter
- In the .modal-backdrop class, I've changed the background color to @white
- In the .modal-content class, I've set text-align to center
- The only other things that have changed are the color and font-size in the .modal a declaration

This completes the updates that you need to perform for the navigation modal. It would probably be a good idea to compile your code and test it out before moving on. However, you may want to complete the footer first and then test out the entire page template at once.

Adding the footer

Like the header, the footer of this project is divided into two sections. The top section has the language selector links. The second part has the footer links and copyright statement. Open up _footer.ejs, which is located in the /partial directory, and insert the following code:

```
<div class="footer-languages">
  <div class="container">
    <div class="row">
      <div class="col-lg-12">
        <ul class="list-inline">
          <li><strong>Language:</strong></li>
          <li><a href="#">English</a></li>
          <li><a href="#">French</a></li>
          <li><a href="#">German</a></li>
          <li><a href="#">Italian</a></li>
          <li><a href="#">Spanish</a></li>
        </ul>
      </div>
    </div>
  </div>
</div>
```

The entire section is wrapped inside a class of .footer-language. Within this section is another inline list component for displaying all the available languages. Let's review the wrapper class styles first:

```
.footer-languages {
  background: @inverse-background;
  color: @bw-black;
  padding: (@padding * 2) 0;
}

.footer-languages ul {
  margin-bottom: 0;
}
```

```
.footer-languages a {
  color: @white;
}

.footer-languages a:hover {
  color: @bw-black;
}
```

Let me summarize what is happening with the footer CSS:

- I've set the background of this section to use the `@inverse-background` color variable

- The text color is set to our custom black so that it really pops out of the background

- I've added some top and bottom padding to give the section some breathing space

- As with the header links, I've removed the bottom margin from `<ul>` so that the spacings above and below the list are equal

- Finally, I've set the links in the section to white, and the hover color is black

The rest of this section depends on default Bootstrap styles, so this part is complete. Let's add the second half of the footer, which is the utility links and the copyright statement. Insert the following markup below the language section:

```
<div class="footer">
  <div class="container">
    <div class="row">
      <div class="col-lg-12">
        <ul class="list-inline">
          <li><a href="#">RSS</a></li>
          <li><a href="#">Terms &amp; Conditions</a></li>
          <li><a href="#">About</a></li>
          <li><a href="#">Contact</a></li>
          <li>Copyright 2015 Bootstrap Wiki</li>
        </ul>
      </div>
    </div>
  </div>
</div>
```

This section is actually the `true` footer of the project. However, I wanted the language picker to appear on every page, so I included it with the footer partial, again saving me some effort if I want to customize it with more languages.

I've wrapped this entire section in a class of .footer. Within that, I'm using—you guessed it—another inline list component to lay out the links. The list component is actually a really powerful/flexible piece of code that you can use for many things. Before you start laying out a bunch of <div>, I encourage you to consider it for your layout challenges. Let's review the .footer styles:

```
.footer {
  color: @bw-light-grey;
  margin: (@margin * 2) 0;
}

.footer a {
  color: @bw-light-grey;
}

.footer a:hover {
  color: @bw-grey;
}
```

The last thing we need to do is review the CSS for the links in the footer:

- I've set the text color for the footer to use our palette's light grey. I've also added some top and bottom margin for whitespace reasons.

- I set the footer links to the same light grey color to make them subtle. On hovering, they will change to darker grey so that they are easy to read.

This completes the footer code. Let's see what the entire thing should look like:

```
<!-- footer //-->
<div class="footer-languages">
  <div class="container">
    <div class="row">
      <div class="col-lg-12">
        <ul class="list-inline">
          <li><strong>Language:</strong></li>
          <li><a href="#">English</a></li>
          <li><a href="#">French</a></li>
          <li><a href="#">German</a></li>
          <li><a href="#">Italian</a></li>
          <li><a href="#">Spanish</a></li>
        </ul>
      </div>
    </div>
  </div>
</div>
```

```
    </div>
    <div class="footer">
      <div class="container">
        <div class="row">
          <div class="col-lg-12">
            <ul class="list-inline">
              <li><a href="#">RSS</a></li>
              <li><a href="#">Terms &amp; Conditions</a></li>
              <li><a href="#">About</a></li>
              <li><a href="#">Contact</a></li>
              <li>Copyright 2015 Bootstrap Wiki</li>
            </ul>
          </div>
        </div>
      </div>
    </div>
```

This completes the updates to the Harp template files for the new project. We'll come back in a moment and fill in the new partials. Next, let's move on to setting up the new home page.

Coding the homepage

The first page that we will tackle in this project is the wiki home page. It consists of a two-column layout. The left side will be a feed of updated pages, and the right side will be our sidebar, which contains a list of categories. We'll also set up a page title and button for adding new content or pages.

Setting up the page title section

Let's go ahead and set up the page title section first. It consists of an `<h1>` heading and an **Add Content** button:

```
<div class="page-title">
    <div class="row">
      <div class="col-lg-6">
        <h1>Featured Pages</h1>
      </div>
      <div class="col-lg-6 add-content">
        <ul class="list-inline pull-right">
          <li>
            <button type="button" class="btn btn-primary">+ Add
              Content</button>
          </li>
```

```
        </ul>
      </div>
    </div>
  </div>
```

I've divided each side into equal-width columns with the .col-lg-6 class. You may want to increase the size of the page title <div> if you anticipate having longer page titles. You'll notice that with the **Add Content** button, I'm using another inline list even though there is only one button. In other pages, there will be multiple buttons, so I'm just being consistent here. Let's review the CSS for this section:

```
.page-title {
  border-bottom: (@border-size * 5) @border-type @border-color;
  padding-bottom: @padding;
}
```

Let me explain how the .page-title CSS works:

- The page title section has a bottom border of 5px so as to divide it from the page content

- I've also added some padding at the bottom of the section so that the border doesn't bump right up against the text:

```
.add-content {
  line-height: 36px;
}
```

I've set the line-height for the add-content section to 36px, which matches the font-size of our <h1> tag. This will force the button to be vertically centered with the page title. Setting the wrapping <div> line-height to match the height of the text is a simple way to achieve the ever-tricky vertical centering. That finishes up this section, but before we go any further, we should add a Less component for our typography styles.

Setting up the type styles

Create a new file called _typography.less and save it in the /css/components directory. Next, open up theme.less and enter the following line of code in the **Modules** section:

```
@import "components/_typography.less";
```

Save `theme.less` and head back to `_typography.less`. Enter this code in the file and save it:

```less
h1 {
  margin: 0;
  color: @bw-primary;
  font-weight: 300;
}

h5 {
  color: @bw-grey;
  text-transform: uppercase;
  font-weight: 700;
}

small {
  color: @bw-light-grey;
}
```

Let's review the values for the typography styles:

- For the `<h1>` tag, I've removed bottom-margin so that the true height of the tag is `36px`. In this way, it will line up perfectly with the **Add Content** button.
- I've set the color of `<h1>` to our primary hue and font-weight will be the light version of Source Sans Pro.
- The `<h5>` tag will be used in the sidebar, and I'm customizing it to use one of the palette's grey values. I've also converted it to uppercase, and font-weight will be bold.
- Finally, we'll be using the `<small>` tag in the content feed, and we've set it to use one of our colors.

Coding the page body

Let's move on to coding the main body of our home page. It's divided into two columns and the wrapping code looks like this:

```
<div class="page-content">
    <div class="row">
      <div class="col-lg-8">
        ..
      </div>
      <%- partial("partial/_sidebar") %>
    </div>
</div>
```

You'll notice that I've included a partial here for the sidebar. Let's go ahead and set up the code for that now.

Coding the sidebar

Open up `_sidebar.ejs`, which is in the `/parital` directory. Once you have it open, insert the following code:

```
<div class="col-lg-4">
  <div class="sidebar">
    <h5>Categories</h5>
    <ul class="list-unstyled">
      <li><a href="#">Arts</a></li>
      <li><a href="#">Cars</a></li>
      <li><a href="#">Computers</a></li>
      <li><a href="#">Education</a></li>
      <li><a href="#">Family</a></li>
      <li><a href="#">Finance</a></li>
      <li><a href="#">Food</a></li>
      <li><a href="#">Health</a></li>
      <li><a href="#">Hobbies</a></li>
      <li><a href="#">Holidays</a></li>
      <li><a href="#">Home &amp; Garden</a></li>
      <li><a href="#">Pets</a></li>
      <li><a href="#">Philosophy</a></li>
      <li><a href="#">Relationships</a></li>
      <li><a href="#">Sports</a></li>
      <li><a href="#">Technology</a></li>
      <li><a href="#">Travel</a></li>
      <li><a href="#">Work</a></li>
    </ul>
  </div>
</div>
```

Make sure you include the grid `<div>` in the partial so that it's a fully contained component. The sidebar makes use of the Bootstrap unstyled list component. We've already set up the custom styles for the `<h5>` header tag, but we do need to add some sidebar styles to `theme.less`:

```
.sidebar {
  background: @secondary-background;
  padding: @padding;
  margin-bottom: (@margin * 2);
}
```

Let me explain further how the sidebar CSS works:

- I'm using the secondary background color here, which is a light grey.

- I've added some padding to the sidebar so that the text has some breathing space.

- Finally, I've added a little margin-bottom in case the sidebar becomes longer than the feed. And we don't want it to bump up right against the footer.

That concludes the setup of the sidebar. Let's move on to setting up the feed portion of the home page.

Coding the home page feed

Head back to the first column that has the class of `.col-lg-8` on it, and insert the following feed code:

```
<div class="feed">
    <div class="post">
        <h3><i class="fa fa-heart"></i> <a href="#">Page name
            goes here</a></h3>
        <p>Lorem ipsum dolor sit amet, consectetur adipiscing
            elit. Proin feugiat sit amet sapien nec tristique.
            Morbi vitae odio mi. Praesent vitae diam ac
                libero tristique viverra. <a
                    href="#">More</a></p>
    </div>
    <div class="post">
        <h3><i class="fa fa-heart favorite"></i> <a
            href="#">Page name goes here</a></h3>
        <p>Lorem ipsum dolor sit amet, consectetur adipiscing
            elit. Proin feugiat sit amet sapien nec tristique.
            Morbi vitae odio mi. Praesent vitae diam ac
                libero tristique viverra. <a
                    href="#">More</a></p>
    </div>
    <div class="post">
        <h3><i class="fa fa-heart favorite"></i> <a
            href="#">Page name goes here</a></h3>
        <p>Lorem ipsum dolor sit amet, consectetur adipiscing
            elit. Proin feugiat sit amet sapien nec tristique.
            Morbi vitae odio mi. Praesent vitae diam ac
                libero tristique viverra. <a
                    href="#">More</a></p>
    </div>
    <div class="post">
```

```
    <h3><i class="fa fa-heart favorite"></i> <a
      href="#">Page name goes here</a></h3>
    <p>Lorem ipsum dolor sit amet, consectetur adipiscing
      elit. Proin feugiat sit amet sapien nec tristique.
        Morbi vitae odio mi. Praesent vitae diam ac
          libero tristique viverra. <a
            href="#">More</a></p>
  </div>
  <div class="post">
    <h3><i class="fa fa-heart"></i> <a href="#">Page name
      goes here</a></h3>
    <p>Lorem ipsum dolor sit amet, consectetur adipiscing
      elit. Proin feugiat sit amet sapien nec tristique.
        Morbi vitae odio mi. Praesent vitae diam ac
          libero tristique viverra. <a
            href="#">More</a></p>
  </div>
  <div class="post">
    <h3><i class="fa fa-heart"></i> <a href="#">Page name
      goes here</a></h3>
    <p>Lorem ipsum dolor sit amet, consectetur adipiscing
      elit. Proin feugiat sit amet sapien nec tristique.
        Morbi vitae odio mi. Praesent vitae diam ac
          libero tristique viverra. <a
            href="#">More</a></p>
  </div>
  <div class="post">
    <h3><i class="fa fa-heart"></i> <a href="#">Page name
      goes here</a></h3>
    <p>Lorem ipsum dolor sit amet, consectetur adipiscing
      elit. Proin feugiat sit amet sapien nec tristique.
        Morbi vitae odio mi. Praesent vitae diam ac
          libero tristique viverra. <a
            href="#">More</a></p>
  </div>
  <div class="post">
    <h3><i class="fa fa-heart"></i> <a href="#">Page name
      goes here</a></h3>
    <p>Lorem ipsum dolor sit amet, consectetur adipiscing
      elit. Proin feugiat sit amet sapien nec tristique.
        Morbi vitae odio mi. Praesent vitae diam ac libero
          tristique viverra. <a href="#">More</a></p>
  </div>
  <div class="feed-pagination">
    <button class="btn btn-primary" type="button">Next
      Page</button>
  </div>
</div>
```

The `feed` wrapping class has a little padding added to it, as I wanted to put some additional whitespace:

```
.feed {
  padding: @padding;
}
```

Within the feed, I've created a new custom component called `.post`. Each page or piece of content is wrapped in this `.post` class. Let's break down an individual instance of this code:

```
<div class="post">
        <h3><i class="fa fa-heart"></i> <a href="#">Page name
          goes here</a></h3>
        <p>Lorem ipsum dolor sit amet, consectetur adipiscing
          elit. Proin feugiat sit amet sapien nec tristique.
            Morbi vitae odio mi. Praesent vitae diam ac
              libero tristique viverra. <a
                href="#">More</a></p>
    </div>
```

The `.post` itself has some styles applied to each entry in the feed:

```
.post {
  margin-top: (@margin * 2);
  border-bottom: @border-size @border-type @border-color;
  padding-bottom: (@padding * 1.5);
}
```

Let's review how the CSS for the .post class works:

- I want to space out the posts, so I've adding some margin-top and padding-bottom
- I've also added a bottom border to each post to create a separator

I don't want to add the top margin to the first post in the feed, so I'm using a pseudo-selector to remove it:

```
.post:firs-child {
  margin-top: 0;
}
```

Within each post, there's an `<h3>` tag with a nested icon and link. Each post has a heart that is inserted from the font awesome library:

```
<i class="fa fa-heart"></i>
```

If you want to make the heart look selected, you need to add the `.favorite` class to the `<i>` tag:

```
<i class="fa fa-heart favorite"></i>
```

The styles for both states of the heart icon are as follows:

```
.post i {
  color: @light-grey;
}

i.favorite {
  color: @red1;
}
```

That's the full breakdown for each post or entry in our feed. The last thing that we need to go over is the pagination for the feed. At the very bottom of the feed, after the last post, you'll see this code:

```
<div class="feed-pagination">
  <button class="btn btn-primary" type="button">Next
    Page</button>
</div>
```

I'm using a next page type pagination to show the next 10 entries in the feed. The following styles are used for the layout:

```
.feed-pagination {
  margin-top: (@margin * 2);
  padding-bottom: (@padding * 2);
  text-align: right;
}
```

Let's breakdown what's happening with the pagination CSS:

- As with the Post component, I'm applying some margin and padding for vertical consistency
- I've set the alignment of this section to right as I want the button to float on the right-hand side of the `<div>`

This completes the layout of the homepage. Here's the code for the entire page for reference:

```
<div class="container">
  <div class="page-title">
    <div class="row">
```

```
        <div class="col-lg-6">
          <h1>Featured Pages</h1>
        </div>
        <div class="col-lg-6 add-content">
          <ul class="list-inline pull-right">
            <li>
              <button type="button" class="btn btn-primary">+ Add
Content</button>
            </li>
          </ul>
        </div>
      </div>
    </div>
    <div class="page-content">
      <div class="row">
        <div class="col-lg-8">
          <div class="feed">
            <div class="post">
              <h3><i class="fa fa-heart"></i> <a href="#">Page name goes
here</a></h3>
              <p>Lorem ipsum dolor sit amet, consectetur adipiscing
elit. Proin feugiat sit amet sapien nec tristique. Morbi vitae
odio mi. Praesent vitae diam ac libero tristique viverra. <a
href="#">More</a></p>
            </div>
            <div class="post">
              <h3><i class="fa fa-heart favorite"></i> <a href="#">Page
name goes here</a></h3>
              <p>Lorem ipsum dolor sit amet, consectetur adipiscing
elit. Proin feugiat sit amet sapien nec tristique. Morbi vitae
odio mi. Praesent vitae diam ac libero tristique viverra. <a
href="#">More</a></p>
            </div>
            <div class="post">
              <h3><i class="fa fa-heart favorite"></i> <a href="#">Page
name goes here</a></h3>
              <p>Lorem ipsum dolor sit amet, consectetur adipiscing
elit. Proin feugiat sit amet sapien nec tristique. Morbi vitae
odio mi. Praesent vitae diam ac libero tristique viverra. <a
href="#">More</a></p>
            </div>
            <div class="post">
              <h3><i class="fa fa-heart favorite"></i> <a href="#">Page
name goes here</a></h3>
              <p>Lorem ipsum dolor sit amet, consectetur adipiscing
elit. Proin feugiat sit amet sapien nec tristique. Morbi vitae
```

```
odio mi. Praesent vitae diam ac libero tristique viverra. <a
href="#">More</a></p>
            </div>
            <div class="post">
                <h3><i class="fa fa-heart"></i> <a href="#">Page name goes
here</a></h3>
                <p>Lorem ipsum dolor sit amet, consectetur adipiscing
elit. Proin feugiat sit amet sapien nec tristique. Morbi vitae
odio mi. Praesent vitae diam ac libero tristique viverra. <a
href="#">More</a></p>
            </div>
            <div class="post">
                <h3><i class="fa fa-heart"></i> <a href="#">Page name goes
here</a></h3>
                <p>Lorem ipsum dolor sit amet, consectetur adipiscing
elit. Proin feugiat sit amet sapien nec tristique. Morbi vitae
odio mi. Praesent vitae diam ac libero tristique viverra. <a
href="#">More</a></p>
            </div>
            <div class="post">
                <h3><i class="fa fa-heart"></i> <a href="#">Page name goes
here</a></h3>
                <p>Lorem ipsum dolor sit amet, consectetur adipiscing
elit. Proin feugiat sit amet sapien nec tristique. Morbi vitae
odio mi. Praesent vitae diam ac libero tristique viverra. <a
href="#">More</a></p>
            </div>
            <div class="post">
                <h3><i class="fa fa-heart"></i> <a href="#">Page name goes
here</a></h3>
                <p>Lorem ipsum dolor sit amet, consectetur adipiscing
elit. Proin feugiat sit amet sapien nec tristique. Morbi vitae
odio mi. Praesent vitae diam ac libero tristique viverra. <a
href="#">More</a></p>
            </div>
            <div class="feed-pagination">
                <button class="btn btn-primary" type="button">Next Page</
button>
            </div>
        </div><!-- feed end //-->
      </div>
      <!-- sidebar //-->
      <%- partial("partial/_sidebar") %>
    </div>
  </div>
</div>
```

The article page template

Now that we've set up the homepage, let's tackle setting up a page for a single article or wiki topic. Here's what the page we're going to build will look like:

First, create a new file called `article.ejs` and save it to the root of your project. If you remember, earlier in this chapter, we added this page to the `_data.json` file. If you name it differently, make sure that the filename matches what was entered in the `_data.json` file. Once you have saved the file, you may want to compile the project to ensure that everything is working correctly. It's a good idea to do a compile every so often so that you catch errors before you are done. Waiting until the very end will make it more complicated to troubleshoot compile errors if you have them.

Start off your new page template by coding a wrapping `.container <div>` for the entire page:

```
<div class="container">
  ..
</div>
```

The first section that we will insert into the container is the page title. This is identical to the page title from the index template, with the addition of one button. First of all, you'd want to update the `<h1>` tag with the title of your page:

```
<h1>Page Title</h1>
```

Next, we'll insert an **Edit** button that will allow the user to edit this wiki page. We're going to insert this button next to the **Add Content** button. Now you see why I decided to use an inline list here. I'm inserting an additional button as a new `<li>`:

```
<li>
  <button type="button" class="btn btn-default">Edit</button>
</li>
```

I've used the `.btn-default` class here as I want the `Add Content` button to stand out more than the **Edit** button. This is a simple design trick to set the hierarchy of our two buttons.

This concludes the changes that we need to make to the page title section of the template.

Coding the article page body

Let's move on to coding the body of the article page. We're going to reuse the `.page-content` and the `.feed <div>` structure that we set up on the index template here. A new addition to the page is the `.post-meta` section, where will add some metadata about this page. After opening `.feed <div>`, add the following block of code:

```
<div class="post-meta">
  <p>
    <small>23 <i class="fa fa-heart favorite"></i> Last edited:
```

```
     January 1, 2015 by <a href="#">John Smith</a></small>
   </p>
 </div>
```

The `.post-meta` class doesn't actually have any custom styles attached to it. It's simply an identifier for the section. However, if you'd like to customize this part of the page, you can easily use the `presetup` class to do so.

Within the `.post-meta` section, I've added a `<p>` tag; this tag actually holds the content. Using the `<p>` tag here will give us a bottom margin to space out the text from the body copy that we'll be adding next. The metadata should be secondary to the actual body text, so I've wrapped it in a `<small>` tag. This will lighten the text and make it a bit smaller. The favorite icon and link at the end will still use the default styles and stand out a bit more, which is what I want. This concludes the `.post-meta` section of the template.

Adding the body content

The next part of the layout is the addition of body content for the page. Here, I'm going to reuse the `.post` class that I created in the previous template. Within that `<div>`, simply enter the content for the page. This can include text tags, headers, images, videos, or whatever you want. I've included some `<p>` tags in the example (shown later) to keep things simple. After you close the `.post` `<div>`, make sure you keep the pagination section so that users can navigate from page to page on your wiki:

```
<div class="feed-pagination">
  <button class="btn btn-primary" type="button">Next
    Page</button>
</div>
```

That concludes the setup of the content section of the page. The last thing that you need to add is the sidebar partial. This is exactly the same as the index template. Insert the partial code in the same location. You can also see the entire page template here:

```
<div class="container">
  <div class="page-title">
    <div class="row">
      <div class="col-lg-6">
        <h1>Page Title</h1>
      </div>
      <div class="col-lg-6 add-content">
        <ul class="list-inline pull-right">
          <li>
```

```
        <button type="button" class="btn btn-default">Edit</
button>
      </li>
      <li>
        <button type="button" class="btn btn-primary">+ Add
Content</button>
      </li>
    </ul>
  </div>
  </div>
  </div>
  <div class="page-content">
    <div class="row">
      <div class="col-lg-8">
        <div class="feed">
          <div class="post-meta">
            <p>
              <small>23 <i class="fa fa-heart favorite"></i> Last
edited: January 1, 2015 by <a href="#">John Smith</a></small>
            </p>
          </div>
          <div class="post">
            <p>Pellentesque habitant morbi tristique senectus et netus
et malesuada fames ac turpis egestas. Vestibulum tortor quam, feugiat
vitae, ultricies eget, tempor sit amet, ante. Donec eu libero sit amet
quam egestas semper. Aenean ultricies mi vitae est. Mauris placerat
eleifend leo. Quisque sit amet est et sapien ullamcorper pharetra.
Vestibulum erat wisi, condimentum sed, commodo vitae, ornare sit amet,
wisi. Aenean fermentum, elit eget tincidunt condimentum, eros ipsum
rutrum orci, sagittis tempus lacus enim ac dui. Donec non enim in
turpis pulvinar facilisis. Ut felis. Praesent dapibus, neque id cursus
faucibus, tortor neque egestas augue, eu vulputate magna eros eu erat.
Aliquam erat volutpat. Nam dui mi, tincidunt quis, accumsan porttitor,
facilisis luctus, metus</p>

            <p>Pellentesque habitant morbi tristique senectus et netus
et malesuada fames ac turpis egestas. Vestibulum tortor quam, feugiat
vitae, ultricies eget, tempor sit amet, ante. Donec eu libero sit amet
quam egestas semper. Aenean ultricies mi vitae est. Mauris placerat
eleifend leo. Quisque sit amet est et sapien ullamcorper pharetra.
Vestibulum erat wisi, condimentum sed, commodo vitae, ornare sit amet,
wisi. Aenean fermentum, elit eget tincidunt condimentum, eros ipsum
rutrum orci, sagittis tempus lacus enim ac dui. Donec non enim in
turpis pulvinar facilisis. Ut felis. Praesent dapibus, neque id cursus
faucibus, tortor neque egestas augue, eu vulputate magna eros eu erat.
Aliquam erat volutpat. Nam dui mi, tincidunt quis, accumsan porttitor,
facilisis luctus, metus</p>
```

```
            <p>Pellentesque habitant morbi tristique senectus et netus
et malesuada fames ac turpis egestas. Vestibulum tortor quam, feugiat
vitae, ultricies eget, tempor sit amet, ante. Donec eu libero sit amet
quam egestas semper. Aenean ultricies mi vitae est. Mauris placerat
eleifend leo. Quisque sit amet est et sapien ullamcorper pharetra.
Vestibulum erat wisi, condimentum sed, commodo vitae, ornare sit amet,
wisi. Aenean fermentum, elit eget tincidunt condimentum, eros ipsum
rutrum orci, sagittis tempus lacus enim ac dui. Donec non enim in
turpis pulvinar facilisis. Ut felis. Praesent dapibus, neque id cursus
faucibus, tortor neque egestas augue, eu vulputate magna eros eu erat.
Aliquam erat volutpat. Nam dui mi, tincidunt quis, accumsan porttitor,
facilisis luctus, metus</p>
            <p>Pellentesque habitant morbi tristique senectus et netus
et malesuada fames ac turpis egestas. Vestibulum tortor quam, feugiat
vitae, ultricies eget, tempor sit amet, ante. Donec eu libero sit amet
quam egestas semper. Aenean ultricies mi vitae est. Mauris placerat
eleifend leo. Quisque sit amet est et sapien ullamcorper pharetra.
Vestibulum erat wisi, condimentum sed, commodo vitae, ornare sit amet,
wisi. Aenean fermentum, elit eget tincidunt condimentum, eros ipsum
rutrum orci, sagittis tempus lacus enim ac dui. Donec non enim in
turpis pulvinar facilisis. Ut felis. Praesent dapibus, neque id cursus
faucibus, tortor neque egestas augue, eu vulputate magna eros eu erat.
Aliquam erat volutpat. Nam dui mi, tincidunt quis, accumsan porttitor,
facilisis luctus, metus</p>
          </div>
          <div class="feed-pagination">
            <button class="btn btn-primary" type="button">Next Page</
button>
          </div>


      </div><!-- feed end //-->
    </div>
    <!-- sidebar //-->
    <%- partial("partial/_sidebar") %>
  </div>
 </div>
</div>
```

This concludes the coding of the article page template. Compile your project and fire up the server. Then enter the following URL in a browser to test it out:

```
http://localhost:9000/article.html
```

Once you're happy with how everything looks, move on to the next section, where I'll show you how to create the search results template.

The search results page template

It's time to create the third template for our wiki project. Create a new file and name it `search-results.ejs`. As with the previous template, make sure you keep the name the same or update the value in `_data.json` for this template. Before we jump into coding the page, let's see what it will look like when we're done:

You'll notice that the search results page is similar to our other pages, but with one major difference. It has a different sidebar. Previously, I had you creating a second sidebar file and as part of this section. We will code it and insert it into the layout. In the case of the search results page, it has some specific search-related content and filters that we want to show in place of the regular categories. That's why I've created a second sidebar for this template.

Updating the page title

Before you jump into the body of the page, you'd want to change the `<h1>` tag to search results. In this case, we won't have an **Edit** button, so the only button to the right will be the add content one. Aside from the change in the page title, everything should be the same as that in the index template.

Updating the post-meta class

Here, I'm again going to use the `.post-meta` section that I set up in the article template. In this case, we'll insert some search-specific data into the section:

```
<div class="post-meta">
  <p>
    <small>About 2,003 results found in 0.45 seconds</small>
  </p>
</div>
```

Adding search posts

Each search entry in our feed will use the same `.post` `<div>` structure that we set up on the home page, but with one exception. I've put an additional `<p>` tag after the page title; it includes the URL of the page:

```
<div class="post">
  <h3><i class="fa fa-heart"></i> <a href="#">Page name goes
    here</a></h3>
  <p><small>http://bootstrapwiki.com/path/to/page/here</small></p>
  <p>Lorem ipsum dolor sit amet, consectetur adipiscing elit.
    Proin feugiat sit amet sapien nec tristique. Morbi vitae odio
      mi. Praesent vitae diam ac libero tristique viverra. <a
        href="#">More</a></p>
</div>
```

Coding the search sidebar

The last part of this template that we need to code is the unique sidebar. First of all, update the partial to use the right file:

```
<%- partial("partial/_sidebar-search") %>
```

Next, open the _sidebar-search.ejs file in /partial and enter the following code:

```
<div class="col-lg-4">
  <div class="sidebar">
    <h5>Related Searches</h5>
    <ul class="list-unstyled">
      <li><a href="#"><strong>Keyword</strong> something</a></li>
      <li><a href="#"><strong>Keyword</strong> something
        else</a></li>
      <li><a href="#"><strong>Keyword</strong> maybe
        this</a></li>
    </ul>
    <hr>
    <h5>Related Tags</h5>
    <ul class="list-unstyled">
      <li><a href="#">Tag 01</a></li>
      <li><a href="#">Tag 02</a></li>
      <li><a href="#">Tag 03</a></li>
      <li><a href="#">Tag 04</a></li>
      <li><a href="#">Tag 05</a></li>
    </ul>
    <hr>
    <h5>Related Topics</h5>
    <ul class="list-unstyled">
      <li><a href="#">Topic 01</a></li>
      <li><a href="#">Topic 02</a></li>
      <li><a href="#">Topic 03</a></li>
      <li><a href="#">Topic 04</a></li>
      <li><a href="#">Topic 05</a></li>
    </ul>
  </div>
</div>
```

The code here should be pretty straightforward. Each section of the sidebar has a heading that uses an `<h5>` tag. Under each heading, I'm using an unstyled list component to list a search-related filter. Finally, each section is divided by an `<hr>`. I have customized the color of the `<hr>` tag on the sidebar with the following styles:

```
.sidebar hr {
  border-color: @bw-light-grey;
}
```

Here's what the entire page template code looks like:

```
<div class="container">
  <div class="page-title">
    <div class="row">
      <div class="col-lg-6">
        <h1>Search Results</h1>
      </div>
      <div class="col-lg-6 add-content">
        <ul class="list-inline pull-right">
          <li>
            <button type="button" class="btn btn-primary">+ Add
Content</button>
          </li>
        </ul>
      </div>
    </div>
  </div>
  <div class="page-content">
    <div class="row">
      <div class="col-lg-8">
        <div class="feed">
          <div class="post-meta">
            <p>
              <small>About 2,003 results found in 0.45 seconds</small>
            </p>
          </div>
          <div class="post">
            <h3><i class="fa fa-heart"></i> <a href="#">Page name goes
here</a></h3>
            <p><small>http://bootstrapwiki.com/path/to/page/here</
small></p>
            <p>Lorem ipsum dolor sit amet, consectetur adipiscing
elit. Proin feugiat sit amet sapien nec tristique. Morbi vitae
odio mi. Praesent vitae diam ac libero tristique viverra. <a
href="#">More</a></p>
```

```
        </div>
        <div class="post">
            <h3><i class="fa fa-heart"></i> <a href="#">Page name goes
here</a></h3>
    <p><small>http://bootstrapwiki.com/path/to/page/here</small></p>
            <p>Lorem ipsum dolor sit amet, consectetur adipiscing
elit. Proin feugiat sit amet sapien nec tristique. Morbi vitae
odio mi. Praesent vitae diam ac libero tristique viverra. <a
href="#">More</a></p>
        </div>
        <div class="post">
            <h3><i class="fa fa-heart"></i> <a href="#">Page name goes
here</a></h3>
            <p><small>http://bootstrapwiki.com/path/to/page/here</
small></p>
            <p>Lorem ipsum dolor sit amet, consectetur adipiscing
elit. Proin feugiat sit amet sapien nec tristique. Morbi vitae
odio mi. Praesent vitae diam ac libero tristique viverra. <a
href="#">More</a></p>
        </div>
        <div class="post">
            <h3><i class="fa fa-heart"></i> <a href="#">Page name goes
here</a></h3>
            <p><small>http://bootstrapwiki.com/path/to/page/here</
small></p>
            <p>Lorem ipsum dolor sit amet, consectetur adipiscing
elit. Proin feugiat sit amet sapien nec tristique. Morbi vitae
odio mi. Praesent vitae diam ac libero tristique viverra. <a
href="#">More</a></p>
        </div>
        <div class="post">
            <h3><i class="fa fa-heart"></i> <a href="#">Page name goes
here</a></h3>
<p><small>http://bootstrapwiki.com/path/to/page/here</small></p>
            <p>Lorem ipsum dolor sit amet, consectetur adipiscing
elit. Proin feugiat sit amet sapien nec tristique. Morbi vitae
odio mi. Praesent vitae diam ac libero tristique viverra. <a
href="#">More</a></p>
        </div>
        <div class="post">
            <h3><i class="fa fa-heart"></i> <a href="#">Page name goes
here</a></h3>
<p><small>http://bootstrapwiki.com/path/to/page/here</small></p>
            <p>Lorem ipsum dolor sit amet, consectetur adipiscing
elit. Proin feugiat sit amet sapien nec tristique. Morbi vitae
odio mi. Praesent vitae diam ac libero tristique viverra. <a
href="#">More</a></p>
        </div>
```

```
            <div class="post">
                <h3><i class="fa fa-heart"></i> <a href="#">Page name goes
here</a></h3>
<p><small>http://bootstrapwiki.com/path/to/page/here</small></p>
                <p>Lorem ipsum dolor sit amet, consectetur adipiscing
elit. Proin feugiat sit amet sapien nec tristique. Morbi vitae
odio mi. Praesent vitae diam ac libero tristique viverra. <a
href="#">More</a></p>
            </div>
            <div class="post">
                <h3><i class="fa fa-heart"></i> <a href="#">Page name goes
here</a></h3>
                <p><small>http://bootstrapwiki.com/path/to/page/here</
small></p>
                <p>Lorem ipsum dolor sit amet, consectetur adipiscing
elit. Proin feugiat sit amet sapien nec tristique. Morbi vitae
odio mi. Praesent vitae diam ac libero tristique viverra. <a
href="#">More</a></p>
            </div>
            <div class="post">
                <h3><i class="fa fa-heart"></i> <a href="#">Page name goes
here</a></h3>
<p><small>http://bootstrapwiki.com/path/to/page/here</small></p>
                <p>Lorem ipsum dolor sit amet, consectetur adipiscing
elit. Proin feugiat sit amet sapien nec tristique. Morbi vitae
odio mi. Praesent vitae diam ac libero tristique viverra. <a
href="#">More</a></p>
            </div>
            <div class="feed-pagination">
                <button class="btn btn-primary" type="button">Next Page</
button>
            </div>

        </div><!-- feed end //-->
      </div>
      <!-- sidebar //-->
      <%- partial("partial/_sidebar-search") %>
    </div>
  </div>
</div>
```

This completes the Search Results page template. You'll notice that we didn't really need to update much CSS for this template. The HTML was also quite straightforward! That was by design and it's an example of making your project modular. When you're coding a project, make sure you think about how to reuse your CSS classes. We could have easily called .post, .feed, or .post-meta something more page-specific, which would have resulted in more CSS than we need. Keep it clean and it will be easier to manage down the road as the project grows.

The Profile template

The last template that we need to create for our wiki is the Profile page. This template will reuse some of the classes that we have already set up and add a bit more to create a complete user profile page. Take a look at this screenshot to understand what we'll be building:

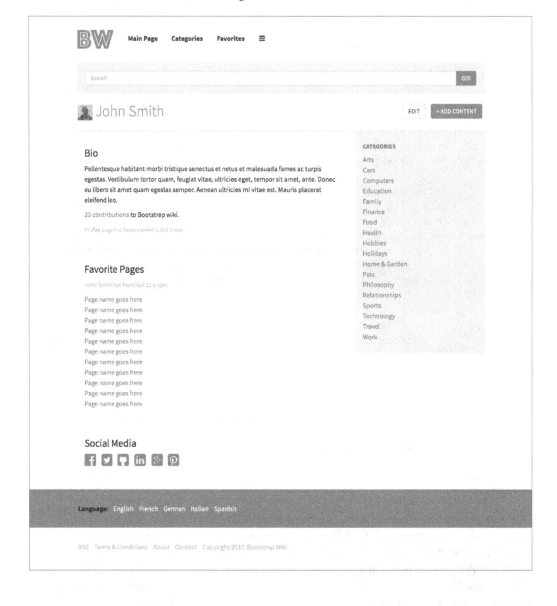

Adding an avatar

We're going to update our page title section to include a user avatar for this page. Update the `<h1>` tag to include an image, as shown in this example:

```
<h1><img src="http://fillmurray.com/36/36" width="36" height="36"
alt="Avatar"> John Smith</h1>
```

Also make sure you change the page title to be your user's name. In this case, I'm using `John Smith`. After you've finished this, add the `Edit` button back to the inline list so that you can allow the user to edit their profile:

```
<li>
  <button type="button" class="btn btn-default">Edit</button>
</li>
```

This concludes the page title setup. Let's move on to the body of the page. It is going to use the same `<div>` structure as all our other templates. In this case, however, we are going to use multiple `.post` `<div>` to separate a few different chunks of content. The first piece of content that we'll insert is a bio for the user:

```
<div class="post">
          <h3>Bio</h3>
          <p>Pellentesque habitant morbi tristique senectus et netus
et malesuada fames ac turpis egestas. Vestibulum tortor quam, feugiat
vitae, ultricies eget, tempor sit amet, ante. Donec eu libero sit amet
quam egestas semper. Aenean ultricies mi vitae est. Mauris placerat
eleifend leo.</p>
          <p><a href="#">23 contributions</a> to Bootstrap wiki.</p>
          <p><small>Profile page has been viewed 1,454 times.</
small></p>
        </div>
```

The next `.post` section will contain a list of the user's favorite pages—pages that they have bookmarked across the wiki:

```
<div class="post">
          <h3>Favorite Pages</h3>
          <p><small>John Smith has favorited 11 pages.</small></p>
          <ul class="list-unstyled">
            <li><a href="#">Page name goes here</a></li>
            <li><a href="#">Page name goes here</a></li>
            <li><a href="#">Page name goes here</a></li>
            <li><a href="#">Page name goes here</a></li>
            <li><a href="#">Page name goes here</a></li>
            <li><a href="#">Page name goes here</a></li>
            <li><a href="#">Page name goes here</a></li>
```

```
            <li><a href="#">Page name goes here</a></li>
            <li><a href="#">Page name goes here</a></li>
            <li><a href="#">Page name goes here</a></li>
            <li><a href="#">Page name goes here</a></li>
        </ul>
    </div>
```

The final section of our page body actually doesn't use the `.post` class. It uses a new `.social-media` class and it will contain links to the user's social media websites. I've created a new section here because I'm going to bump up the size of the icons and I want to isolate these styles:

```
<div class="social-media">
        <h3>Social Media</h3>
        <ul class="list-inline">
          <li><a href="#"><i class="fa fa-facebook-official"></i></a></li>
          <li><a href="#"><i class="fa fa-twitter-square"></i></a></li>
          <li><a href="#"><i class="fa fa-github-square"></i></a></li>
          <li><a href="#"><i class="fa fa-linkedin-square"></i></a></li>
          <li><a href="#"><i class="fa fa-google-plus-square"></i></a></li>
          <li><a href="#"><i class="fa fa-pinterest-square"></i></a></li>
        </ul>
    </div>
```

There are a few custom styles associated with this section, as shown in the following code:

```
.social-media {
  margin-top: (@margin * 2);
  padding-bottom: (@padding * 1.5);
}

.social-media i {
  font-size: (@font-size * 2);
}
```

Let's review the CSS for the `.social-media` section:

- The `.social-media` class has some simple margin and padding added to it to match the post layout styles
- I've bumped up the size of the icons with the next declaration so they really stand out on the page

The last thing we need to add to this page is the regular sidebar partial, as we did on the `index` template. Here's what the entire template looks like:

```
<div class="container">
  <div class="page-title">
    <div class="row">
      <div class="col-lg-6">
        <h1><img src="http://fillmurray.com/36/36" width="36"
height="36" alt="Avatar"> John Smith</h1>
      </div>
      <div class="col-lg-6 add-content">
        <ul class="list-inline pull-right">
          <li>
            <button type="button" class="btn btn-default">Edit</
button>
          </li>
          <li>
            <button type="button" class="btn btn-primary">+ Add
Content</button>
          </li>
        </ul>
      </div>
    </div>
  </div>
  <div class="page-content">
    <div class="row">
      <div class="col-lg-8">
        <div class="feed">
          <div class="post">
            <h3>Bio</h3>
            <p>Pellentesque habitant morbi tristique senectus et netus
et malesuada fames ac turpis egestas. Vestibulum tortor quam, feugiat
vitae, ultricies eget, tempor sit amet, ante. Donec eu libero sit amet
quam egestas semper. Aenean ultricies mi vitae est. Mauris placerat
eleifend leo.</p>
            <p><a href="#">23 contributions</a> to Bootstrap wiki.</p>
```

```
            <p><small>Profile page has been viewed 1,454 times.</
small></p>
          </div>
          <div class="post">
            <h3>Favorite Pages</h3>
            <p><small>John Smith has favorited 11 pages.</small></p>
            <ul class="list-unstyled">
              <li><a href="#">Page name goes here</a></li>
              <li><a href="#">Page name goes here</a></li>
              <li><a href="#">Page name goes here</a></li>
              <li><a href="#">Page name goes here</a></li>
              <li><a href="#">Page name goes here</a></li>
              <li><a href="#">Page name goes here</a></li>
              <li><a href="#">Page name goes here</a></li>
              <li><a href="#">Page name goes here</a></li>
              <li><a href="#">Page name goes here</a></li>
              <li><a href="#">Page name goes here</a></li>
              <li><a href="#">Page name goes here</a></li>
            </ul>
          </div>
          <div class="social-media">
            <h3>Social Media</h3>
            <ul class="list-inline">
              <li><a href="#"><i class="fa fa-facebook-official"></
i></a></li>
              <li><a href="#"><i class="fa fa-twitter-square"></i></
a></li>
              <li><a href="#"><i class="fa fa-github-square"></i></
a></li>
              <li><a href="#"><i class="fa fa-linkedin-square"></i></
a></li>
              <li><a href="#"><i class="fa fa-google-plus-square"></
i></a></li>
              <li><a href="#"><i class="fa fa-pinterest-square"></i></
a></li>
            </ul>
          </div>
        </div><!-- feed end //-->
      </div>
      <!-- sidebar //-->
      <%- partial("partial/_sidebar") %>
    </div>
  </div>
</div>
```

Mobile-specific styling

The last thing I'll cover in this chapter is some specific mobile styles that I applied to the layout. You will need to insert these styles at the bottom of `theme.less` in the `/css` directory. Before I explain the code, here's a preview of what the mobile version will look like on a phone:

Now, let's review the custom styles that go into the making of this layout:

```
@media (max-width: 768px) {
  .container {
    padding-right: @padding;
    padding-left: @padding;
  }

  .add-content {
    float: left;
    margin-top: @margin;
  }

  li.desktop-only {
    display: none;
  }

  .modal a {
    font-size: (@font-size * 2);
  }
}
```

Let me explain how the mobile specific styles work for this project:

- I'm using the value of `768px` in the media query to target tablets and phones with these mobile-specific styles.
- The styles in the `.container` class reset the left and right padding. I've added more padding to our desktop containers to squeeze the layout.
- I want the **Add Content** button to left align in mobiles, so adding the float will accomplish this. The margin will ensure that the button doesn't bump into the page title.
- The `.desktop-only` class will hide some of the header links that aren't as important. Those links are only for the desktop version of the user will have to rely on the navigation modal to navigate on a phone.
- I've shrunk the text down for the links that appear in the modal to make it more suitable for smaller view ports.

Summary

That brings the fourth chapter to a close. We've successfully created our own wiki layout using Bootstrap. Anything is possible with this framework if you use a little creativity. Let's review what you learned: how to create a wiki layout with Bootstrap, how to add multiple templates to a project in Harp, how to customize the navigation modal that we made in the previous chapter, how to use Harp partials for more than just the header and footer, and how to code our template in a modular fashion to save time and produce Less code.

5
Bootstrap News Magazine

In this chapter, I'm going to show you how to create an art-and-design Bootstrap magazine website. We'll be creating a home page and an article template that you can use to create your own blog or magazine. As part of this chapter, I'm going to show you how to use a flexbox layout within the Bootstrap grid. Like the previous projects, I'll use a minimal design with lots of whitespace, and to make things interesting, I'll you show you how to implement Disqus comments.

Before we jump into updating our template, let's take a look at the home page:

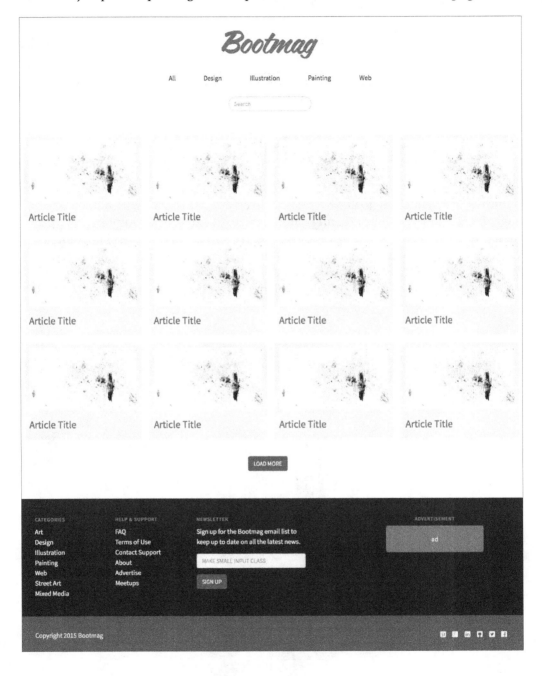

Customizing the template

As in our previous projects, we start by copying our Boilerplate project and create a new one called `Chapter 5`. Open up the `_data.json` file and insert the following code:

```
{
  "index": {
    "pageTitle": "Home"
  },
  "article": {
    "pageTitle": "Article",
    "layout": "_layout-article"
  }
}
```

For this project, we are going to create two page templates. Let's start by creating two new files in the root of our project. For now, they can just be blank and we'll start to fill them in a little later:

- `index.ejs`
- `article.ejs`

Updating _layout.ejs

Let's start by updating the `_layout.ejs` file in the root of our new project. The layout for the home page is pretty straightforward. Make sure you include the line of code that will import Source Sans Pro as our web font. Yep, we're going to use it again in this project:

```
<link
href='http://fonts.googleapis.com/css?family=Source+Sans+Pro:300,
400,700' rel='stylesheet' type='text/css'>
```

This will import three type weights: Light (`300`), Regular (`400`), and Bold (`700`). When we get to the article template, we're actually going to create a unique layout for it. However, we'll cover that a little later, after the home page. For now, simply create another file in the root of the project, called `_layout-article.ejs`. This completes the customizations of our base layout file. Here's what the entire file should look like:

```
<!DOCTYPE html>
<html lang="en">
<head>
  <meta charset="utf-8">
  <meta http-equiv="X-UA-Compatible" content="IE=edge">
```

```html
<meta name="viewport" content="width=device-width, initial-
scale=1">
<title><%- pageTitle %> | <%- siteTitle %></title>

<link rel="stylesheet" type="text/css"
href="css/bootstrap.min.css">
<link rel="stylesheet" type="text/css" href="css/font-
awesome.min.css">
<link rel="stylesheet" type="text/css" href="css/theme.css">
<link
href='http://fonts.googleapis.com/css?family=Source+Sans+Pro:
300,400,700' rel='stylesheet' type='text/css'>

<!-- HTML5 shim and Respond.js for IE8 support of HTML5 elements
and media queries -->
<!-- WARNING: Respond.js doesn't work if you view the page via
file:// -->
<!--[if lt IE 9]>
  <script
  src="https://oss.maxcdn.com/html5shiv/3.7.2/html5shiv.min.js">
   </script>
  <script
  src="https://oss.maxcdn.com/respond/1.4.2/respond.min.js">
  </script>
<![endif]-->
</head>
<body>

  <%- partial("partial/_header") %>

  <%- yield %>

  <%- partial("partial/_footer") %>

  <!-- javascript //-->
  <script
  src="//ajax.googleapis.com/ajax/libs/jquery/1.11.1/
  jquery.min.js"></script>
  <script src="js/bootstrap.min.js"
  type="text/javascript"></script>
</body>
</html>
```

Setting up the Less variables

The next step will be to set up the new Less variables for the magazine project. Open the `_variables.less` file, which is found in `css/components`. Let's go through each section that you need to update:

```
@bm-primary: #673ab7;
@bm-dark-primary: #512da8;
@bm-light-primary: #d1c4e9;
@bm-accent: #e040fb;
@bm-black: #212121;
@bm-grey: #727272;
@bm-light-grey: #b6b6b6;
```

As we did in the previous wiki project, we're going to use the primary naming convention for our custom colors. Each one is prepended with `bm-` in order to make it easily identifiable.

Background colors

Next, let's update our background color variables to use our new color values:

```
@primary-background: @white;
@secondary-background: @bm-grey;
@inverse-background: @bm-black;
```

Text colors

After setting up the background, let's move on to updating our text color variables to use the new values:

```
@primary-text: @bm-grey;
@light-text: @bm-light-grey;
@loud-text: @bm-black;
@inverse-text: @white;
@heading-text: @bm-black;
```

Link colors

For the links, we're going to use our primary color for the link and the dark primary color for the hover state:

```
@primary-link-color: @bm-primary;
@primary-link-color-hover: @bm-dark-primary;
```

Borders

For the project's borders, we're only going to update the colors for the primary and focus border states. The size and type values will stay the same:

```
@border-color: @light-grey;
@border-size: 1px;
@border-type: solid;
@border-focus: @bm-accent;
```

Typography

The typography values will more or less be the same, but with one change. Since this is a magazine, I'm going to bump up the base font size to 16px. We want our magazine to be easy to read, so it makes sense that we should make the type larger. Also make sure that the font stack is set up properly, with Source Sans Pro spelled properly:

```
@body-copy: "Source Sans Pro", "Helvetica Neue", helvetica, arial,
verdana, sans-serif;
@heading-copy: "Source Sans Pro", "Helvetica Neue", helvetica,
arial, verdana, sans-serif;
@base-font-size: 16px; //new
@font-size: 1em;
@base-line-height: 1.5;
```

Border radius

The last thing that I'm going to do is change the border-radius value to 5px. I thought I'd mix up the look a little by making our corners more rounded:

```
.round-corners (@radius: 5px) {
  -moz-border-radius: @radius;
  -ms-border-radius: @radius;
  border-radius: @radius;
}
```

This completes the updates that you need to make to the variables' Less file. Before we move on to setting up the header and footer, let's review the entire content of the file:

```
// color palette
@black: #000;
@dark-grey: #333;
@grey: #ccc;
```

```less
@light-grey: #ebebeb;
@off-white: #f5f5f5;
@white: #ffffff;

@blue1: #3498db;
@blue2: #2980b9;
@red1: #e74c3c;
@red2: #c0392b;
@yellow1: #f1c40f;
@yellow2: #f39c12;
@green1: #2ecc71;
@green2: #27ae60;
@orange1: #e67e22;
@orange2: #d35400;
@aqua1: #1abc9c;
@aqua2: #16a085;
@purple1: #9b59b6;
@purple2: #8e44ad;
@navy1: #34495e;
@navy2: #2c3e50;

// custom colors prepended with bm-
@bm-primary: #673ab7;
@bm-dark-primary: #512da8;
@bm-light-primary: #d1c4e9;
@bm-accent: #e040fb;
@bm-black: #212121;
@bm-grey: #727272;
@bm-light-grey: #b6b6b6;


// background colors
@primary-background: @white;
@secondary-background: @bm-grey;
@inverse-background: @bm-black;

// text colors
@primary-text: @bm-grey;
@light-text: @bm-light-grey;
@loud-text: @bm-black;
@inverse-text: @white;
@heading-text: @bm-black;
```

```less
// link colors
@primary-link-color: @bm-primary;
@primary-link-color-hover: @bm-dark-primary;

// primary border properties
@border-color: @light-grey;
@border-size: 1px;
@border-type: solid;
@border-focus: @bm-accent;

// typography
@body-copy: "Source Sans Pro", "Helvetica Neue", helvetica, arial,
verdana, sans-serif;
@heading-copy: "Source Sans Pro", "Helvetica Neue", helvetica,
arial, verdana, sans-serif;
@base-font-size: 16px;
@font-size: 1em;
@base-line-height: 1.5;

// layout
@margin: 1em;
@padding: 1em;

// MIXINS

// round corners or Border radius
.round-corners (@radius: 5px) {
  -moz-border-radius: @radius;
  -ms-border-radius: @radius;
  border-radius: @radius;
}

// animation transitions
.transition (@transition: background .1s linear) {
  -moz-transition: @transition;
  -webkit-transition: @transition;
  transition: background @transition;
}
```

Coding the header and footer

The header for this project is fairly minimal in design. It will include a logo, some post filter links, and a search field. The footer for this project, however, is the most complex one we've done yet. It will include two sections, a number of links, an e-mail sign-up form, and space for an advertisement—any good magazine design will include some space for ads.

Updating the header

Let's start with updating the header first. For this project, I'm going to use a couple of HTML5 tags to mix things up. For each project in this book, I try to change how I build the header to show you that there are several ways by which you can construct a header. Some will use the default Bootstrap header, but some will be totally custom. The first thing that we're going to do is wrap the entire header in the `<header>` tag:

```
<header>
  ...
</header>
```

Everything contained within the header is going to be centered horizontally, so let's apply a single style to this tag:

```
header {
  text-align: center;
}
```

Inserting the logo

Next we'll insert a new `<div>` tag for the logo. Once you've inserted the following HTML, open up the `theme.less` file and insert the corresponding styles:

```
<div class="logo">
  <a href="/"><img src="img/bootmag-logo.png" width="234"
  height="67" alt="Bootmag"></a>
</div>
```

The logo needs a top margin so that it doesn't bump against the top edge of the browser. It will inherit the center styling from the `<header>` tag:

```
.logo {
  margin-top: (@margin * 2);
}
```

Adding the filters

Directly after the logo, we are going to insert a second `<div>` tag for our filters. Within the wrapping parent `<div>` tag, I've inserted a number of child `<div>` tags, one for each filter:

```
<div class="filters">
        <div class="selected"><a href="#">All</a></div>
        <div><a href="#">Design</a></div>
        <div><a href="#">Illustration</a></div>
        <div><a href="#">Painting</a></div>
        <div><a href="#">Web</a></div>
</div>
```

For the wrapping `.filters` `<div>`, we are going to add top and bottom margins:

```
.filters {
  margin: (@margin * 2) 0;
}
```

We want the child `<div>` tags to be displayed in a line horizontally and centered within the overall layout. To achieve this, we will use the `display` property with a value of `inline-block`. We'll then add left and right margins to each to space them out:

```
.filters div {
  display: inline-block;
  margin: 0 (@margin * 2);
}
```

I'm going to change the appearance of the filter links to be different from that of our primary links. Add the following styles to `theme.less`:

```
.filters a {
  color: @bm-black;
}

.filters a:hover {
  color: @bm-accent;
}
```

Adding the search field

The last piece of the header that we need to add is the search field. Immediately after the `filters` `<div>` tag, insert the following block of code:

```
<div class="search">
        <form>
          <div class="form-group">
            <input type="text" class="form-control"
            placeholder="Search">
          </div>
        </form>
      </div>
```

For this component, we're wrapping a generic Bootstrap form within a `<div>` tag with a class of `.search` on it. We'll need to add some custom styles to the form to achieve the look that we want:

```
.search form {
  width: 200px;
  margin: 0 auto;
}

.search input {
  width: 200px;

  -moz-border-radius: 20px;
  border-radius: 20px;
}
```

Let's breakdown the CSS for the search form:

- I've set `width` of `form` and `input` to `200px`, so it isn't too long.
- Setting `text-align` to `center` won't work with a form. So, I've set the left and right `margin` to `auto` to center it in the layout.
- I've bumped up the `border-radius` on the actual input to `20px` so that I get the circular look at the ends of the field.

Adding the form Less component

For the search field, we need to customize one of the default Bootstrap form styles. When the input is in focus, I want the border to use our color palette. Create a new file in `css/components` called `_forms.less` and insert the following code:

```less
.form-control:focus {
  border-color: @border-focus;
  box-shadow: none;
}
```

Don't forget to `@import` the new `_forms.less` file into `theme.less`. That completes the design of our header. As I explained, this should've been pretty straightforward. Before we move on to the footer, let's review the entire code for the header:

```html
<header>
  <div class="container">
    <div class="row">
      <div class="col-lg-12">
        <div class="logo">
          <a href="/"><img src="img/bootmag-logo.png" width="234"
          height="67" alt="Bootmag"></a>
        </div>
        <div class="filters">
          <div class="selected"><a href="#">All</a></div>
          <div><a href="#">Design</a></div>
          <div><a href="#">Illustration</a></div>
          <div><a href="#">Painting</a></div>
          <div><a href="#">Web</a></div>
        </div>
        <div class="search">
          <form>
            <div class="form-group">
              <input type="text" class="form-control"
              placeholder="Search">
            </div>
          </form>
        </div>
      </div>
    </div>
  </div>
</header>
```

Updating the footer

As I mentioned early in this chapter, the footer for this project is the most complicated one yet. It will be divided into a top and a bottom section and the design is in line with footers that you would see on other magazine-style websites. Similar to the header design, I want to strive to give you something that is a little different in each project. As we did with the header, we're going to wrap the entire footer in the HTML5 `<footer>` tag:

```
<footer>
  ..
</footer>
```

The actual `<footer>` tag doesn't have any styles attached to it, but it's a good way to group the top and bottom sections of the overall section. Before we jump into the footer sections, let's customize the links styles for both in `theme.less`:

```
.footer-top a,
.footer-bottom a {
  color: @white;
  text-decoration: none;
}

.footer-top a:hover,
.footer-bottom a:hover {
  color: @bm-light-grey;
}
```

Coding the top of the footer

The top section of the footer is divided into four columns. The first two columns contain unordered lists of links, the third column will hold a newsletter sign-up form, and the final column will be a placeholder for an advertisement. We want the footer to stretch across the full width of the browser, so we won't use the `.container` `<div>` here. I'll wrap the top section in a `.footer-top` `<div>` and then start a regular Bootstrap grid within it:

```
<div class="footer-top">
  <div class="row">
    <div class="col-lg-2">
      ..
    </div>
    <div class="col-lg-2">
      ..
    </div>
```

```
        <div class="col-lg-3">
          ..
        </div>
        <div class="col-lg-4 col-lg-offset-1 advertisement">
          ..
        </div>
      </div>
    </div>
```

Let's breakdown the CSS for the footer:

- The first two columns use the `.col-lg-2` class. They don't need to be very wide as they just have a list of links.

- The third column is a bit wider in order to allow more space for our newsletter sign-up form. As part of this section, we'll update our Button styles.

- The final column is the widest and is offset by `1` to give some space around for our ad. As part of this section, we'll update our Well styles.

At this point, let's set up the styles for the `.footer-top` class, which wraps this entire section. We're going to set the background to black, set the text to white, and add some padding:

```
.footer-top {
  background: @bm-black;
  color: @white;
  padding: (@padding * 2);
}
```

Adding the first two columns

The first two columns are pretty simple—just a couple of unordered lists that use the Bootstrap unstyled list class:

```
<div class="col-lg-2">
  <h5>Categories</h5>
  <ul class="list-unstyled">
    <li><a href="#">Art</a></li>
    <li><a href="#">Design</a></li>
    <li><a href="#">Illustration</a></li>
    <li><a href="#">Painting</a></li>
    <li><a href="#">Web</a></li>
    <li><a href="#">Street Art</a></li>
```

```
      <li><a href="#">Mixed Media</a></li>
   </ul>
</div>
<div class="col-lg-2">
   <h5>Help &amp; Support</h5>
   <ul class="list-unstyled">
      <li><a href="#">FAQ</a></li>
      <li><a href="#">Terms of Use</a></li>
      <li><a href="#">Contact Support</a></li>
      <li><a href="#">About</a></li>
      <li><a href="#">Advertise</a></li>
      <li><a href="#">Meetups</a></li>
   </ul>
</div>
```

This section is straightforward, but I will add some custom styles to the `<h5>` tag, which are shown here:

```
.footer-top h5 {
   text-transform: uppercase;
   color: @bm-accent;
   font-size: (@font-size - 0.25);
   letter-spacing: 1px;
}
```

Adding the newsletter form

Let's move on to the third column and add the form for the newsletter. Insert the following code after the first two columns:

```
<div class="col-lg-3">
   <h5>Newsletter</h5>
   <p>Sign up for the Bootmag email list to keep up to date on all
   the latest news.</p>
   <form>
      <div class="form-group">
         <input type="text" class="form-control">
      </div>
      <button type="submit" class="btn btn-primary">Sign Up</button>
   </form>
</div>
```

This section should also be pretty easy to understand. We're using a basic Bootstrap form combined with some type tags. One thing that we need to do here is update our button styles.

Updating the button styles

The button used in the form is the first instance in this project, so let's go ahead and update our styles. Create a new file called `_buttons.less` and save it in `css/components`. Next, head to `theme.less` and `@import` it into `theme.less`. Once that's set up, insert the following code into the new Less file:

```
.btn {
  text-transform: uppercase;
}

.btn-primary {
  background: @bm-primary;
  border-color: @bm-primary;
  color: @white;
}

.btn-primary:hover {
  background: @bm-dark-primary;
  border-color: @bm-dark-primary;
}
```

Let's breakdown the CSS for the button component:

* All the buttons are going to be uppercase
* I have reset the primary button static and hover states to use the color palette

This completes the third column in the first part of footer. Let's move on to the final column, which holds the advertisement.

Coding the advertisement section

We're going to make the advertisement section the widest so that it can support a larger ad if needed. We're also going to offset it by 1 to add some space. This will make the ad more noticeable, which is what you would want if you're using an ad on your magazine website:

```
<div class="col-lg-4 col-lg-offset-1 advertisement">
  <h5>Advertisement</h5>
  <div class="well">
      ad
  </div>
</div>
```

I'm using a .advertisement class here and some other custom styles, so let's take a look at what's going on:

```
.advertisement {
  text-align: center;
}

.advertisement .well {
  margin: 0 (@margin * 4);
}
```

Let's breakdown the CSS for the .advertisement class:

- I want to center this section, so I've added the text-align property to the .advertisement class.

- I also want to add some more margin to the Well component that holds the advertisement. Speaking of the Well component, we need to update it.

Updating the well styles

Create a new file named _well.less and save it in css/components. Next, open theme.less and @import the new Less file into theme.less. Once you've done that, insert the following styles:

```
.well {
  border: 0;
  box-shadow: none;
  background-color: @secondary-background;
  .round-corners;
}
```

Let's breakdown the CSS for the .well component:

- I've removed the well's border and box-shadow
- Next, we'll want to use our background-color variable
- Finally, let's reset border-radius to use our Less mixin

This brings the fourth column to a close, as well as the top of the footer. Let's move on to the bottom of this section to finish it.

Coding the bottom of the footer

The bottom part of the footer is simpler than its top. This section is divided into two equal columns. On the left, we have the standard copyright statement, and on the right, we have social media icon links. Let's take a look at the code:

```
<div class="footer-bottom">
  <div class="row">
    <div class="col-lg-6">
      Copyright 2015 Bootmag
    </div>
    <div class="col-lg-6">
      <div class="social-media">
        <div><a href="#"><i class="fa fa-facebook-
        official"></i></a></div>
        <div><a href="#"><i class="fa fa-twitter-
        square"></i></a></div>
        <div><a href="#"><i class="fa fa-github-
        square"></i></a></div>
        <div><a href="#"><i class="fa fa-linkedin-
        square"></i></a></div>
        <div><a href="#"><i class="fa fa-google-plus-
        square"></i></a></div>
        <div><a href="#"><i class="fa fa-pinterest-
        square"></i></a></div>
      </div>
    </div>
  </div>
</div>
```

As with the top of the footer, we have some styles specific to the bottom. The background will use our primary color, white text, and the same padding as the top:

```
.footer-bottom {
  background: @bm-primary;
  color: @white;
  padding: (@padding * 2);
}
```

The last thing that we should cover is the social media links. As with the header section, I'm using a collection of `<div>`s here, which are displayed as `inline-block`. This `<div>` tag also floats to the right, so it aligns to the right side of the column:

```
.social-media div {
  display: inline-block;
  margin: 0 (@margin - 0.5);
  float: right;
}
```

This brings the footer to a close. Let's review all of the markup together before we move on to coding the `Homepage` template:

```
<footer>
  <div class="footer-top">
    <div class="row">
      <div class="col-lg-2">
        <h5>Categories</h5>
        <ul class="list-unstyled">
          <li><a href="#">Art</a></li>
          <li><a href="#">Design</a></li>
          <li><a href="#">Illustration</a></li>
          <li><a href="#">Painting</a></li>
          <li><a href="#">Web</a></li>
          <li><a href="#">Street Art</a></li>
          <li><a href="#">Mixed Media</a></li>
        </ul>
      </div>
      <div class="col-lg-2">
        <h5>Help &amp; Support</h5>
        <ul class="list-unstyled">
          <li><a href="#">FAQ</a></li>
          <li><a href="#">Terms of Use</a></li>
          <li><a href="#">Contact Support</a></li>
          <li><a href="#">About</a></li>
          <li><a href="#">Advertise</a></li>
          <li><a href="#">Meetups</a></li>
        </ul>
      </div>
      <div class="col-lg-3">
        <h5>Newsletter</h5>
        <p>Sign up for the Bootmag email list to keep up to date
        on all the latest news.</p>
        <form>
          <div class="form-group">
            <input type="text" class="form-control">
          </div>
          <button type="submit" class="btn btn-primary">Sign
          Up</button>
        </form>
      </div>
      <div class="col-lg-4 col-lg-offset-1 advertisement">
        <h5>Advertisement</h5>
        <div class="well">
```

```
                ad
              </div>
            </div>
          </div>
        </div>
        <div class="footer-bottom">
          <div class="row">
            <div class="col-lg-6">
              Copyright 2015 Bootmag
            </div>
            <div class="col-lg-6">
              <div class="social-media">
                <div><a href="#"><i class="fa fa-facebook-
                official"></i></a></div>
                <div><a href="#"><i class="fa fa-twitter-
                square"></i></a></div>
                <div><a href="#"><i class="fa fa-github-
                square"></i></a></div>
                <div><a href="#"><i class="fa fa-linkedin-
                square"></i></a></div>
                <div><a href="#"><i class="fa fa-google-plus-
                square"></i></a></div>
                <div><a href="#"><i class="fa fa-pinterest-
                square"></i></a></div>
              </div>
            </div>
          </div>
        </div>
      </footer>
```

One last thing before you move on to the next section — it would be a good idea to compile and test your project to make sure that you aren't getting any Harp errors. Once you have confirmed that your project is set up properly, you can move on to the Homepage layout.

Coding the home page

The first of two templates for this project is the home page. This page is made up of a flexbox grid that is wrapped into the Bootstrap grid code. Following the grid, we'll add a pagination section. The entire body of the page is wrapped in the following HTML:

```
<div class="page-body">
  ..
</div>
```

This section has top and bottom margins attached to it. This is the same spacing that we'll use on the article page, so you'll see `.article` class in there as well:

```
.page-body,
.article {
  margin: (@margin * 2) 0;
}
```

Creating a post grid with flexbox

Before we jump fully into the flexbox code, let's outline the basic structure of a row of posts. Each row of our grid will have four posts in it. As with the footer, we want rows to stretch across the width of the layout, so we'll be omitting the `.container` `<div>`. Here's the basic structure of a row:

```
<div class="row">
  <div class="col-lg-12">
    <div class="flex-parent">
      <div class="flex-child">
        ..
      </div>
      <div class="flex-child">
        ..
      </div>
      <div class="flex-child">
        ..
      </div>
      <div class="flex-child">
        ..
      </div>
    </div>
  </div>
</div>
```

Let's breakdown the CSS for the flexbox layout:

- We're wrapping a full-width Bootstrap grid around our flexbox layout
- The `.flex-parent` is the wrapper for this row of posts
- The `.flex-child` is the class for every post or child of `.flex-parent`

The code for each flex child `<div>` looks like what is shown next. It's made up of an image and a post title. You can easily add more content to the section if you like:

```
<div class="flex-child">
  <a href="#"><img src="img/article1.jpg"></a>
  <h3><a href="#">Article Title</a></h3>
</div>
```

Let's take a look at the styles that power this section of the layout. There are a few things that we need to review to get our flexbox to work properly. First, create a new file called `_flexbox.less` and save it in `css/components`. After that, open `theme.less` and `@import` the new file. Go back to the Less file and insert the following code:

```
.flex-parent {
  display: flex;
  display: -webkit-flex;
}

.flex-child {
  width: 100%;
  flex: 1;
  background: @off-white;
  margin: 10px;
  height: auto;
  padding: 10px;

  .round-corners;
}

.flex-child img {
  width: 100%;

  .round-corners;
}
```

Let's breakdown the CSS for the flexbox layout:

- Our `.flex-parent` class simply needs to have its display property set to `flex`. Don't forget the webkit value too.

- The child needs a little more work. Set `width` to `100%` so that the `@off-white` background fills the width of the column. We set `flex` to `1`, and we'll need to add some `margin` and `padding` since this is not a regular Bootstrap grid. Finally, set `height` to `auto` so that the background will grow to fit its content. Don't forget to reset `border-radius` too.

- We also need to add some styles for the image that appears in each column. It's a good idea to use a larger image here as the width of this column is fluid. By setting the image `width` to `100%`, we can be sure that the image will fit in the box properly. Setting `height` to `auto` will allow it to resize properly.

Now that we've finished a single row of four posts, it's just a matter of adding more rows of four. We need to add the pagination controls to this layout next. Then I'll show you what all of the markup should look like.

Adding the pagination section

For the pagination of this project, we're going to use a mobile pattern. Instead of traditional pagination, which has a page count, we're just going to insert a `Load More` button and use an infinite scrolling pattern. Start by adding the following HTML after the grid code:

```
<div class="container">
  <div class="row">
    <div class="col-lg-12 pagination">
      <div class="">
        <button class="btn btn-primary">Load More</button>
      </div>
    </div>
  </div>
</div>
```

You'd see that I'm using a container here, which is perfectly fine. I don't need this part of the layout to stretch the width of the browser. You'll notice that on the grid class `<div>`, I've also added a class of `.pagination`. The following styles apply to this class:

```
.pagination {
  text-align: center;
  margin: (@margin * 2) 0;
}
```

I've centered the entire section and added top and bottom margins for spacing. This brings the pagination section to an end. The idea here is that you would click on the button and another row or two of posts would load in. This will go on infinitely or until you run out of posts to show. Let's take a look at the entire HTML code for this template:

```
<div class="page-body">
  <div class="row">
    <div class="col-lg-12">
      <div class="flex-parent">
```

```
        <div class="flex-child">
          <a href="#"><img src="img/article1.jpg"></a>
          <h3><a href="#">Article Title</a></h3>
        </div>
        <div class="flex-child">
          <a href="#"><img src="img/article1.jpg"></a>
          <h3><a href="#">Article Title</a></h3>
        </div>
        <div class="flex-child">
          <a href="#"><img src="img/article1.jpg"></a>
          <h3><a href="#">Article Title</a></h3>
        </div>
        <div class="flex-child">
          <a href="#"><img src="img/article1.jpg"></a>
          <h3><a href="#">Article Title</a></h3>
        </div>
      </div>
    </div>
  </div>
  <div class="row">
    <div class="col-lg-12">
      <div class="flex-parent">
        <div class="flex-child">
          <a href="#"><img src="img/article1.jpg"></a>
          <h3><a href="#">Article Title</a></h3>
        </div>
        <div class="flex-child">
          <a href="#"><img src="img/article1.jpg"></a>
          <h3><a href="#">Article Title</a></h3>
        </div>
        <div class="flex-child">
          <a href="#"><img src="img/article1.jpg"></a>
          <h3><a href="#">Article Title</a></h3>
        </div>
        <div class="flex-child">
          <a href="#"><img src="img/article1.jpg"></a>
          <h3><a href="#">Article Title</a></h3>
        </div>
      </div>
    </div>
  </div>
  <div class="row">
```

```
<div class="col-lg-12">
  <div class="flex-parent">
    <div class="flex-child">
      <a href="#"><img src="img/article1.jpg"></a>
      <h3><a href="#">Article Title</a></h3>
    </div>
    <div class="flex-child">
      <a href="#"><img src="img/article1.jpg"></a>
      <h3><a href="#">Article Title</a></h3>
    </div>
    <div class="flex-child">
      <a href="#"><img src="img/article1.jpg"></a>
      <h3><a href="#">Article Title</a></h3>
    </div>
    <div class="flex-child">
      <a href="#"><img src="img/article1.jpg"></a>
      <h3><a href="#">Article Title</a></h3>
    </div>
  </div>
</div>
</div>

<!-- pagination //-->
<div class="container">
  <div class="row">
    <div class="col-lg-12 pagination">
      <div class="">
        <button class="btn btn-primary">Load More</button>
      </div>
    </div>
  </div>
</div>
</div>
```

Coding the article template

The second template in this project is the article or post template. It will contain the detailed view and content for a magazine story. Before we start coding the page, let's see what it will look like:

The layout here is narrower, which allows easier readability of a large amount of content. I've also followed my regular minimal style to keep the page looking really clean. The entire page template is wrapped in a `<div>` tag with a class of `.article` so that we can apply some styling:

```
<div class="article">
  ..
</div>
```

We had already added the styles for this when we set up our `.page-body` class in the previous template. However, there is a container class inside of the `.article` class that needs some customization:

```
.article .container {
  padding-left: (@padding * 18);
  padding-right: (@padding * 18);
}
```

This might look like a decent amount of padding, and it is. This is how we will achieve the narrower column layout that we want for better readability.

Adding the article title

First things first, let's add our page title. Like any good page title, ours is wrapped in an `<h1>` tag:

```
<h1>This is the title for the story it can get kinda big if we want it
to eh.</h1>
```

Let's take a look at the styles that are being applied to this header tag:

```
.article h1 {
  text-align: center;
  margin: 0;
  margin-bottom: (@margin - 0.5);
  line-height: 1.3;
  font-weight: 700;
  color: @bm-black;
}
```

Let's breakdown the CSS for our article section of the page:

- The `text-align` is set to `center` for the entire title
- I've removed the default Bootstrap `margin` on the `<h1>` tag and then re-added a bottom margin
- I've tweaked the default `line-height` a bit to make it more readable
- Finally, the type is set to bold and our black

Adding the article metadata

After finishing the page title, let's cover the article or post meta markup. The meta section lists the post category as a link, and the author's name:

```
<div class="article-meta">
  Posted in <a href="#">Design</a> by John Smith
</div>
```

There are also a few styles that you need to add for the metadata section:

- I've added a bottom margin to the section
- The text-align here is centered again, and the text color is set to use our palette

```
.article-meta {
  margin-bottom: (@margin * 2);
  text-align: center;
  color: @bm-light-grey;
}
```

Adding the article content

We're now ready to jump into the actual content section of a post. There is no special wrapper for this section, but I will add a bottom margin to each image in this section to create more space:

```
.article img {
  margin-bottom: (@margin * 2);
}
```

Following this, it's simply an exercise of entering content for the actual article. At the end of this section, I'll insert the entire page code so that you can see some sample content. For now, let's move on to the comments section of the post.

Adding the comment section

The comment section of the article template is going to be a two-part exercise. First, we're going to use some jQuery to reveal the comment feed at the click of a button. Then we're going to implement a Disqus comment system. Let's start with the custom jQuery that we'll need to power the button effect.

Creating the custom article layout

To start, open the `_layout-article.ejs` file in the root of the project that I had you create earlier in the chapter. Also open up `_layout.ejs`. Copy the entire content of the file and then paste it in the new layout file. Scroll to the bottom of the template, and after the line where we import `bootstrap.min.js`, insert a new `<script>` tag. Within the `<script>` tag, insert the following jQuery code. Then we'll go over each line:

```
<script>
    $(document).ready(function() {
        $("#comment-container").hide();
        $("#comment-trigger").click(function(){
            $("#comment-container").fadeIn();
            $("#comment-trigger").fadeOut();
        });
    });
</script>
```

I'm going to assume that you know a little bit about jQuery and know what `(document).ready` does. If not, just insert that line and move on to the next one. You're going to see some IDs here that we haven't set up yet in our template. After I review the jQuery, we'll insert the related code into `article.ejs`:

```
$("#comment-container").hide();
```

In this line, we're going to target the `#comment-container` `<div>` and hide it using the `.hide()` method. When the page first loads, we don't want the comment section to show up, so we need to hide it:

```
$("#comment-trigger").click(function(){
    ..
});
```

Next, we need to set up a click function that will be attached to a button with the `#comment-trigger` ID. The code inside this function will be executed once the user clicks on the button. Here's what the entire function looks like:

```
$("#comment-trigger").click(function(){
  $("#comment-container").fadeIn();
   $("#comment-trigger").fadeOut();
});
```

We're doing two things here on the button click. The first thing we want to do is reveal the `#comment-container` `<div>`, and I'm using the `.fadeIn()` method for a subtle effect. The next thing I'm going to do is remove the `Load Comments` button, and I'll use the `.fadeOut()` method to do this. This completes the jQuery code that you need to include in the layout. Let's save the file, get back to the `article.ejs` template, and insert the corresponding HTML code.

Adding the trigger button

Scroll to the bottom of the template, and at the end of your post content, insert the following code:

```
<div class="center">
  <button id="comment-trigger" class="btn btn-primary">Load
  Comments</button>
</div>
```

The first thing I've done here is creating a new `<div>` with a class of `.center` on it. This is a new utility class that you can use to center anything in your templates. Jump over to `theme.less` quickly and insert this CSS for the utility class:

```
.center {
  text-align: center;
}
```

Since the button is inside of our post column, this class will center the button in the layout. Next, I've created a button, and note that it's using the `#comment-trigger` ID that we added in the layout. This part is critical for the button click to work.

Adding the Disqus content component

Now that the button is ready to roll, let's set up the comments container `<div>`. After our button code, we insert the following markup:

```
<div id="comment-container">
  ..
</div>
```

As I mentioned, this is going to be the container for our comments. Note that the ID matches the one that we set up in the layout. Again, this is critical to making the effect work. The next thing you need to do is register for a Disqus account to get the code that will generate your comments feed for you. Head over to `https://publishers.disqus.com` and sign up for an account if you don't already have one. Once you've signed up, follow these steps:

- Enter your website details when prompted to do so
- Click on the **Universal Code** option
- Copy the code that appears and paste it in the `#comments-container <div>`
- Insert the second piece of code from the Disqus page in `_layout-article.ejs`, at the bottom right before the closing `</body>` tag

Now save your template and the layout and compile your code. Open the article template in the browser and refresh the page. Hit the **Load Comments** button and wait for a couple seconds the first time for the comment feed to load. If all goes well, your Disqus comments feed should load, and you now have a great component that you can use. Here's an example of what the entire section should look like in your template. Please keep in mind that this code is configured for my website, so you can't do a straight copy and paste. You need to use the code snippet that is provided when you sign up for your account:

```html
<div class="center">
  <button id="comment-trigger" class="btn btn-primary">Load Comments</button>
</div>
<div id="comment-container">
  <div id="disqus_thread"></div>
  <script type="text/javascript">
      /* * * CONFIGURATION VARIABLES * * */
      var disqus_shortname = 'bootstrapblueprints';

      /* * * DON'T EDIT BELOW THIS LINE * * */
      (function() {
          var dsq = document.createElement('script'); dsq.type =
          'text/javascript'; dsq.async = true;
          dsq.src = '//' + disqus_shortname +
          '.disqus.com/embed.js';
          (document.getElementsByTagName('head')[0] ||
          document.getElementsByTagName('body')[0])
          .appendChild(dsq);
      })();
  </script>
```

```
<noscript>Please enable JavaScript to view the <a
href="https://disqus.com/?ref_noscript" rel="nofollow">comments
powered by Disqus.</a></noscript>
</div>
```

That completes the article template and the project. Before we move on to the chapter's summary, let's review the code for the entire `article.ejs` file:

```
<div class="article">
  <div class="container">
    <div class="row">
      <div class="col-lg-12">
        <h1>This is the title for the story it can get kinda big
          if we want it to eh.</h1>
        <div class="article-meta">
          Posted in <a href="#">Design</a> by John Smith
        </div>
        <img src="/img/article1.jpg" width="600" height="335"
          alt="image 1" class="border">
        <p>Lorem ipsum dolor ...</p>
        <p>Quisque luctus eget ...</p>
        <p>Mauris turpis justo ...</p>
        <img src="/img/article2.jpg" width="600" height="466"
          alt="image 2" class="border">
        <p>Quisque luctus eget ...</p>
        <p>Mauris turpis justo ...</p>
        <div class="center">
          <button id="comment-trigger" class="btn btn-
            primary">Load Comments</button>
        </div>
        <div id="comment-container">
          <div id="disqus_thread"></div>
            <script type="text/javascript">
                /* * * CONFIGURATION VARIABLES * * */
                var disqus_shortname = 'bootstrapblueprints';

                /* * * DON'T EDIT BELOW THIS LINE * * */
                (function() {
                    var dsq = document.createElement('script');
                      dsq.type = 'text/javascript'; dsq.async =
                        true;
                    dsq.src = '//' + disqus_shortname +
                      '.disqus.com/embed.js';
```

```
                        (document.getElementsByTagName('head')[0] ||
                           document.getElementsByTagName('body')[0]).
    appendChild(dsq);
                        })();
                </script>
                <noscript>Please enable JavaScript to view the <a
                    href="https://disqus.com/?ref_noscript"
                        rel="nofollow">comments powered by
                            Disqus.</a></noscript>
            </div>
          </div>
        </div>
      </div>
    </div>
```

Summary

That brings the fifth chapter to a close. Let's review what you learned: how to create a magazine website using Bootstrap, a new way to lay out a header using inline `div`, how to construct a complex footer using multiple parts, how to use flexbox with a Bootstrap grid, how to use some basic jQuery to improve the experience of your article page, and how to implement a Disqus-powered comments section.

6
Bootstrap Dashboard

In this chapter, I'm going to show you how to create a dashboard using Bootstrap. For a change, we'll make a dark-colored design and implement a number of components commonly found on a dashboard. Part of this exercise will teach you how to integrate a third-party chart library and customize it to work in Bootstrap. We'll also cover customizations of a few components that we have not used yet, such as navigation pills, panels, and tables.

Before we dive into updating our template, let's take a look at what we'll be creating:

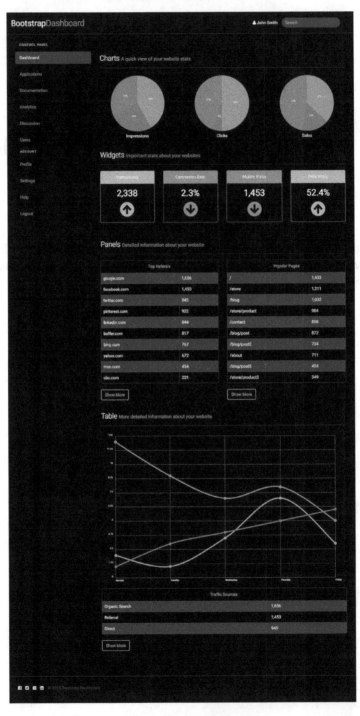

Customizing the template

As in our other projects, we start by copying our boilerplate project to a new directory called chapter6. Open the _data.json file and insert the following code:

```
{
  "index": {
    "pageTitle": "Dashboard"
  }
}
```

For this project, we're only creating one page template. Let's start by creating a file in the root of our project. For now, just leave the file blank; we'll fill it in a bit later: index.ejs.

Updating _layout.ejs

Next, let's update the _layout.ejs file in the root of our new project. The layout for this project will need a few more things that we haven't seen before. First of all, insert the following line of code to import the Google web font Roboto, which we'll be using for our dashboard:

```
<link href='https://fonts.googleapis.com/
css?family=Roboto:400,300,700' rel='stylesheet' type='text/css'>
```

For this project, we're going to use a third-party chart library to draw some pie charts and line graphs. I've decided to use a library called Chartist. This library is a simple, responsive charts option that will give us exactly what we need. Head over to the following URL and download the library:

https://gionkunz.github.io/chartist-js/

Once you've downloaded the library, unzip it and then copy a couple of files to your project. Locate the file named chartist.min.css and copy it to your /css directory. Also, find the file named chartist.min.js and copy it to the /js directory. Once you've copied the files, you need to insert them into the layout. Add the following line of code to the layout after font-awesome.min.css. Also make sure that your theme.css is inserted after the Chartist CSS. Later on, we're going to overwrite some of the styles in the library:

```
<link rel="stylesheet" type="text/css" href="css/chartist.min.css">
```

Next, we need to include the JavaScript library file. Insert the following line of code after bootstrap.min.js:

```
<script src="js/chartist.min.js" type="text/javascript"></script>
```

We also need to include another JavaScript file. This file will hold our custom code that will render our charts on the **dashboard** page. First, create a file named `bootboard-charts.js` in the `/js` directory. You can leave it blank for now. Next, go back to the layout and insert the following line of code after `chartist.min.js`:

```
<script src="js/bootboard-charts.js" type="text/javascript"></script>
```

This completes the updates we need for the layout. Let's check out what the entire file looks like:

```
<!DOCTYPE html>
<html lang="en">
<head>
  <meta charset="utf-8">
  <meta http-equiv="X-UA-Compatible" content="IE=edge">
  <meta name="viewport" content="width=device-width, initial-scale=1">
  <title><%- pageTitle %> | <%- siteTitle %></title>

  <link rel="stylesheet" type="text/css" href="css/bootstrap.min.css">
  <link rel="stylesheet" type="text/css" href="css/font-awesome.min.
css">
  <link rel="stylesheet" type="text/css" href="css/chartist.min.css">
  <link rel="stylesheet" type="text/css" href="css/theme.css">
  <link href='https://fonts.googleapis.com/
css?family=Roboto:400,300,700' rel='stylesheet' type='text/css'>

  <!-- HTML5 shim and Respond.js for IE8 support of HTML5 elements and
media queries -->
  <!-- WARNING: Respond.js doesn't work if you view the page via
file:// -->
  <!--[if lt IE 9]>
    <script src="https://oss.maxcdn.com/html5shiv/3.7.2/html5shiv.min.
js"></script>
    <script src="https://oss.maxcdn.com/respond/1.4.2/respond.min.
js"></script>
  <![endif]-->
</head>
<body>

  <%- partial("partial/_header") %>

  <%- yield %>

  <%- partial("partial/_footer") %>
```

```
<!-- javascript //-->
<script src="//ajax.googleapis.com/ajax/libs/jquery/1.11.1/jquery.
min.js"></script>
<script src="js/bootstrap.min.js" type="text/javascript"></script>
<script src="js/chartist.min.js" type="text/javascript"></script>
<script src="js/bootboard-charts.js" type="text/javascript"></
script>
</body>
</html>
```

Setting up the Less variables

Now that we've finished our layout, it's time to move on to updating our Less variables. For this project, I'm not going to add any new colors. We're going to fall back to the colors from our original boilerplate. I want to give you a good example of how it's useful to have these stock colors for use on a project.

Background colors

Let's start by updating our background colors to use our boilerplate color values. As you'll see, I'm using @black for the primary background. This is because we're going to make this a dark colored design:

```
@primary-background: @black;
@secondary-background: @dark-grey;
@inverse-background: @white;
```

Text colors

Next, let's update our text colors and invert them to be readable on a dark background:

```
@primary-text: @white;
@light-text: @dark-grey;
@loud-text: @white;
@inverse-text: @white;
@heading-text: @light-grey;
```

Link colors

The same inverse color approach will be used to set the values for our links:

```
@primary-link-color: @light-grey;
@primary-link-color-hover: @white;
```

Borders

Again, we'll update the border colors to match our new dark design:

```
@border-color: @dark-grey;
@border-size: 1px;
@border-type: solid;
@border-focus: @light-grey;
```

Typography

For the typography of this project, I've decided to switch the font to Roboto. You'll need to update the two typeface variables to reflect this:

```
@body-copy: "Roboto", helvetica, arial, verdana, sans-serif;
@heading-copy: "Roboto", helvetica, arial, verdana, sans-serif;
```

This completes the updates that you need to make to the variables Less file. Look how easy it was using the stock color values! You didn't even need to think about the colors; you only had to think how you wanted to apply them. That process was super easy too! If you are working on a large number of projects or themes, this type of time saver will be invaluable to you. Let's take a look at the entire variables file before we move on to the header and footer:

```
// color palette

@black: #000;
@dark-grey: #333;
@grey: #777;
@light-grey: #ebebeb;
@off-white: #f5f5f5;
@white: #ffffff;

@blue1: #3498db;
@blue2: #2980b9;
@red1: #e74c3c;
@red2: #c0392b;
@yellow1: #f1c40f;
@yellow2: #f39c12;
@green1: #2ecc71;
@green2: #27ae60;
@orange1: #e67e22;
@orange2: #d35400;
@aqua1: #1abc9c;
@aqua2: #16a085;
@purple1: #9b59b6;
```

```less
@purple2: #8e44ad;
@navy1: #34495e;
@navy2: #2c3e50;

// background colors
@primary-background: @black;
@secondary-background: @dark-grey;
@inverse-background: @white;

// text colors
@primary-text: @white;
@light-text: @dark-grey;
@loud-text: @white;
@inverse-text: @white;
@heading-text: @light-grey;

// link colors
@primary-link-color: @light-grey;
@primary-link-color-hover: @white;

// primary border properties
@border-color: @dark-grey;
@border-size: 1px;
@border-type: solid;
@border-focus: @light-grey;

// typography NEW fonts
@body-copy: "Roboto", helvetica, arial, verdana, sans-serif;
@heading-copy: "Roboto", helvetica, arial, verdana, sans-serif;
@base-font-size: 14px;
@font-size: 1em;
@base-line-height: 1.5;

// layout
@margin: 1em;
@padding: 1em;

// MIXINS

// round corners or Border radius
.round-corners (@radius: 2px) {
  -moz-border-radius: @radius;
  -ms-border-radius: @radius;
  border-radius: @radius;
```

```
}

// animation transitions
.transition (@transition: background .1s linear) {
  -moz-transition: @transition;
  -webkit-transition: @transition;
  transition: background @transition;
}
```

Coding the header and footer

Let's now proceed to code the header and footer for the project. The header will use the default Bootstrap `navbar` with some color customizations. We'll also be inserting a search form and some other text into the header. Our footer will be super basic, with only a few social media icons and a copyright statement.

Updating the header

Let's start out by creating the header, and then we'll customize it. Here's the code for the entire thing:

```
<nav class="navbar navbar-default" role="navigation">
  <div class="container">
    <div class="navbar-header">
      <button type="button" class="navbar-toggle" data-
toggle="collapse" data-target="#bootboard-nav">
        <span class="sr-only">Toggle navigation</span>
        <span class="icon-bar"></span>
        <span class="icon-bar"></span>
        <span class="icon-bar"></span>
      </button>
      <a class="navbar-brand" href="#">Bootstrap<span>Dashboard</
span></a>
    </div>

    <form class="navbar-form navbar-right" role="search">
      <div class="form-group">
        <input type="text" class="form-control" placeholder="Search">
      </div>
    </form>

    <ul class="nav navbar-nav navbar-right">
      <li>
        <i class="fa fa-user"></i>
```

```
        John Smith
      </li>
    </ul>
  </div>
</nav>
```

The first important thing to note here is the responsive button line of code. You'll notice the `data-target` attribute is pointing to `#bootboard-nav`. This `nav` is not actually in the header; it will be the sidebar navigation. If you're viewing this on a mobile device, the sidebar will disappear and the links will be rolled into the mobile navigation list of links:

```
<button type="button" class="navbar-toggle" data-toggle="collapse"
data-target="#bootboard-nav">
```

The next part that we should review is the markup for the search input:

```
<form class="navbar-form navbar-right" role="search">
  <div class="form-group">
    <input type="text" class="form-control" placeholder="Search">
  </div>
</form>
```

This is our standard `navbar` search field, but I've applied some custom styles to the field to give it round corners. Create a new file called `_navbar.less` and save it in the `css/components` directory. Also, don't forget to import `_navbar.less` into `theme.less`. In `_navbar.less`, insert the following code:

```
.navbar-form input {
  -moz-border-radius: 20px;
  border-radius: 20px;
  border: 0;
  background: @dark-grey;
  color: @white;
  margin-top: -5px;
}
```

Here, you'll see that I've set `border-radius` to `20px` to get that rounded ends look. I've also customized the colors to match our dark color scheme, and I need to apply a bit of negative margin to vertically center the field in the `navbar`. I'll get deeper into the customization of the `navbar` component a little later. The last things that we should review are the username and icon on the right-hand side of the `navbar`:

```
<ul class="nav navbar-nav navbar-right">
  <li>
    <i class="fa fa-user"></i>
```

```
        John Smith
    </li>
</ul>
```

On the `<ul>` tag, I've added the `.navbar-right` Bootstrap utility class, which will align the list on the right-hand side of the page. I'm also using a Font Awesome icon here for the user. The last three points are the key things you need to keep in mind while coding this component. Now, let's move on to all the styles required to customize the look and feel of the navigation bar.

Customizing the navbar component

Go back to the `_navbar.less` file that you recently created. We're going to insert some more styles for our component:

```
.navbar {
  background: @primary-background;
  margin-bottom: @margin;
}
```

I've set the background of the `navbar` to use our primary background color, which is black. I've also reset the margins to use our global value. We're going to use the default Bootstrap `navbar`, but we'll need to make a bunch of changes:

```
.navbar-default .navbar-brand {
  font-family: @heading-copy;
  font-weight: 400;
  font-size: (@font-size * 2);
  height: 72px;
  line-height: 72px;
  padding: 0;
}
```

Let's breakdown the CSS for the `.navbar` component:

- Using the `.brand` class, I'm going to set it to use our heading copy variable.
- We'll set font-weight to regular and double the font-size.
- I'm going to set the `height` and `line-height` of the brand to 72px. This is a little trick to vertically center everything in our `navbar`.
- Finally, I'm going to remove the default padding so that everything lines up vertically.

Let's continue editing the brand by setting up some hover and color styles. You'll notice in the HTML that part of the title is wrapped in a `<span>` tag. This will allow me to target that word and give it a different color:

```
.navbar-default .navbar-brand:hover,
.navbar-default .navbar-brand:hover span {
  color: @blue1;
}

.navbar-default .navbar-brand span {
  color: @blue1;
  font-weight: 300;
}
```

I've also reduced the `font-weight` of the `brand` `<span>` to light or `300`. On hovering over the brand, both words will turn blue. This creates a subtle but attractive little effect. Let's continue and customize the actual default `navbar` styles:

```
.navbar-default {
  border: 0;
  border-bottom: @border-size @border-type @border-color;
  margin: 0;
  margin-bottom: (@margin * 2);
  line-height: 72px;
  height: 72px;

  border-radius: 0;
  -moz-border-radius: 0;
}
```

Let's breakdown the CSS for the `.navbar` a little more:

- I've removed all borders from the `navbar`, but then I've added the bottom-border back in. I did it this way because I first want to neutralize the Bootstrap styles before I apply my own.
- I've also removed the margin so that the vertical centering doesn't get messed up. However, I've added some `bottom-margin` to create some space below the `navbar`.
- Again, I set the height and line-height to `72px` so that everything is centered vertically.

- Finally, I removed border-radius. This is because I want the `navbar` and background to blend in together perfectly:

```
.navbar-collapse {
  padding-left: 0;
  padding-right: 0;
}
```

I've removed the default left and right padding from the collapsible `navbar` for the same reasons as I removed border-radius. There's one last style that we need to add:

```
.navbar-form {
  margin: 0;
}
```

Finally, I've removed the margin from the `navbar` form so that it doesn't mess up the vertical centering of the component. This brings the `navbar` component customization to an end. Let's proceed to set up the footer, and then we can move on to the actual body of our dashboard.

Updating the footer

The footer for the dashboard project is pretty straightforward. It's made up of a copyright statement and social media links. Let's take a look at the HTML:

```
<!-- footer //-->
<footer>
  <div class="container">
    <div class="row">
      <div class="col-lg-12">
        <ul class="list-inline">
          <li><a href="#"><i class="fa fa-facebook-official"></i></
a></li>
          <li><a href="#"><i class="fa fa-twitter-square"></i></a></
li>
          <li><a href="#"><i class="fa fa-pinterest-square"></i></a></
li>
          <li><a href="#"><i class="fa fa-linkedin-square"></i></a></
li>
          <li>&copy; 2015 Bootstrap Dashboard</li>
        </ul>
      </div>
    </div>
  </div>
</footer>
```

I've wrapped the entire footer in the HTML5 `<footer>` tag. Within that is a container with a Bootstrap inline list. Each list item uses the Font Awesome icon set and then a copyright statement. There are also a few footer styles to review:

```
footer {
  margin-top: (@padding * 6);
  padding-bottom: (@padding * 2);
  padding-top: (@padding * 2);
  border-top: @border-size @border-color @border-type;
  color: @light-text;
}
```

Let's breakdown the CSS for the footer:

- I've added a top margin in order to add some spacing between the content and the footer
- I've also added a little bottom padding for breathing space
- Then, I've added a top border to act as a divider
- There is some top padding so as to add space between the list and the border
- Finally, I set the text color to light

This completes the updates to all our standard template pieces. Next, we'll move on to coding the main content section of the dashboard.

Coding the dashboard

The main body of the dashboard is going to hold the main portion of this project. We'll start by setting up the two-column layout, followed by inserting the sidebar with pill-based navigation. Next, we'll update the typography styles and insert pie charts. Finally, we'll customize the Bootstrap `panel` and `table` components and add a line chart for good measure.

Setting up the layout

The dashboard is going to use a two-column layout. The left column will be our sidebar navigation, and it will use the Bootstrap `pill` component. The right-side will hold our page content with charts, panels, and tables. If you haven't already done so, create a file named `index.ejs` in the root of your project and enter the layout code:

```
<div class="container">
  <div class="row">
```

```
        <div class="col-lg-3">
          <!-- sidebar //-->
        </div>
        <div class="col-lg-9">
          <!-- content //-->
        </div>
      </div>
    </div>
```

This layout code is very straightforward. I've created a 1:4 grid system. Let's move on to setting up the sidebar.

Creating the sidebar

The sidebar is going to use the Bootstrap pill `navigation` component. Let's start by coding a basic list of pages first. Then, we'll add the custom pill styles that we need to update:

```
<div class="col-lg-3">
  <div class="collapse navbar-collapse" id="bootboard-nav">
    <ul class="nav nav-pills nav-stacked">
      <li class="navigation-header">Control Panel</li>
      <li class="active"><a href="#">Dashboard</a></li>
      <li><a href="#">Applications</a></li>
      <li><a href="#">Documentation</a></li>
      <li><a href="#">Analytics</a></li>
      <li><a href="#">Discussion</a></li>
      <li><a href="#">Users</a></li>
      <li class="navigation-header">Account</li>
      <li><a href="#">Profile</a></li>
      <li><a href="#">Settings</a></li>
      <li><a href="#">Help</a></li>
      <li><a href="#">Logout</a></li>
    </ul>
  </div>
</div>
```

- Within the parent `<div>`, there is `<div>` with the Bootstrap collapsible navigation classes. In a mobile viewport, this list of links will be grabbed and inserted into the mobile menu. It's important to note that you can grab any list of links and make it a mobile navigation if you use the write code structure. You aren't restricted to using only the default navigation bar.

- Inside that collapsible `<div>`, there is a `<ul>` with some nav pill classes on the `<ul>`. These are the classes that will change the regular list into a pill navigation.

- Some `<li>` tags have a class of `.navigation-header` on them. These are the category names for our navigation, and they will be styled differently.

Customizing the nav pills component

Thus, we have completed the HTML for the navigation. Let's now take a look at the custom styles that we need to add. Start by creating a new Less file called `_navs.less` and save it to the `css/components` directory. Before we code the pill-specific CSS, we need to update this global nav component. We'll customize the actual pill styles next. For now, insert the following CSS into the nav file:

```
.nav-stacked > li + li {
  margin-top: @margin;
}

.nav > li > a:focus,
.nav > li > a:hover {
  background-color: @blue1;
  color: @white;
}
```

Let's breakdown the CSS for the navigation links:

- The first selector will add a top margin to each list item.

- The second set of styles will set the link colors for our navigation list. As you can see, we're using our color palette variables here.

Next, let's create the pills CSS. Create another Less file and name it `_pills.less`. Import it into `theme.less`. Within `_pills.less`, insert the following CSS:

```
.nav-pills > li > a {
  color: @grey;
}

.nav-pills > li.active > a,
.nav-pills > li.active > a:focus,
.nav-pills > li.active > a:hover {
  background-color: @dark-grey;
}
```

These styles set the link text and background colors for the active pill or page in our navigation. You can set the active link by adding a class of .active to the `<li>` tag for the current page. In this case, it should be set to `Dashboard`.

Before we can complete the sidebar, we need to add styles for our navigation category headers. Open `theme.less`, scroll down to the **Layout** section, and insert the following CSS:

```
li.navigation-header {
  color: @blue1;
  text-transform: uppercase;
  font-size: (@font-size - 0.25);
  letter-spacing: 1px;
  font-weight: 700;
  margin-bottom: @margin 0;
  padding-left: 15px;
}
```

These styles will give the navigation category headers a unique look so that they stand out from the regular navigation links.

That completes the sidebar navigation portion of the dashboard. Next, I'll go over how to build the content section of the project.

Creating the content section

The content section of the dashboard will be made up of pie charts, panels, tables, and line charts. We'll also use the Bootstrap page header component and customize some other text styles. Let's start with the page section headers.

Customizing the typography

There is a page header component in Bootstrap that will add some spacing and a border to a section header so that it stands out more. Let's take a look at the HTML for this component:

```
<div class="row">
  <div class="col-lg-12">
    <div class="page-header">
      <h3>Charts <small>A quick view of your website stats</small></
h3>
    </div>
  </div>
</div>
```

Let's breakdown the CSS for the project's typography:

- Within my content section, using the col-lg-9 grid class, I'm going to insert a number of new row classes for each part of the page body. Since we want the section header to span the entire width of the parent <div>, we'll use the col-lg-12 grid class here.

- Within that <div>, we'll use the .page-header class to invoke that component.

- Then, within the page header, I'll use an <h3> tag for my section title.

- You'll also notice a <small> tag nested in <h3>, which is a feature of the page header component. This allows you to add a smaller piece of text next to the title. This is great for adding a short description, as I've done here.

Before we move on to the pie charts, we need to customize the page header styles a little. Create a new Less file called _typography.less and save it to the css/components directory. Don't forget to import it into theme.less. Within _typography.less, insert the following CSS:

```
.page-header {
  border-bottom: @border-size @border-type @border-color;
}
```

All I've done here is normalized the border for this component so that it uses our look and feel. Let's move on to the pie chart section of the dashboard.

Writing the pie chart HTML

The pie chart portion of the dashboard is rendered using a JavaScript chart library called **Chartist**. We previously included the **Chartist** library when we set up our layout. Now we actually need to use it. We're going to divide the section into three equal columns and then insert a chart into each:

```
<div class="charts">
  <div class="row">
    <div class="col-lg-4">
      <div class="ct-chart-one ct-perfect-fourth"></div>
      Impressions
    </div>
    <div class="col-lg-4">
      <div class="ct-chart-two ct-perfect-fourth"></div>
      Clicks
    </div>
    <div class="col-lg-4">
      <div class="ct-chart-three ct-perfect-fourth"></div>
      Sales
    </div>
  </div>
</div>
```

Let's breakdown the HTML for the pie charts:

- I've wrapped the entire row in a class of .charts, which we'll use to add some styling a little later.

- I divided the row into three equal columns using the col-lg-4 grid class.

- Within each column is a <div> for a chart. These <div> will be empty as we'll be loading in the chart with JavaScript.

- Note that each <div> has a unique class for each chart, for example, ch-chart-one. This is required so that we can make each chart different.

- There is a second class called ct-perfect-fourth that defines the type of chart we want to use. Check out the Chartist documentation for more information on how this works at https://gionkunz.github.io/chartist-js/getting-started.html.

Now that we've coded the HTML for the pie charts, we need to move on to the JavaScript. Following that, we'll customize the pie chart look and feel with some CSS.

Writing the pie chart JavaScript

This project marks the first time we'll write some custom JavaScript. Start by creating a new file called `bootboard-chart.js` and save it to the `/js` directory in your project. Next, we insert the following JavaScript for our first chart:

```
// first pie chart
var data = {
  series: [5, 3, 4]
};

var sum = function(a, b) { return a + b };

new Chartist.Pie('.ct-chart-one', data, {
  labelInterpolationFnc: function(value) {
    return Math.round(value / data.series.reduce(sum) * 100) + '%';
  }
});
```

Let's breakdown the JavaScript for the chart:

- Don't let the JavaScript intimidate you. There is actually very little that we need to change here.

- Take a look at the series: line of code and you'll see three numerical values. This is how our chart will be divided. It doesn't really matter what these numbers are; you just need three of them.

- Next, jump to the new `Chartist.Pie` line. Notice that there is a CSS class on this line. This is the class that we entered in our first chart `<div>`. Make sure that the class name matches and save your file. That's all you need to update.

Let's take a look at the JavaScript for the second pie chart. It's very similar to the first pie chart, but we're going to change a few values:

```
// second pie chart
var data = {
  series: [8, 1, 7]
};

var sum = function(a, b) { return a + b };

new Chartist.Pie('.ct-chart-two', data, {
  labelInterpolationFnc: function(value) {
```

```
      return Math.round(value / data.series.reduce(sum) * 100) + '%';
    }
  });
```

Let's breakdown the second pie chart:

- Note that the values in the `series:` array have changed, so the chart will be divided differently
- I've also changed the class to point to our second <div>

Finally, let's check out the JavaScript for the last chart:

```
// third pie chart
var data = {
  series: [7, 3, 9]
};

var sum = function(a, b) { return a + b };

new Chartist.Pie('.ct-chart-three', data, {
  labelInterpolationFnc: function(value) {
    return Math.round(value / data.series.reduce(sum) * 100) + '%';
  }
});
```

Let's breakdown the last pie chart:

- Like the previous two, I've updated the numbers in the series: array to be different
- I've also changed the class name to make it unique and match our third <div>

Let's take a look at all of the chart code together:

```
// first pie chart
var data = {
  series: [5, 3, 4]
};

var sum = function(a, b) { return a + b };

new Chartist.Pie('.ct-chart-one', data, {
```

```
    labelInterpolationFnc: function(value) {
      return Math.round(value / data.series.reduce(sum) * 100) + '%';
    }
});

// second pie chart
var data = {
  series: [8, 1, 7]
};

var sum = function(a, b) { return a + b };

new Chartist.Pie('.ct-chart-two', data, {
    labelInterpolationFnc: function(value) {
      return Math.round(value / data.series.reduce(sum) * 100) + '%';
    }
});

// third pie chart
var data = {
  series: [7, 3, 9]
};

var sum = function(a, b) { return a + b };

new Chartist.Pie('.ct-chart-three', data, {
    labelInterpolationFnc: function(value) {
      return Math.round(value / data.series.reduce(sum) * 100) + '%';
    }
});
```

That's it! The pie chart JavaScript is done. Pretty straightforward if you ask me! Keep the file open as we'll add a line chart later on in this chapter. At this point, I'd recommend that you save all your files and compile them. Open up the project in the browser and make sure that your charts are loading in. If they are, it's great! However, you'll notice that they don't quite look right. We need to apply some custom CSS styles.

Creating a Less component for the charts

Just like all of our Bootstrap components, we're going to create a new Less file named `_charts.less` and save it to the `css/components` directory. Also, don't forget to import all of these new Less files into `theme.less`. Otherwise, the CSS changes won't be overwritten. Within the new charts less file, insert the following code:

```
// pie charts

.ct-series-a .ct-area,
.ct-series-a .ct-slice-pie {
  fill: @blue1;
}

.ct-series-b .ct-area,
.ct-series-b .ct-slice-pie {
  fill: (@blue1 - #222);
}

.ct-series-c .ct-area,
.ct-series-c .ct-slice-pie {
  fill: @blue2;
}
```

Let's breakdown the CSS for the customizing the chart colors:

- We're using pie charts with three sections, so note the class naming: `ct-series-a`, `ct-series-b`, and `ct-series-c`. Each one of these will map to a piece of pie.

- For each different piece of pie, I've assigned a unique color: `@blue1` for the first piece, `(@blue1 - #222)` for the second piece (this is by using a Less operator), and `@blue2` for the third piece.

That's all you need to change to adjust the look and feel. Compile your code again and test it in your browser. You can also keep this file open, as we'll be adding more styles for our line chart later. Before we move on to the widgets section of the dashboard, we don't want to forget about styling the `.charts` container that we previously set up. Open `theme.less` and scroll down to the **Layout** section of the theme. Once you get there, insert the following CSS:

```
.charts {
  text-align: center;
}
```

I want each chart to be centered in its <div>, so I've set text-align to center for everything nested under .charts.

That completes the pie chart section of the dashboard. Let's move on to the next section—widgets.

Setting up the widgets section

The widgets section of the dashboard is going to be built using the Bootstrap panels component. However, before we get that far, let's insert another page header component for this new section. This will be just like the pie charts section but with a new title and description:

```
<div class="row">
  <div class="col-lg-12">
    <div class="page-header">
      <h3>Widgets <small>Important stats about your websites</small></h3>
    </div>
  </div>
</div>
```

Writing the widgets HTML

With that complete, let's move on to the content of this section. The widget row is going to be divided into four equal columns using the col-lg-3 Bootstrap grid class. Within each column, we'll insert one panel component, which we'll then customize. Let's check out the HTML for the entire section:

```
<div class="row widgets">
  <div class="col-lg-3">
    <div class="panel panel-success">
      <div class="panel-heading">Impressions</div>
      <div class="panel-body">
        <h2>2,338</h2>
        <i class="fa fa-arrow-circle-up"></i>
      </div>
    </div>
  </div>
  <div class="col-lg-3">
    <div class="panel panel-danger">
      <div class="panel-heading">Conversion Rate</div>
      <div class="panel-body">
        <h2>2.3%</h2>
```

```
              <i class="fa fa-arrow-circle-down"></i>
          </div>
        </div>
      </div>
      <div class="col-lg-3">
        <div class="panel panel-danger">
          <div class="panel-heading">Mobile Visits</div>
          <div class="panel-body">
            <h2>1,453</h2>
            <i class="fa fa-arrow-circle-down"></i>
          </div>
        </div>
      </div>
      <div class="col-lg-3">
        <div class="panel panel-success">
          <div class="panel-heading">New Visits</div>
          <div class="panel-body">
            <h2>52.4%</h2>
            <i class="fa fa-arrow-circle-up"></i>
          </div>
        </div>
      </div>
    </div>
```

Let's breakdown the HTML for the `widgets/`:

- I've added a class of `.widgets` to the `.row` `<div>` so that I can add some styling later.

- You'll notice that I'm using two types of panels here: `.panel-success` and `.panel-danger`. We're going to be creating some simple analytics widgets, so if a value is up, with positive and down with negative.

- Within the body of each panel, we have a value and a Font Awesome up or down arrow icon, depending on whether the number has increased or decreased based on the previous day. Of course, this content is fictional, but it can easily be applied to an actual dashboard.

Reviewing the success panel

Let's take a closer look at the success panel HTML and the styles that we need to customize for this component:

```
<div class="panel panel-success">
  <div class="panel-heading">Impressions</div>
    <div class="panel-body">
       <h2>2,338</h2>
       <i class="fa fa-arrow-circle-up"></i>
    </div>
  </div>
</div>
```

Let's breakdown the HTML for the panel component:

- As you can see, the first `<div>` has a class of `.panel` and `.panel-success`. The `.panel` class is required, and the second class can change depending on what type you want to use.

- Each panel has a `.panel-heading` `<div>`, which is the title for that panel. In this case, I've named it `Impressions`.

- Each panel also has a `.panel-body` `<div>` for the body of the component.

- The first thing that I inserted in the body is an `<h2>` tag with a value. I used `<h2>` so that the text would be larger in size. Feel free to use a different tag if you like.

- Next, there is a Font Awesome up arrow icon, since this is a success panel.

Before we can move on to the danger panel, we need to add some custom styles for the success version. Create a new Less file called `_panels.less` and save it in the `css/components` directory. Also, don't forgot to import this file into `theme.less`. Insert the following code into the new panel Less file:

```
.panel {
  background: transparent;
}

.panel h2 {
  margin-top: 0;
}

.panel i {
  font-size: (@font-size * 4);
}
```

Let's breakdown the CSS for the .panel component:

- Let's start with some styles consistent in all panel components. By default, the background of all panels is white, but I want to remove that. So, I've reset it to transparent.

- I removed the top margin for the <h2> in the body of the panel so that the vertical alignment is equal.

- Finally, I set the font-size of the icon to four times the normal size, as I want the arrows to be quite large.

Now, let's add a few more styles that are specific to the success panel:

```
.panel-success {
  border-color: @green1;
}

.panel-success > .panel-heading {
  color: @white;
  background: @green1;
  border-color: @green1;
}

.panel-success i {
  color: @green1;
}
```

Let's review the CSS for setting up the different panel colors:

- The first selector will reset the border of the success panel to use the color green from our palette

- We'll also reset the colors of the panel heading to use our palette's colors

- Finally, I'll set the arrow icon color to green to match the rest of the panel

Reviewing the danger panel

The `danger` panel is just like the success one, but it will be red. This panel styling should be used for an analytical value that has gone down since the last time of measure. The only change in HTML here will be the `.panel-danger` class on the parent `<div>`:

```
<div class="panel panel-danger">
  <div class="panel-heading">Conversion Rate</div>
    <div class="panel-body">
      <h2>2.3%</h2>
      <i class="fa fa-arrow-circle-down"></i>
    </div>
  </div>
</div>
```

We will need to add some more custom CSS to our panels component. Go back to `_panels.less` and insert the following danger panel styles:

```
.panel-danger {
  border-color: @red1;
}

.panel-danger > .panel-heading {
  color: @white;
  background: @red1;
  border-color: @red1;
}

.panel-danger i {
  color: @red1;
}
```

As with the success panel, these styles will reset the panel to use the red shade from our color palette. This will also set the down arrow icon that appears in the body of the component to red.

This completes the widgets section of the dashboard. Next, I'll teach you how to code the **Panels** section (not to be confused with the `panels` component).

Writing the panels HTML

The next section of the dashboard will also use the panel component, but we will extend it further by including a table. Let's first look at the HTML for the first panel. Then, we'll go over the styles that need customizing. First of all, we'll include a full-width row with our section header:

```
<div class="row">
  <div class="col-lg-12">
    <div class="page-header">
      <h3>Panels <small>Detailed information about your website</small></h3>
    </div>
  </div>
</div>
```

This is the same as the previous section headers. Next, we'll divide a row into two equal columns and insert our first panel with a table inside:

```
<div class="panel panel-default">
  <div class="panel-heading">Top Referals</div>
  <table class="table table-striped table-bordered table-hover">
    <tbody>
      <tr>
        <td>google.com</td>
        <td>1,656</td>
      </tr>
      <tr>
        <td>facebook.com</td>
        <td>1,453</td>
      </tr>
      <tr>
        <td>twitter.com</td>
        <td>945</td>
      </tr>
      <tr>
        <td>pinterest.com</td>
        <td>922</td>
      </tr>
      <tr>
        <td>linkedin.com</td>
        <td>844</td>
      </tr>
      <tr>
        <td>buffer.com</td>
```

```
        <td>817</td>
    </tr>
    <tr>
        <td>bing.com</td>
        <td>767</td>
    </tr>
    <tr>
        <td>yahoo.com</td>
        <td>672</td>
    </tr>
    <tr>
        <td>msn.com</td>
        <td>454</td>
    </tr>
    <tr>
        <td>cbc.com</td>
        <td>231</td>
    </tr>
    </tbody>
  </table>
</div>
```

Let's breakdown the HTML for the table:

- I'm using the `.panel-default` class again.
- Inside my panel body, I inserted a `<table>` with some classes in it. The `.table-striped` will zebra stripe the table, `.table-bordered` will add borders, and `.table-hover` will add a hover state to each row.

Next, let's review the styles that we need to add for this variation of the `panel` component.

Customizing the table component

Start by creating a new file called `_tables.less` and save it at `css/components` directory. Next, open up `theme.less` and import the `table` component Less file. Let's start breaking down the custom table styles:

```
table,
tr,
tbody {
  border-color: @dark-grey;
}
```

I've reset the table borders to use a color from our palette. Otherwise, they'll be the default light gray, which we don't want:

```
.table-bordered > tbody > tr > td,
.table-bordered > tbody > tr > th,
.table-bordered > tfoot > tr > td,
.table-bordered > tfoot > tr > th,
.table-bordered > thead > tr > td,
.table-bordered > thead > tr > th {
  border: @border-size @border-type @border-color;
}
```

We also need to customize the border values for the `.table-bordered` class, which we added to our `<table>` tag. We'll want those values to match the global variables that we set up previously:

```
.table-striped > tbody > tr:nth-of-type(odd) {
  background-color: @dark-grey;
}
```

For the `.table-striped` class, which adds the zebra striping effect, we need to change `background-color` to use the dark gray shade from our color palette. Again, if you don't change this, it will be a light gray background:

```
.table-hover > tbody > tr:hover {
  background-color: @blue1;
}
```

Finally, we need to set a hover color for the `.table-hover` class. In this case, I'm going to use the same blue that I used for the global links. This will give us some color consistency throughout the dashboard.

Adding the button

You'll notice below the panel that I've inserted a button. This could allow the user to go to an inside page that shows an expanded report. Insert the following button code after the panel:

```
<button class="btn btn-primary">Show More</button>
```

I'm using a basic primary button here. We'll need to update the CSS for the buttons to match our design.

Customizing the button component

Create a new file called `_buttons.less` and save it at `css/components` directory. Next, open up `theme.less` and import the new button component into the master theme. Insert the following styles into the button style sheet to apply the proper look and feel:

```
.btn-primary {
  background: @black;
  border: (@border-size * 2) @border-type @blue1;
  color: @blue1;
}

.btn-primary:hover {
  background-color: @black;
  border: (@border-size * 2) @border-type @blue1;
  color: @white;
}
```

Let's breakdown the CSS for the button component:

- I've set `background-color` to `black` so that it blends with our page background. You can set it to transparent if you prefer.

- I've increased the border-width a bit so that it really pops.

- The border-color is set to the same blue that we've been using throughout the dashboard.

- On hover, the only thing that will change is the color of the text in the button, which will go from blue to white. This creates a nice, subtle button effect.

Inserting a line chart

We've made it to the last part of the dashboard project. Now we're going to step back and insert another chart here using the chartist library. However, in this case, we are going to insert a line chart instead of a pie chart. The first thing that we need to do is code the HTML for the chart. Next, we'll add some more JavaScript to render the chart. Finally, we'll need to update some more CSS to control the look and feel of the lines in our chart.

Adding the HTML for the line chart

This final section of the dashboard is made up of three parts. The first is the section header, the second is the line chart, and the third is a table that will appear below the line chart. Let's start by first inserting the section header. Insert the following HTML after the panel tables section that you just completed:

```
<div class="row">
  <div class="col-lg-12">
    <div class="page-header">
      <h3>Table <small>More detailed information about your website</
small></h3>
    </div>
  </div>
</div>
```

This section is the same as that of the previous headers. I'm just changing the name and description. Let's move on to the next part of this section, which is the line chart container. Remember that as in our previous charts, we just need to code a container `<div>` in which the chart will be loaded via our JavaScript. Insert the following HTML after the section header code:

```
<div class="row">
  <div class="col-lg-12">
     <div class="ct-chart-table ct-golden-section"></div>
  </div>
</div>
```

Let's breakdown the HTML for the line chart:

- For this chart, I'm using the `.ct-chart-table` class, which will render a line chart.

- I'm also using the `.ct-golden-section` class, which determines what aspect ratio should be used for the chart. There are many different options that you can use here. For more information, check out the documentation at `https://gionkunz.github.io/chartist-js/getting-started.html`.

Finally, let's insert the HTML for the table that will appear below the line chart. Also note that there is a button directly below the table in the layout:

```
<div class="row">
  <div class="col-lg-12">
    <div class="panel panel-default">
      <div class="panel-heading">Traffic Sources</div>
```

```
<table class="table table-striped table-bordered table-hover">
  <tbody>
    <tr>
      <td>Organic Search</td>
      <td>1,656</td>
    </tr>
    <tr>
      <td>Referral</td>
      <td>1,453</td>
    </tr>
    <tr>
      <td>Direct</td>
      <td>945</td>
    </tr>
  </tbody>
</table>
</div>
<button class="btn btn-primary">Show More</button>
</div>
</div>
```

As in the previous section, I'm using a panel here with a table nested inside. The only difference is that this table stretches the width of the layout to fill the entire column. The **Show More** button at the bottom is also the same as that in the previous section. Now that all of the HTML is written, let's move on to coding the JavaScript for the line chart.

Updating the chart JavaScript

For the line chart, we'll need to insert some additional code into the `bootboard-charts.js` file, which is found in the `/js` directory. This is the same file that we created when we made the pie charts earlier in this chapter. Open it again and insert the following JavaScript code:

```
// table chart
new Chartist.Line('.ct-chart-table', {
  labels: ['Monday', 'Tuesday', 'Wednesday', 'Thursday', 'Friday'],
  series: [
    [12, 9, 7, 8, 5],
    [2, 1, 3.5, 7, 3],
    [1, 3, 4, 5, 6]
  ]
}, {
  fullWidth: true,
```

```
    chartPadding: {
      right: 40
    }
  });
```

Let's breakdown the CSS for the line chart:

- The labels array contains the labels that will appear along the *x* axis of the chart. They are displayed at the bottom of the chart.

- The `series` array will plot the dots for your line. In this chart, there will be three lines, so there are three sets of values. Feel free to use more or less.

- I've included the `fullWidth` property as I want the chart to span the width of its container.

- Finally, I've added some padding around the chart with the `chartPadding` property.

After you've finished customizing these values, save your JavaScript file and compile. Let's do a compilation here to make sure that everything is working before we do the CSS updates. Take a look at your page to make sure that a line chart is being loaded in. It will likely look messed up, but don't worry about that. The last step will be to customize the CSS and get our chart to look right.

Updating the chart CSS

So, the last thing that we need to do for our line chart is update the associated CSS so that it matches the look and feel of the dashboard. Open `_charts.less`, which is located in the `css/components` directory. Let's go step by step through the CSS changes that are required:

```
.ct-series-a .ct-line,
.ct-series-a .ct-point {
  stroke: @blue1;
}
```

Similar to the pie charts, each section of our line chart will be represented by a letter — a, b, and c — and we can assign a color to each one of them. The first line in our chart will be blue. You'll also notice there is a class for the line and the point. The line should be self-explanatory, but you could break that point class out to be on its own if you want to give the chart points a color different from that of the line. In this case, I'm making them the same:

```
.ct-series-b .ct-line,
.ct-series-b .ct-point {
```

```less
  stroke: @aqua1;
}
```

The second line in the chart will use the aqua color from the global color palette. Let's move on to the third and final line:

```less
.ct-series-c .ct-line,
.ct-series-c .ct-point {
  stroke: @purple1;
}
```

We'll set the final point to purple from the global color palette. Don't forget that the second line used -b in the class name and the third used -c. Save the CSS, compile again, and go back to the dashboard in your browser. Refresh the page, and your line chart should load in and match the proper color scheme.

That brings the dashboard design and coding to a close! Let's now take a look at the code for the entire page:

```html
<div class="container">
  <div class="row">
    <!-- sidebar //-->
    <div class="col-lg-3">
      <div class="collapse navbar-collapse" id="bootboard-nav">
        <ul class="nav nav-pills nav-stacked">
          <li class="navigation-header">Control Panel</li>
          <li class="active"><a href="#">Dashboard</a></li>
          <li><a href="#">Applications</a></li>
          <li><a href="#">Documentation</a></li>
          <li><a href="#">Analytics</a></li>
          <li><a href="#">Discussion</a></li>
          <li><a href="#">Users</a></li>
          <li class="navigation-header">Account</li>
          <li><a href="#">Profile</a></li>
          <li><a href="#">Settings</a></li>
          <li><a href="#">Help</a></li>
          <li><a href="#">Logout</a></li>
        </ul>
      </div>
    </div>
    <!-- content //-->
    <div class="col-lg-9">
      <!-- chart row //-->
      <div class="row">
        <div class="col-lg-12">
          <div class="page-header">
```

```
            <h3>Charts <small>A quick view of your website stats</
small></h3>
          </div>
        </div>
      </div>
      <div class="charts">
        <div class="row">
          <div class="col-lg-4">
            <div class="ct-chart-one ct-perfect-fourth"></div>
            Impressions
          </div>
          <div class="col-lg-4">
            <div class="ct-chart-two ct-perfect-fourth"></div>
            Clicks
          </div>
          <div class="col-lg-4">
            <div class="ct-chart-three ct-perfect-fourth"></div>
            Sales
          </div>
        </div>
      </div>
      <!-- widget row //-->
      <div class="row">
        <div class="col-lg-12">
          <div class="page-header">
            <h3>Widgets <small>Important stats about your websites</
small></h3>
          </div>
        </div>
      </div>
      <div class="row widgets">
        <div class="col-lg-3">
          <div class="panel panel-success">
            <div class="panel-heading">Impressions</div>
            <div class="panel-body">
              <h2>2,338</h2>
              <i class="fa fa-arrow-circle-up"></i>
            </div>
          </div>
        </div>
        <div class="col-lg-3">
          <div class="panel panel-danger">
            <div class="panel-heading">Conversion Rate</div>
            <div class="panel-body">
```

```
            <h2>2.3%</h2>
            <i class="fa fa-arrow-circle-down"></i>
          </div>
        </div>
      </div>
      <div class="col-lg-3">
        <div class="panel panel-danger">
          <div class="panel-heading">Mobile Visits</div>
          <div class="panel-body">
            <h2>1,453</h2>
            <i class="fa fa-arrow-circle-down"></i>
          </div>
        </div>
      </div>
      <div class="col-lg-3">
        <div class="panel panel-success">
          <div class="panel-heading">New Visits</div>
          <div class="panel-body">
            <h2>52.4%</h2>
            <i class="fa fa-arrow-circle-up"></i>
          </div>
        </div>
      </div>
    </div>
    <!-- panels //-->
    <div class="row">
      <div class="col-lg-12">
        <div class="page-header">
          <h3>Panels <small>Detailed information about your
website</small></h3>
        </div>
      </div>
    </div>
    <div class="row">
      <div class="col-lg-6">
        <div class="panel panel-default">
          <div class="panel-heading">Top Referals</div>
          <table class="table table-striped table-bordered table-
hover">
            <tbody>
              <tr>
                <td>google.com</td>
                <td>1,656</td>
              </tr>
```

```
                    <tr>
                      <td>facebook.com</td>
                      <td>1,453</td>
                    </tr>
                    <tr>
                      <td>twitter.com</td>
                      <td>945</td>
                    </tr>
                    <tr>
                      <td>pinterest.com</td>
                      <td>922</td>
                    </tr>
                    <tr>
                      <td>linkedin.com</td>
                      <td>844</td>
                    </tr>
                    <tr>
                      <td>buffer.com</td>
                      <td>817</td>
                    </tr>
                    <tr>
                      <td>bing.com</td>
                      <td>767</td>
                    </tr>
                    <tr>
                      <td>yahoo.com</td>
                      <td>672</td>
                    </tr>
                    <tr>
                      <td>msn.com</td>
                      <td>454</td>
                    </tr>
                    <tr>
                      <td>cbc.com</td>
                      <td>231</td>
                    </tr>
                  </tbody>
                </table>
              </div>
              <button class="btn btn-primary">Show More</button>
            </div>
            <div class="col-lg-6">
              <div class="panel panel-default">
                <div class="panel-heading">Popular Pages</div>
                <table class="table table-striped table-bordered table-
hover">
```

```
      <tbody>
        <tr>
          <td>/</td>
          <td>1,433</td>
        </tr>
        <tr>
          <td>/store</td>
          <td>1,211</td>
        </tr>
        <tr>
          <td>/blog</td>
          <td>1,032</td>
        </tr>
        <tr>
          <td>/store/product</td>
          <td>984</td>
        </tr>
        <tr>
          <td>/contact</td>
          <td>898</td>
        </tr>
        <tr>
          <td>/blog/post</td>
          <td>872</td>
        </tr>
        <tr>
          <td>/blog/post2</td>
          <td>734</td>
        </tr>
        <tr>
          <td>/about</td>
          <td>711</td>
        </tr>
        <tr>
          <td>/blog/post3</td>
          <td>454</td>
        </tr>
        <tr>
          <td>/store/product2</td>
          <td>349</td>
        </tr>
      </tbody>
    </table>
  </div>
</div>
<button class="btn btn-primary">Show More</button>
```

```
        </div>
      </div>
      <!-- table row 2 //-->
      <div class="row">
        <div class="col-lg-12">
          <div class="page-header">
            <h3>Table <small>More detailed information about your
website</small></h3>
          </div>
        </div>
      </div>
      <div class="row">
        <div class="col-lg-12">
          <div class="ct-chart-table ct-golden-section"></div>
        </div>
      </div>
      <div class="row">
        <div class="col-lg-12">
          <div class="panel panel-default">
            <div class="panel-heading">Traffic Sources</div>
            <table class="table table-striped table-bordered table-
hover">
              <tbody>
                <tr>
                  <td>Organic Search</td>
                  <td>1,656</td>
                </tr>
                <tr>
                  <td>Referral</td>
                  <td>1,453</td>
                </tr>
                <tr>
                  <td>Direct</td>
                  <td>945</td>
                </tr>
              </tbody>
            </table>
          </div>
          <button class="btn btn-primary">Show More</button>
        </div>
      </div>
    </div>
  </div>
</div>
```

Mobile considerations

To optimize the dashboard for mobiles, we need to insert a few mobile-specific styles into `theme.less`. Head over to the bottom of the stylesheet and insert the following code:

```
@media (max-width: 768px) {
  .container {
    padding-right: @padding;
    padding-left: @padding;
  }

  .navbar-form {
    display: none;
  }

  ul.nav.navbar-nav.navbar-right {
    display: none;
  }
}
```

Let's breakdown the mobile specific CSS for the project:

- I've added some left and right padding to the overall layout for tablets and phones
- I've removed the search field, username, and icon in the navbar for mobile devices

Summary

This brings the sixth chapter to a close. We covered how to code your own dashboard using Bootstrap. Let's review what you learned, which is as follows— how to code a dashboard using Bootstrap; how to create a project with a dark look and feel; how to implement and customize the Chartist JavaScript library; how to customize the Bootstrap `panels` component, `table` component, `nav` component, and `navbar` component; and how to use a mobile `nav` outside of the default `navbar`.

7
Bootstrap Social Network

Welcome to the last chapter of this book, where you're going to learn how to build a social networking site using Bootstrap! This project will include a public profile, an activity feed, notifications, friends, and private message pages. As part of this chapter, we'll use much of what you learned in the book to create a complex project with a minimal look.

Before we jump into updating our template, let's take a look at the public profile page, which will be like this:

Customizing the template

Let's start the last blueprint by copying our boilerplate project and creating a new one called `Chapter 7`. Open the `_data.json` file and insert the following code:

```
{
  "index": {
    "pageTitle": "Home"
  },
  "activity-feed": {
    "pageTitle": "Activity Feed"
  },
  "notifications": {
    "pageTitle": "Notifications"
  },
  "messages": {
    "pageTitle": "Messages"
  },
  "friends": {
    "pageTitle": "Friends"
  }
}
```

For this project, we are going to create five page templates. Let's start by creating the files in the root of our project. For now, they can just be blank, and we'll start to fill them in a little later:

- `index.ejs`
- `activity-feed.ejs`
- `notifications.ejs`
- `messages.ejs`
- `friends.ejs`

Updating _layout.ejs

Next, let's update the `_layout.ejs` file in the root of our new project. The layout for the profile page doesn't have any major differences. Make sure you include the line of code that will import `Roboto` as your web font:

```
<link
href='https://fonts.googleapis.com/css?family=Roboto:400,700,300'
rel='stylesheet' type='text/css'>
```

This will import three type weights: light (300), regular (400), and bold (700). That's all we need to do to customize the layout for this project. Here's what the entire file should look like:

```html
<!DOCTYPE html>
<html lang="en">
<head>
  <meta charset="utf-8">
  <meta http-equiv="X-UA-Compatible" content="IE=edge">
  <meta name="viewport" content="width=device-width, initial-scale=1">
  <title><%- pageTitle %> | <%- siteTitle %></title>

  <link rel="stylesheet" type="text/css"
href="css/bootstrap.min.css">
  <link rel="stylesheet" type="text/css" href="css/font-awesome.min.
css">
  <link
href='https://fonts.googleapis.com/css?family=Roboto:400,700,300'
rel='stylesheet' type='text/css'>
  <link rel="stylesheet" type="text/css" href="css/theme.css">

  <!-- HTML5 shim and Respond.js for IE8 support of HTML5 elements
and media queries -->
  <!-- WARNING: Respond.js doesn't work if you view the page via
file:// -->
  <!--[if lt IE 9]>
    <script
src="https://oss.maxcdn.com/html5shiv/3.7.2/html5shiv.min.js"></
script>
    <script
src="https://oss.maxcdn.com/respond/1.4.2/respond.min.js"></script>
  <![endif]-->
</head>
<body>

  <%- partial("partial/_header") %>

  <%- yield %>

  <%- partial("partial/_footer") %>

  <!-- javascript //-->
  <script
src="//ajax.googleapis.com/ajax/libs/jquery/1.11.1/jquery.min.js"></
script>
```

```
    <script src="js/bootstrap.min.js"
type="text/javascript"></script>
</body>
</html>
```

Setting up the Less variables

The process of setting up your Less variables should feel pretty familiar now. Let's go ahead and set up the Less variables for the social network. As in the previous project, we're going to use the colors included with the boilerplate.

Background colors

For the background color section, we only need to update the value of the inverse background variable:

```
@inverse-background: @navy1;
```

Text colors

The only text color that we are going to change is the heading text variable:

```
@heading-text: @navy1;
```

Link colors

Let's change both the link color variables to match the color scheme for our new project:

```
@primary-link-color: @aqua1;
@primary-link-color-hover: @aqua2;
```

Border colors

For the borders, everything will stay the same except for the focus color. This is the property that controls the border color of an input when it is in focus:

```
@border-focus: @aqua1;
```

Typography

Earlier, we imported `Roboto` from Google Web Fonts. Let's now set up our text variables to use the typeface:

```
@body-copy: "Roboto", "Helvetica Neue", helvetica, arial, verdana,
sans-serif;
@heading-copy: "Roboto", "Helvetica Neue", helvetica, arial,
verdana, sans-serif;
```

Border radius

Finally, let's update the `border-radius` variable to 5px, which will make our buttons a little rounder:

```
.round-corners (@radius: 5px) { // new
  -moz-border-radius: @radius;
  -ms-border-radius: @radius;
  border-radius: @radius;
}
```

These are all the updates for the Less variables. Let's take a look at the entire file before we move on to setting up the header and footer:

```
// color palette

@black: #000;
@dark-grey: #333;
@grey: #ccc;
@light-grey: #ebebeb;
@off-white: #f5f5f5;
@white: #ffffff;

@blue1: #3498db;
@blue2: #2980b9;
@red1: #e74c3c;
@red2: #c0392b;
@yellow1: #f1c40f;
@yellow2: #f39c12;
@green1: #2ecc71;
@green2: #27ae60;
@orange1: #e67e22;
@orange2: #d35400;
@aqua1: #1abc9c;
@aqua2: #16a085;
```

```less
@purple1: #9b59b6;
@purple2: #8e44ad;
@navy1: #34495e;
@navy2: #2c3e50;

// background colors
@primary-background: @white;
@secondary-background: @off-white;
@inverse-background: @navy1;

// text colors
@primary-text: @dark-grey;
@light-text: @light-grey;
@loud-text: @black;
@inverse-text: @white;
@heading-text: @navy1;

// link colors
@primary-link-color: @aqua1;
@primary-link-color-hover: @aqua2;

// primary border properties
@border-color: @light-grey;
@border-size: 1px;
@border-type: solid;
@border-focus: @aqua1;

// typography
@body-copy: "Roboto", "Helvetica Neue", helvetica, arial, verdana,
sans-serif;
@heading-copy: "Roboto", "Helvetica Neue", helvetica, arial, verdana,
sans-serif;
@base-font-size: 14px;
@font-size: 1em;
@base-line-height: 1.5;

// layout
@margin: 1em;
@padding: 1em;

// MIXINS

// round corners or Border radius
.round-corners (@radius: 5px) {
```

```
  -moz-border-radius: @radius;
  -ms-border-radius: @radius;
  border-radius: @radius;
}

// animation transitions
.transition (@transition: background .1s linear) {
  -moz-transition: @transition;
  -webkit-transition: @transition;
  transition: background @transition;
}
```

Coding the header and footer

Let's set up the header and footer for our social networking website. It's going to be made up of the regular Bootstrap `navbar` component, with some new customizations. The main new items will be an icon-based navigation, a search bar, a utility drop-down menu, and some mobile-specific styling.

Updating the header

I'll start out by showing you the code for the entire header, and then we'll dissect the parts that we need to update. Start off by creating a file called `_header.ejs`, and save it in the `/partial` directory. Then, insert this code:

```
<nav class="navbar navbar-default" role="navigation">
  <div class="container-fluid">
    <div class="navbar-header">
      <button type="button" class="navbar-toggle collapsed" data-toggle="collapse" data-target="#navbar1">
        <span class="sr-only">Toggle navigation</span>
        <span class="icon-bar"></span>
        <span class="icon-bar"></span>
        <span class="icon-bar"></span>
      </button>
      <a href="index.html" class="navbar-brand"><span>Soc</span>Strap</a>
    </div>

    <div class="collapse navbar-collapse" id="navbar1">
      <ul class="nav navbar-nav">
        <li><a href="activity-feed.html"><i class="fa fa-home"></i></a></li>
```

```
        <li><a href="notifications.html"><i class="fa fa-bell"></i></
a></li>
        <li><a href="messages.html"><i class="fa fa-envelope"></i></
a></li>
        <li><a href="friends.html"><i class="fa fa-user"></i></a></li>
      </ul>
      <form class="navbar-form navbar-right" role="search">
        <div class="form-group">
          <input type="text" class="form-control"
placeholder="Search">
        </div>
      </form>
      <ul class="nav navbar-nav navbar-right">
        <li class="dropdown">
          <a href="#" class="dropdown-toggle" data-toggle="dropdown"
role="button" aria-haspopup="true" aria-expanded="false">Username
<span class="caret"></span></a>
          <ul class="dropdown-menu">
            <li><a href="#">View Profile</a></li>
            <li><a href="#">Settings</a></li>
            <li><a href="#">Help</a></li>
            <li><a href="#">Logout</a></li>
          </ul>
        </li>
      </ul>
    </div>
  </div>
</nav>
```

Inserting the brand

Head down to the Soc Strap brand line of code as shown in the following code. You'll notice that part of the brand is wrapped in a `<span>` tag. This is for styling reasons, which I'll cover next:

```
<a href="index.html" class="navbar-brand"><span>Soc</span>Strap</a>
```

Creating the navbar Less file

We need to create a new Less file for the navbar component. Open up a new file, name it _navbar.less, and save it in the css/components directory. Insert the following styles into the file and save it:

```
//navbar
.navbar-default {
  background-color: @inverse-background;
```

```
    border-color: transparent;

    -moz-border-radius: 0;
    border-radius: 0;
}
```

This first section of styles is actually for the `navbar`, not the `brand`. I've set the background to a different color and removed the bottom border and round corners:

```
// brand
.navbar-default .navbar-brand {
  font-weight: 300;
  color: @inverse-text;
}
```

Here's our base `brand` class. I've set the font weight to `light` and set the color to use the inverse variable for the text:

```
.navbar-default .navbar-brand:focus,
.navbar-default .navbar-brand:hover {
  color: @aqua1;
}
```

At the same time, let's set up the hover and focus states for the `brand` to use our color palette:

```
.navbar-brand span {
  font-weight: 700;
  color: @aqua1;
}
```

Finally, I've set some different styles for the portion of the brand text that appears in the `<span>` tag. This will make the text bold and give it a different color. This is a easy way of making your brand or logo look a little unique without having to use an image. Once you've saved the file, don't forget to import it back into `theme.less` in the modules section:

```
@import "components/_navbar.less";
```

Setting up the icon navigation

For this project, we're going to use Font Awesome icons for the primary navigation links. Check out the following HTML for rendering the icons:

```
<ul class="nav navbar-nav">
  <li><a href="activity-feed.html"><i class="fa fa-home"></i></a></li>
  <li><a href="notifications.html"><i class="fa fa-bell"></i></a></li>
```

```
    <li><a href="messages.html"><i class="fa fa-envelope"></i></a></li>
    <li><a href="friends.html"><i class="fa fa-user"></i></a></li>
</ul>
```

The HTML portion here should be easy to understand. However, we need to add some custom styles for our navbar links as well. Head back to the navbar Less file and insert the following styles:

```
// navbar links
.navbar-default .navbar-nav > li > a {
  color: @aqua1;
}

.navbar-default .navbar-nav > li > a:focus,
.navbar-default .navbar-nav > li > a:hover {
  color: @inverse-text;
}
```

These styles will simply customize the icons and all the links in the navbar to use our color palette.

Adding the search bar

For the search bar in the navbar, we're going to insert a form. This is a basic Bootstrap navbar form, but I'll go over what's happening:

```
<form class="navbar-form navbar-right" role="search">
  <div class="form-group">
    <input type="text" class="form-control" placeholder="Search">
  </div>
</form>
```

I've inserted a basic Bootstrap form. Make sure you include the navbar-form class to get some custom header styling. Also, don't forget the navbar-right class as we want the form to be aligned right in the header. From there on, it is just your basic Bootstrap form code, with the exception of a couple of custom styles:

```
// search form
.navbar-form .form-control {
  border-color: @navy1;
}

.form-control:focus {
  border-color: @border-focus;
}
```

- I've changed the border color of the form input to navy blue
- The next class applies the custom `border-focus` variable that we previously set up

Adding the utility drop-down menu

The last piece of HTML that we need to include is the portion that will include the utility drop-down menu. Here's what it looks like:

```
<ul class="nav navbar-nav navbar-right">
  <li class="dropdown">
    <a href="#" class="dropdown-toggle" data-toggle="dropdown"
role="button" aria-haspopup="true" aria-expanded="false">Username
<span class="caret"></span></a>
    <ul class="dropdown-menu">
      <li><a href="#">View Profile</a></li>
      <li><a href="#">Settings</a></li>
      <li><a href="#">Help</a></li>
      <li><a href="#">Logout</a></li>
    </ul>
  </li>
</ul>
```

Like the search field, the HTML here is straight out of the Bootstrap box. If you need more of an explanation, check out the docs at `http://getbootstrap.com`.

Adding some mobile-specific styles

The final thing that we need to do before finishing our header is include some mobile-specific styles. Head back to the navbar Less file and paste the following code in it:

```
// mobile trigger
.navbar-default .navbar-toggle {
  border-color: @white;
}

.navbar-toggle {
  background: @navy2;
  border: none;
  .round-corners;
}
```

```
.navbar-default .navbar-toggle:focus,
.navbar-default .navbar-toggle:hover {
  background-color: @aqua1;
}

.navbar-default .navbar-toggle .icon-bar {
  background-color: @white;
}
```

The preceding styles control the color of the mobile toggle button that will appear on tablets and phones. I'm simply switched them to match the project's color scheme. Before we move on to the footer, we need to add some more mobile styles to `theme.less`. Open up that file and head to the bottom, where the media queries appear. Then, insert the following:

```
@media (max-width: 767px) {
  .navbar-default .navbar-nav .open .dropdown-menu > li > a {
    color: @primary-link-color;
  }

  .navbar-default .navbar-nav .open .dropdown-menu > li >a:focus,
  .navbar-default .navbar-nav .open .dropdown-menu > li >a:hover {
    color: @white;
  }
}
```

We need to switch some of the utility drop-down menu's colors when it's in the mobile view. Otherwise, the colors will be lost in the background. That's it for our header; let's move on to the footer:

Updating the footer

The footer for this project is purposely simple. Create a new file called `_footer.ejs` and save it in the `/partial` directory. Then, insert the following code:

```
<!-- footer //-->
<div class="container-fluid">
  <div class="row">
    <div class="col-lg-12">
      <div class="footer">
        &copy; SocStrap
      </div>
    </div>
  </div>
</div>
```

As I mentioned, the footer is really simple. We do need to add a few custom styles, however, to give it a proper look and feel. Insert the following code into `theme.less`:

```less
.footer {
  margin-top: (@padding * 6);
  padding-bottom: (@padding * 6);
  padding-top: @padding;
  border-top: @border-size @border-color @border-type;
  color: @grey;
}
```

Here, I'm giving the footer some margin and padding. I've also added a top border and set the text to a lighter color. That completes the setup of the header and the footer. Let's move on to the first template for our project, which will be the public-facing profile page.

Coding the profile page

The profile page is the public-facing page of your social network. If someone is searching for you on the website, this is the page that they will see. In this first template, we will define a three-column layout that will be used through all the pages of this project. We'll also set up some new partials for the sidebar elements of the profile. In this way, we can modularize the design and reuse some of the parts where it makes sense. Let's start by creating a new file called `index.ejs` and saving it to the root of the project. As I mentioned, our project will have a three-column layout built upon the following grid:

- I'm using the `container-fluid` class here because I want the layout to span the entire width of the viewport
- I'm using a three-column grid of 25%, 50%, and 25%

```html
<div class="container-fluid">
  <div class="row">
    <!-- left side //-->
    <div class="col-lg-3">
      ..
    </div>
    <div class="col-lg-6">
      ..
    </div>
    <div class="col-lg-3">
```

```
    ..
  </div>
  </div>
 </div>
```

Setting up the left sidebar

The left sidebar of our project is going to have a couple of versions. One will be for public-facing pages such as this profile. The second will be for internal pages, which only the logged-in user can see. This second version will have some different actions that make sense for the user. First of all, let's insert the code for the first column into the profile page:

```
<div class="col-lg-3">
  <div class="sidebar-left">
    <%- partial("partial/_sidebar-left-home") %>
  </div>
</div>
```

To make the code more modular, I've broken the sidebar into a partial. Create a new file called _sidebar-left-home.ejs and save it in the /partial directory. Let's open the file and go over the code.

Adding the avatar

This first line of the code will render the user's avatar for their profile. Here's the code:

```
<div><img src="img/main-avatar.jpg" class="main-avatar"></div>
```

It's linking to an image that has a class of .main-avatar on it. We need to add some custom styles for this class:

- I've set the width of the image to 100% so that it will stretch the entire width of the column. It's a good idea to make sure that your image is a little bigger than you think the maximum size will be so that no pixelation occurrs.

- The height property is set to auto so that the image will automatically resize depending on the width the column.

- I've added a `border-radius` to the image to give it a more polished look.

```
img.main-avatar {
  width: 100%;
  height: auto;

  .round-corners;
}
```

Adding the name and description

The next block of code will render our user's name and description. Here's the HTML code:

```
<h2><a href="index.html">John Smith</a></h2>
<p>Pellentesque habitant morbi tristique senectus et netus et
malesuada fames ac turpis egestas. Vestibulum tortor quam, feugiat
vitae, ultricies eget, tempor sit amet, ante. Donec eu libero sit
amet quam egestas semper. Aenean ultricies mi vitae est. Mauris
placerat eleifend leo.</p>
<ul class="list-unstyled">
  <li><i class="fa fa-map-marker"></i> Vancouver, BC</li>
  <li><i class="fa fa-desktop"></i> <a href="#">website.com</a></li>
</ul>
```

The first line is our user's name, and there are a couple of styles that we need to add to `theme.less`. I'm going to remove `line-height` and manually set the top and bottom margins that are exact:

```
.sidebar-left h2 {
  margin-top: (@margin * 1.5);
  margin-bottom: (@margin * 1.5);
  line-height: 0;
}
```

We also need to add a few styles for the unordered list of properties at the bottom of the description. The following are some simple layout tweaks meant to tighten up the look and feel:

```
.sidebar-left li {
  margin-bottom: (@margin - 0.5);
}
```

```
.sidebar-left li i {
  margin-right: 5px;
}
```

This completes all of the code for the first sidebar partial. Let's take a look at the entire thing before we move on:

```
<div><img src="img/main-avatar.jpg" class="main-avatar"></div>
<h2><a href="index.html">John Smith</a></h2>
<p>Pellentesque habitant morbi tristique senectus et netus et
malesuada fames ac turpis egestas. Vestibulum tortor quam, feugiat
vitae, ultricies eget, tempor sit amet, ante. Donec eu libero sit
amet quam egestas semper. Aenean ultricies mi vitae est. Mauris
placerat eleifend leo.</p>
<ul class="list-unstyled">
  <li><i class="fa fa-map-marker"></i> Vancouver, BC</li>
  <li><i class="fa fa-desktop"></i> <a
href="#">website.com</a></li>
</ul>
```

Adding the content column

Let's move on to the second column in the layout, which will hold the main content (or feed) for the page. Here's the basic structure of the column:

```
<div class="col-lg-6">
  <div class="content-feed">
    <!-- post //-->
    <div class="well">
      ..
    </div>
  </div>
</div>
```

Let's take a closer look at what's happening with the structure of the column:

- Within the column, there is a `<div>` with a wrapping class of `content-feed`.
- Inside the content feed will be a series of well. Each post on the feed will be a new `well` component.

The following code shows the contents of a single well post in the feed:

```
<div class="well">
  <div class="row">
    <div class="col-lg-2">
```

```
        <p><img src="img/avatar1.jpg" width="70" height="70"
class="avatar"></p>
    </div>
    <div class="col-lg-10">
        <h3><a href="#">Mike Michaels</a></h3>
        <p>Pellentesque habitant morbi tristique senectus et netus
et malesuada fames ac turpis egestas.</p>
        <div class="feed-meta">
          <ul class="list-inline">
            <li>About 3 minutes ago</li>
            <li><a href="#"><i class="fa fa-reply"></i>
Reply</a></li>
            <li><a href="#"><i class="fa fa-heart"></i>
Like</a></li>
          </ul>
        </div>
    </div>
  </div>
</div>
```

Let's take a closer look at the contents of a single well post in the feed:

- Each well is divided into two-column grid
- The left column holds the user's avatar image
- The right column holds the content of the post
- Within the content section, there is some post metadata at the bottom

Each well comes with some custom styling that we need to add. Let's first start with the global styles that we need to add to theme.less:

```
.content-feed h3 {
  margin-top: 0;
  margin-bottom: (@margin - 0.5);
}
```

The following margin styles tweak the default Bootstrap margins on an <h3> tag to make them work with our layout:

```
img.avatar {
  .round-corners;
}
```

Like our main profile avatar, we want each of the post avatars to also have round corners. However, this image doesn't need to stretch the width of its column, so I've created a more general `.avatar` class to apply `border-radius`:

```
.feed-meta {
  font-size: (@font-size - 0.25);
}
```

The preceding style will shrink the `font-size` of the `meta` text by 25%:

```
.feed-meta ul {
  margin-bottom: 0;
}
```

Finally, I've removed the bottom margin from the `meta` unordered list so that I don't have extra spacing on the inside of the `well` component. Before we can finish this column, we need to customize the `well` component.

Customizing the well component

We'll be using the `well` on multiple pages, so let's create a new Less file named `_well.less` and save it in `/css/components`. Once you've completed that, insert the following code into the Less file:

```
.well {
  background: @secondary-background;
  border: none;
  padding: (@padding * 2);
  box-shadow: none;

  .round-corners;
}
```

Let's take a closer look at what's happening in the Less file:

- I've updated the `background` color to use our palette
- I've removed the well's border
- I added some more padding to the well
- I've also removed the default `box-shadow` and added round corners using the property value of 5px

Now this `well` component can be used across multiple templates. We will come back a little later and add an alternate styling option for a different well. Once you've saved the file, don't forget to import it back into `theme.less` in the `modules` section:

```
@import "components/_well.less";
```

Adding the third column

The third column of the profile page is similar to the first. It will also use a partial to make our project more modular. Here's the HTML code:

```
<div class="col-lg-3">
  <div class="sidebar-right">
    <%- partial("partial/_sidebar-right") %>
  </div>
</div>
```

I've created another sidebar partial here that we need to fill in. Create a new file called `_sidebar-right.ejs` and save it to the `/partial` directory. Here's the code for the right sidebar:

```
<div class="well">
  <h5>Trends</h5>
  <div>
    <p><a href="#">#Trend1</a></p>
    <p><small>Pellentesque habitant morbi tristique senectus et
netus et malesuada fames ac turpis egestas.</small></p>
  </div>
  <div>
    <p><a href="#">#Trend1</a></p>
    <p><small>Pellentesque habitant morbi tristique senectus et
netus et malesuada fames ac turpis egestas.</small></p>
  </div>
  <div>
    <p><a href="#">#Trend1</a></p>
    <p><small>Pellentesque habitant morbi tristique senectus et
netus et malesuada fames ac turpis egestas.</small></p>
  </div>
  <div>
    <p><a href="#">#Trend1</a></p>
    <p><small>Pellentesque habitant morbi tristique senectus et
netus et malesuada fames ac turpis egestas.</small></p>
  </div>
</div>
<div class="well">
```

```
<h5>Linkage</h5>
<ul class="list-unstyled">
  <li><a href="#">About</a></li>
  <li><a href="#">Help</a></li>
  <li><a href="#">Terms</a></li>
  <li><a href="#">Privacy</a></li>
  <li><a href="#">Ads</a></li>
  <li><a href="#">Apps</a></li>
  <li><a href="#">Jobs</a></li>
  <li><a href="#">Advertise</a></li>
  <li><a href="#">Contact</a></li>
</ul>
</div>
```

The same `well` component is being used to create a boxed or card-type layout feel for our profile page. However, there are some custom styles that we need to apply to these wells. Open up `theme.less` and insert the following CSS under the `layout` section:

```
.sidebar-right .well div {
  margin-bottom: @margin;
}
```

I want to space out each `<div>` element within the well consistently, so I've added the preceding styling to do this:

```
.sidebar-right .well div p {
  margin-bottom: 0;
}
```

Since I've added a margin to the wrapping `<div>`, I've removed the bottom margin from any `<p>` tags in these wells. This is because I don't want extra spacing there:

```
.sidebar-right h5 {
  font-weight: 700;
  margin-top: 0;
  margin-bottom: (@margin * 1.5);
  color: @heading-text;
}
```

Finally, I added some custom styling to the `<h5>` tag that is used for the header in each well.

Completing the template

The rest of the HTML in the template is basic Bootstrap code. Save the `index.ejs` file and the first template is complete! Let's take a look at the entire file together:

```
<div class="container-fluid">
  <div class="row">
    <!-- left side //-->
    <div class="col-lg-3">
      <div class="sidebar-left">
        <%- partial("partial/_sidebar-left-home") %>
      </div>
    </div>
    <!-- content //-->
    <div class="col-lg-6">
      <div class="content-feed">
        <!-- post //-->
        <div class="well">
          <div class="row">
            <div class="col-lg-2">
              <p><img src="img/avatar1.jpg" width="70" height="70"
class="avatar"></p>
            </div>
            <div class="col-lg-10">
              <h3><a href="#">Mike Michaels</a></h3>
              <p>Pellentesque habitant morbi tristique senectus et
netus et malesuada fames ac turpis egestas.</p>
              <div class="feed-meta">
                <ul class="list-inline">
                  <li>About 3 minutes ago</li>
                  <li><a href="#"><i class="fa fa-reply"></i>
Reply</a></li>
                  <li><a href="#"><i class="fa fa-heart"></i>
Like</a></li>
                </ul>
              </div>
            </div>
          </div>
        </div>
        <!-- post //-->
        <div class="well">
          <div class="row">
```

```
            <div class="col-lg-2">
                <p><img src="img/avatar2.jpg" width="70" height="70"
class="avatar"></p>
            </div>
            <div class="col-lg-10">
                <h3><a href="#">John Smith</a></h3>
                <p>Pellentesque habitant morbi tristique senectus et
netus et malesuada fames ac turpis egestas.</p>
                <div class="feed-meta">
                    <ul class="list-inline">
                        <li>About 3 minutes ago</li>
                        <li><a href="#"><i class="fa fa-reply"></i>
Reply</a></li>
                        <li><a href="#"><i class="fa fa-heart"></i>
Like</a></li>
                    </ul>
                </div>
            </div>
        </div>
    </div>
    <!-- post //-->
    <div class="well">
        <div class="row">
            <div class="col-lg-2">
                <p><img src="img/avatar3.jpg" width="70" height="70"
class="avatar"></p>
            </div>
            <div class="col-lg-10">
                <h3><a href="#">Chris Christopher</a></h3>
                <p>Pellentesque habitant morbi tristique senectus et
netus et malesuada fames ac turpis egestas.</p>
                <div class="feed-meta">
                    <ul class="list-inline">
                        <li>About 3 minutes ago</li>
                        <li><a href="#"><i class="fa fa-reply"></i>
Reply</a></li>
                        <li><a href="#"><i class="fa fa-heart"></i>
Like</a></li>
                    </ul>
                </div>
            </div>
        </div>
```

```
            </div>
            <!-- post //-->
            <div class="well">
              <div class="row">
                <div class="col-lg-2">
                  <p><img src="img/avatar4.jpg" width="70" height="70"
class="avatar"></p>
                </div>
                <div class="col-lg-10">
                  <h3><a href="#">Matt Matthews</a></h3>
                  <p>Pellentesque habitant morbi tristique senectus et
netus et malesuada fames ac turpis egestas.</p>
                  <div class="feed-meta">
                    <ul class="list-inline">
                      <li>About 3 minutes ago</li>
                      <li><a href="#"><i class="fa fa-reply"></i>
Reply</a></li>
                      <li><a href="#"><i class="fa fa-heart"></i>
Like</a></li>
                    </ul>
                  </div>
                </div>
              </div>
            </div>
            <!-- post //-->
            <div class="well">
              <div class="row">
                <div class="col-lg-2">
                  <p><img src="img/avatar5.jpg" width="70" height="70"
class="avatar"></p>
                </div>
                <div class="col-lg-10">
                  <h3><a href="#">John Johnson</a></h3>
                  <p>Pellentesque habitant morbi tristique senectus et
netus et malesuada fames ac turpis egestas.</p>
                  <div class="feed-meta">
                    <ul class="list-inline">
                      <li>About 3 minutes ago</li>
                      <li><a href="#"><i class="fa fa-reply"></i>
Reply</a></li>
                      <li><a href="#"><i class="fa fa-heart"></i>
Like</a></li>
```

```
            </ul>
          </div>
        </div>
      </div>
    </div>
    <div class="center">
      <p><button class="btn btn-primary">Load More
Posts</button></p>
    </div>
  </div>
</div>
<!-- right side //-->
<div class="col-lg-3">
  <div class="sidebar-right">
    <%- partial("partial/_sidebar-right") %>
  </div>
</div>
</div>
</div>
</div>
```

Before you move on to the activity feed template, it would be a good idea to compile your project and make sure that there are no errors. Also make sure you test the first page in the browser to ensure that it looks good.

Coding the activity feed

The next template in the project that we're going to tackle is the activity feed. This is the page that you would see when you log in to your account. The main differences compared to the public profile are the form for posting an update and some changes to the right sidebar.

Let's see what this page will look like:

Customizing the first column

As I mentioned earlier, the first column in this template is going to be different compared to the public profile. The second left sidebar will be the one used for the remaining templates as they are all pages that are viewable by the logged-in user only. Start by creating a new file called `_sidebar-left.ejs` and save it to the /partial directory. The top of the sidebar, which includes the avatar and description, will remain the same. Here's the code again, or you can copy it from the first file:

```
<div><img src="img/main-avatar.jpg" class="main-avatar"></div>
<h2><a href="#">John Smith</a></h2>
<p>Pellentesque habitant morbi tristique senectus et netus et
malesuada fames ac turpis egestas. Vestibulum tortor quam, feugiat
vitae, ultricies eget, tempor sit amet, ante. Donec eu libero sit
amet quam egestas semper. Aenean ultricies mi vitae est. Mauris
placerat eleifend leo.</p>
```

The new portion of this file is a set of action buttons. These buttons are designed as a quick way to get to other pages or sections of the social network. Insert the following HTML after the avatar and description code:

```
<div>
   <button class="btn btn-primary btn-block"><i class="fa fa-user"></i>
Friends</button>
</div>
<div>
   <button class="btn btn-primary btn-block"><i class="fa fa-bell"></i>
Notifications</button>
</div>
<div>
   <button class="btn btn-primary btn-block"><i class="fa fa-
envelope"></i> Messages</button>
</div>
<div>
   <button class="btn btn-primary btn-block"><i class="fa fa-cog"></i>
Edit Profile</button>
</div>
```

This is your standard Bootstrap button code. However, note that I'm using the `.btn-block` class on each button as I want them to be treated as block elements that will span the width of the column.

Adding button styles

Since we're using the Bootstrap button component, we need to create a new Less component file to style its look and feel. Create a new file called `_buttons.less` and save it to the `/css/components` directory. Insert the following code into the file and save:

```
.btn-primary {
  background-color: @navy1;
  border-color: @navy1;
}

.btn-primary.active,
.btn-primary.focus,
.btn-primary:active,
.btn-primary:focus,
.btn-primary:hover,
.open > .dropdown-toggle.btn-primary {
  background-color: @navy2;
  border-color: @navy2;
}
```

I'm only going to customize the `.btn-primary` button variation. This is because we'll only be using one button style in the project. All I've done here is changed the colors to match our palette. Note that I've also included some dropdown classes so that the navbar dropdown will have the same colors. Once you've saved the file, don't forget to import it back into `theme.less` in the `modules` section:

```
@import "components/_buttons.less";
```

Adding the post form

The second main element of the activity feed is the form for posting an update. This will be inserted at the top of the center column above the feed of updates. The update list code is the same as that for the public profile, so feel free to paste that in. Next, you'll want to insert the following code above the feed entries:

```
<!-- post form //-->
<div class="well alternate">
  <form>
    <div class="form-group">
      <input type="text" class="form-control" placeholder="What's
Up?">
    </div>
    <div class="row">
```

```
            <div class="col-lg-6">
               <ul class="list-inline">
                 <li><a href="#"><i class="fa fa-camera"></i>
Media</a></li>
                 <li><a href="#"><i class="fa fa-map-marker"></i>
Location</a></li>
               </ul>
            </div>
            <div class="col-lg-6">
               <div class="pull-right">
                 <button class="btn btn-primary">Post Update</button>
               </div>
            </div>
         </div>
      </form>
   </div>
```

The entire form is wrapped inside a `well` component. However, note that there is
also a `.alternate` class on that `<div>` element. What I've done here is created a
variation of the well with a different look and feel for the form. This will require you
to add some more styles to your `well` component. Open `_well.less` again and paste
the following code:

```
.well.alternate {
    background: @inverse-background;
}
```

First, I've set the alternate well to use the `inverse-background` color variable, which
happens to be the navy blue color:

```
.well.alternate ul.list-inline {
  margin-top: 10px;
  margin-bottom: 0;
}
```

Next, note the **Media** and **Location** links in the form. These are displayed using an
inline `list` component, and I had to adjust their margins so that they fit perfectly
in the well. These two items also take advantage of using a Font Awesome icon to
improve the design. Finally, we're using our button again and the `.pull-right`
Bootstrap class to align it on the right within the well.

Adding the new post notification bar

The last element that we need to add to this template is the new post notification bar. This is the aqua colored bar that appears below the form in the layout. The idea here is similar to Twitter, where you likely have an Ajax call updating you if there are new posts to view while you are on this page. We're going to implement this using the Bootstrap `alert` component. First of all, insert the following HTML code after the form you just created:

```
<div class="alert alert-info">
  <a href="#"><i class="fa fa-arrow-down"></i> View 10 new
posts</a>
</div>
```

This should be straightforward. We're using the `alert-info` variation of the component, which we will style next. Within the alert, there is a link that wraps another Font Awesome icon and a label indicating how many new posts are available.

Styling the alert bar

Create another Less file called `_alert.less` and save it to `/css/components`. Next, insert the following code into the file and save it:

```
.alert {
  .round-corners;
  padding: @padding;
}
```

Let's take a closer look at what's happening with the alert bar:

- I've added our `border-radius` mixing to normalize the round corners
- I've also added our `padding` variable so that it is a consistent value throughout the project:

```
.alert-info {
  background: @aqua1;
  text-align: center;
  border-color: @aqua1;
  color: @white;
}
```

- I reset the background to use the aqua color from our palette
- I've set the text alignment as `center` for the entire bar
- I've also set the border color to the same as the background, as I want them to be the same
- The text color is set to `white` so that it's easy to read on the aqua background

```
.alert-info a {
  color: @white;
}
```

- Any links within the alert bar have also been set to `white` for consistency

Once you've saved the file, don't forget to import it back into `theme.less` in the `modules` section:

```
@import "components/_alert.less";
```

All the templates in this project will use the same partial for the third column. Thus, you're done with the activity feed template. Compile your code and make sure that you don't have any errors. If all is good, test the page in the browser. Then, let's start off with the notifications template. Before we go there, however, here's the code for the entire activity feed page:

```
<div class="container-fluid">
  <div class="row">
    <!-- left side //-->
    <div class="col-lg-3">
      <div class="sidebar-left">
        <%- partial("partial/_sidebar-left") %>
      </div>
    </div>
    <!-- content //-->
    <div class="col-lg-6">
      <div class="content-feed">
        <!-- post form //-->
        <div class="well alternate">
          <form>
            <div class="form-group">
              <input type="text" class="form-control"
placeholder="What's Up?">
            </div>
```

```
          <div class="row">
            <div class="col-lg-6">
              <ul class="list-inline">
                <li><a href="#"><i class="fa fa-camera"></i>
Media</a></li>
                <li><a href="#"><i class="fa fa-map-marker"></i>
Location</a></li>
              </ul>
            </div>
            <div class="col-lg-6">
              <div class="pull-right">
                <button class="btn btn-primary">Post
Update</button>
              </div>
            </div>
          </div>
        </form>
      </div>
      <div class="alert alert-info">
        <a href="#"><i class="fa fa-arrow-down"></i> View 10 new
posts</a>
      </div>
      <!-- post //-->
      <div class="well">
        <div class="row">
          <div class="col-lg-2">
            <p><img src="img/avatar1.jpg" width="70" height="70"
class="avatar"></p>
          </div>
          <div class="col-lg-10">
            <h3><a href="#">Mike Michaels</a></h3>
            <p>Pellentesque habitant morbi tristique senectus et
netus et malesuada fames ac turpis egestas.</p>
            <div class="feed-meta">
              <ul class="list-inline">
                <li>About 3 minutes ago</li>
                <li><a href="#"><i class="fa fa-reply"></i>
Reply</a></li>
                <li><a href="#"><i class="fa fa-heart"></i>
Like</a></li>
              </ul>
            </div>
          </div>
        </div>
```

```
            </div>
          </div>
          <!-- post //-->
          <div class="well">
            <div class="row">
              <div class="col-lg-2">
                <p><img src="img/avatar2.jpg" width="70" height="70"
class="avatar"></p>
              </div>
              <div class="col-lg-10">
                <h3><a href="#">John Smith</a></h3>
                <p>Pellentesque habitant morbi tristique senectus et
netus et malesuada fames ac turpis egestas.</p>
                <div class="feed-meta">
                  <ul class="list-inline">
                    <li>About 3 minutes ago</li>
                    <li><a href="#"><i class="fa fa-reply"></i>
Reply</a></li>
                    <li><a href="#"><i class="fa fa-heart"></i>
Like</a></li>
                  </ul>
                </div>
              </div>
            </div>
          </div>
          <!-- post //-->
          <div class="well">
            <div class="row">
              <div class="col-lg-2">
                <p><img src="img/avatar3.jpg" width="70" height="70"
class="avatar"></p>
              </div>
              <div class="col-lg-10">
                <h3><a href="#">Chris Christopher</a></h3>
                <p>Pellentesque habitant morbi tristique senectus et
netus et malesuada fames ac turpis egestas.</p>
                <div class="feed-meta">
                  <ul class="list-inline">
                    <li>About 3 minutes ago</li>
                    <li><a href="#"><i class="fa fa-reply"></i>
Reply</a></li>
                    <li><a href="#"><i class="fa fa-heart"></i>
Like</a></li>
```

```
                 </ul>
               </div>
             </div>
           </div>
         </div>
         <!-- post //-->
         <div class="well">
           <div class="row">
             <div class="col-lg-2">
               <p><img src="img/avatar4.jpg" width="70" height="70"
class="avatar"></p>
             </div>
             <div class="col-lg-10">
               <h3><a href="#">Matt Matthews</a></h3>
               <p>Pellentesque habitant morbi tristique senectus et
netus et malesuada fames ac turpis egestas.</p>
               <div class="feed-meta">
                 <ul class="list-inline">
                   <li>About 3 minutes ago</li>
                   <li><a href="#"><i class="fa fa-reply"></i>
Reply</a></li>
                   <li><a href="#"><i class="fa fa-heart"></i>
Like</a></li>
                 </ul>
               </div>
             </div>
           </div>
         </div>
         <!-- post //-->
         <div class="well">
           <div class="row">
             <div class="col-lg-2">
               <p><img src="img/avatar5.jpg" width="70" height="70"
class="avatar"></p>
             </div>
             <div class="col-lg-10">
               <h3><a href="#">John Johnson</a></h3>
               <p>Pellentesque habitant morbi tristique senectus et
netus et malesuada fames ac turpis egestas.</p>
               <div class="feed-meta">
                 <ul class="list-inline">
                   <li>About 3 minutes ago</li>
```

```
                    <li><a href="#"><i class="fa fa-reply"></i>
Reply</a></li>
                    <li><a href="#"><i class="fa fa-heart"></i>
Like</a></li>
                </ul>
              </div>
            </div>
          </div>
        </div>
        <div class="center">
          <p><button class="btn btn-primary">Load More
Posts</button></p>
        </div>
      </div>
    </div>
    <!-- right side //-->
    <div class="col-lg-3">
      <div class="sidebar-right">
        <%- partial("partial/_sidebar-right") %>
      </div>
    </div>
  </div>
</div>
```

Coding the notifications section

The notifications template for the social network is a collection of actions that apply directly to the user. Here, you might see things such as the confirmation of a new friend following you, someone who has liked one of your posts, or a public reply to a post from another user. Like the previous template, we are going to use the same code for the first column. The main changes will be to the second column, where the content will change to reflect the types of notifications you might receive.

Before we start, let's see what this page will look like:

Open the notifications.ejs file and insert the partial for the first column. Here's the code again, just in case you need it:

```
<!-- left side //-->
<div class="col-lg-3">
  <div class="sidebar-left">
    <%- partial("partial/_sidebar-left") %>
  </div>
</div>
```

Updating the center column

The layout code for this column will not change. However, the content of the column will be different. The first new part will be the introduction of a page header for this template. Insert the following code at the top of the column:

```
<h1 class="page-header">Notifications</h1>
```

You'll notice that I'm using the Bootstrap `.page-header` class here. Before we move on, let's style this component to match our design. Create a new Less file called `_typography.less` and save it to `/css/components`. Then, paste the following code:

```
.page-header {
  margin-top: 0;
}

h1 {
  font-weight: 300;
  color: @heading-text;
}

.center {
  text-align: center;
}
```

Let's take a closer look at what's happening with the center column:

- I've removed the top margin from the `page-header` class, as I want my title to align horizontally with the top of the avatar.

- I customized the `<h1>` tag to use the lightweight of our font and applied the `heading-text` color variable.

- Lastly, I added a utility centering class that can be used anywhere in the project. We're not actually using this in the header, but this is a good time to add it since we're creating the typography Less file.

Save the Less file, and don't forget to import it to `theme.less` under the `modules` section:

```
@import "components/_typography.less";
```

Adding an alert bar

As we did with the activity feed, we're going to add a new notification alert bar to the top of the feed for this page. Insert the following code after the page header:

```
<div class="alert alert-info">
  <i class="fa fa-bell"></i> 5 New Notifications
</div>
```

I've swapped in a different Font Awesome icon and label here, but otherwise the code is the same as that of the previous page.

Adding a notification entry

There are multiple types of notifications that you could have on your social networking website. However, the code for all of them will be the same, with only the content changing. Let's check out what one of them will look like, in this case, when a new friend adds you. Insert the following code after the alert bar:

```
<!-- notification //-->
<div class="well">
  <div class="row">
    <div class="col-lg-2">
      <img src="img/avatar1.jpg" width="70" height="70"
class="avatar">
    </div>
    <div class="col-lg-10">
      <h3><a href="#">Mike Michaels</a></h3>
      <div>Added you as a friend. <small>About 3 minutes
ago</small></div>
    </div>
  </div>
</div>
```

We're using the same two-column grid here as in the other templates. On the avatar `<img>` tag, I've applied the `.avatar` class to give the image round corners. Make sure that you add these styles to `theme.less` so that the styles are applied:

```
img.avatar {
  .round-corners;
}
```

The rest of the CSS for this section has been set up in previous templates, so this is just an exercise of changing the content to be notification-specific. Let's take a look at the entire page code before we move on to the private messages section:

```
<div class="container-fluid">
  <div class="row">
    <!-- left side //-->
    <div class="col-lg-3">
      <div class="sidebar-left">
        <%- partial("partial/_sidebar-left") %>
      </div>
    </div>
    <!-- content //-->
    <div class="col-lg-6">
      <div class="content-feed">
        <h1 class="page-header">Notifications</h1>
        <div class="alert alert-info">
          <i class="fa fa-bell"></i> 5 New Notifications
        </div>
        <!-- notification //-->
        <div class="well">
          <div class="row">
            <div class="col-lg-2">
              <img src="img/avatar1.jpg" width="70" height="70"
class="avatar">
            </div>
            <div class="col-lg-10">
              <h3><a href="#">Mike Michaels</a></h3>
              <div>Added you as a friend. <small>About 3 minutes
ago</small></div>
            </div>
          </div>
        </div>
        <!-- notification //-->
        <div class="well">
          <div class="row">
            <div class="col-lg-2">
              <img src="img/avatar3.jpg" width="70" height="70"
class="avatar">
            </div>
            <div class="col-lg-10">
```

```
            <h3><a href="#">Chris Christopher</a></h3>
            <div>Liked your <a href="#">post</a>. <small>About
33 minutes ago</small></div>
          </div>
        </div>
      </div>
      <!-- notification //-->
      <div class="well">
        <div class="row">
          <div class="col-lg-2">
            <img src="img/avatar4.jpg" width="70" height="70"
class="avatar">
          </div>
          <div class="col-lg-10">
            <h3><a href="#">Matt Matthews</a></h3>
            <p>"Pellentesque habitant morbi tristique senectus
et netus et malesuada fames ac turpis egestas."</p>
            <div>Replied to your <a href="#">post</a>.
<small>About 56 minutes ago</small></div>
          </div>
        </div>
      </div>
      <!-- notification //-->
      <div class="well">
        <div class="row">
          <div class="col-lg-2">
            <img src="img/avatar5.jpg" width="70" height="70"
class="avatar">
          </div>
          <div class="col-lg-10">
            <h3><a href="#">John Johnson</a></h3>
            <div>Added you as a friend. <small>About 2 hours
ago</small></div>
          </div>
        </div>
      </div>
      <!-- notification //-->
      <div class="well">
        <div class="row">
          <div class="col-lg-2">
```

```
            <img src="img/avatar4.jpg" width="70" height="70"
class="avatar">
            </div>
            <div class="col-lg-10">
              <h3><a href="#">Matt Matthews</a></h3>
              <p>"Pellentesque habitant morbi tristique senectus
et netus et malesuada fames ac turpis egestas."</p>
              <div>Replied to your <a href="#">post</a>.
<small>About 2 days ago</small></div>
            </div>
          </div>
        </div>
        <div class="center">
          <p><button class="btn btn-primary">Load Older
Notifications</button>
        </div>
      </div>
    </div>
    <!-- right side //-->
    <div class="col-lg-3">
      <div class="sidebar-right">
        <%- partial("partial/_sidebar-right") %>
      </div>
    </div>
  </div>
</div>
```

Coding the private messages section

The next page that we are going to tackle is the private messages template. This is where you would come to send a direct message to one of your friends on the social network—a message that you want to keep private and hidden from other users. The left and right sidebars will remain the same; only the content of the center column will change.

Before we start, let's see what this page will look like:

Open the `messages.ejs` file and paste the `page-header` code at the top of the column:

```
<h1 class="page-header">
  Messages
  <span class="pull-right">
    <button class="btn btn-primary">New Message</button>
  </span>
</h1>
```

Note that in this header, I've added a `<span>` tag that is right aligned with a button inside of it. This is the button that a user would click on to start a new message. The span needs to be nested inside the `<h1>` tag as it's a block element, but we don't want to break the button onto a new line.

Adding a conversation

In previous templates, we were happy to have a single entry in a single `well` component. For a conversation, however, there may be multiple entries and we would want to group them all into one well so that the user can see where conversations start and end. To do this, I've decided to use the Bootstrap `media` component. This is a flexible component that can be used to display different types of content, such as feeds, conversations, and card-type layouts. Let's start by looking at the code for a single conversation:

```
<!-- message//-->
<div class="well">
  <div class="media">
    <div class="media-left">
      <img src="img/avatar1.jpg" class="media-object avatar">
    </div>
    <div class="media-body">
      <h4 class="media-heading"><a href="#">Mike Michaels</a></h4>
      <p>Pellentesque habitant morbi tristique senectus et netus
et malesuada fames ac turpis egestas. Vestibulum tortor quam,
feugiat vitae, ultricies eget, tempor sit amet, ante. Donec eu
libero sit amet quam egestas semper. Aenean ultricies mi vitae
est. Mauris placerat eleifend leo.</p>
    </div>
  </div>
  <hr />
  <div class="media">
    <div class="media-left">
      <img src="img/avatar2.jpg" class="media-object avatar">
```

```
    </div>
    <div class="media-body">
      <h4 class="media-heading"><a href="#">John Smith</a></h4>
      <p>Pellentesque habitant morbi tristique senectus et netus
et malesuada fames ac turpis egestas. Vestibulum tortor quam,
feugiat vitae, ultricies eget, tempor sit amet, ante. Donec eu
libero sit amet quam egestas semper. Aenean ultricies mi vitae
est. Mauris placerat eleifend leo.</p>
      <span class="pull-right">
        <button class="btn btn-primary"><i class="fa fa-reply"></i>
Reply</button>
        <button class="btn btn-danger"><i class="fa fa-trash"></i>
Delete</button>
      </span>
    </div>
  </div>
</div>
```

Let's take a closer look at what's happening with the single conversation:

- Note that there is a `well` component that wraps the entire conversation.
- Each entry or response in the conversation is wrapped into a `media` component. In the case of this component, you don't need to use the standard Bootstrap grid classes; you can simply use the predefined class names.
- At the bottom of the well are some action buttons. They are wrapped in a `<span>` tag with the `pull-right` class in order to right-align them.
- I'm using the primary button style for the **Reply** button and the danger button style as a "delete this conversation" button.
- Each button makes use of a Font Awesome icon to better indicate its assigned action.

That completes the design of the private messages section. Let's look at all of the HTML before moving on to the final friends template:

```
<div class="container-fluid">
  <div class="row">
    <!-- left side //-->
    <div class="col-lg-3">
      <div class="sidebar-left">
        <%- partial("partial/_sidebar-left") %>
      </div>
    </div>
    <!-- content //-->
```

```
<div class="col-lg-6">
  <div class="content-feed">
    <h1 class="page-header">
      Messages
      <span class="pull-right">
        <button class="btn btn-primary">New Message</button>
      </span>
    </h1>
    <!-- message//-->
    <div class="well">
      <div class="media">
        <div class="media-left">
          <img src="img/avatar1.jpg" class="media-object
avatar">
        </div>
        <div class="media-body">
          <h4 class="media-heading"><a href="#">Mike
Michaels</a></h4>
          <p>Pellentesque habitant morbi tristique senectus et
netus et malesuada fames ac turpis egestas. Vestibulum tortor
quam, feugiat vitae, ultricies eget, tempor sit amet, ante. Donec
eu libero sit amet quam egestas semper. Aenean ultricies mi vitae
est. Mauris placerat eleifend leo.</p>
        </div>
      </div>
      <hr />
      <div class="media">
        <div class="media-left">
          <img src="img/avatar2.jpg" class="media-object
avatar">
        </div>
        <div class="media-body">
          <h4 class="media-heading"><a href="#">John
Smith</a></h4>
          <p>Pellentesque habitant morbi tristique senectus et
netus et malesuada fames ac turpis egestas. Vestibulum tortor
quam, feugiat vitae, ultricies eget, tempor sit amet, ante. Donec
eu libero sit amet quam egestas semper. Aenean ultricies mi vitae
est. Mauris placerat eleifend leo.</p>
          <span class="pull-right">
            <button class="btn btn-primary"><i class="fa fa-
reply"></i> Reply</button>
            <button class="btn btn-danger"><i class="fa fa-
trash"></i> Delete</button>
          </span>
```

```
          </div>
        </div>
      </div>
      <!-- message//-->
      <div class="well">
        <div class="media">
          <div class="media-left">
            <img src="img/avatar3.jpg" class="media-object
avatar">
          </div>
          <div class="media-body">
            <h4 class="media-heading"><a href="#">Chris
Christopher</a></h4>
              <p>Pellentesque habitant morbi tristique senectus et
netus et malesuada fames ac turpis egestas. Vestibulum tortor
quam, feugiat vitae, ultricies eget, tempor sit amet, ante. Donec
eu libero sit amet quam egestas semper. Aenean ultricies mi vitae
est. Mauris placerat eleifend leo.</p>
          </div>
        </div>
        <hr />
        <div class="media">
          <div class="media-left">
            <img src="img/avatar2.jpg" class="media-object
avatar">
          </div>
          <div class="media-body">
            <h4 class="media-heading"><a href="#">John
Smith</a></h4>
              <p>Pellentesque habitant morbi tristique senectus et
netus et malesuada fames ac turpis egestas. Vestibulum tortor quam,
feugiat vitae, ultricies eget, tempor sit amet, ante. Donec
eu libero sit amet quam egestas semper. Aenean ultricies mi vitae
est. Mauris placerat eleifend leo.</p>
          </div>
        </div>
        <hr />
        <div class="media">
          <div class="media-left">
            <img src="img/avatar3.jpg" class="media-object
avatar">
          </div>
          <div class="media-body">
            <h4 class="media-heading"><a href="#">Chris
Christopher</a></h4>
```

```html
        <p>Pellentesque habitant morbi tristique senectus et
netus et malesuada fames ac turpis egestas. Vestibulum tortor
quam, feugiat vitae, ultricies eget, tempor sit amet, ante. Donec
eu libero sit amet quam egestas semper. Aenean ultricies mi vitae
est. Mauris placerat eleifend leo.</p>
        </div>
      </div>
      <hr />
      <div class="media">
        <div class="media-left">
          <img src="img/avatar2.jpg" class="media-object
avatar">
        </div>
        <div class="media-body">
          <h4 class="media-heading"><a href="#">John
Smith</a></h4>
          <p>Pellentesque habitant morbi tristique senectus et
netus et malesuada fames ac turpis egestas. Vestibulum tortor
quam, feugiat vitae, ultricies eget, tempor sit amet, ante. Donec
eu libero sit amet quam egestas semper. Aenean ultricies mi vitae
est. Mauris placerat eleifend leo.</p>
          <span class="pull-right">
            <button class="btn btn-primary"><i class="fa fa-
reply"></i> Reply</button>
            <button class="btn btn-danger"><i class="fa fa-
trash"></i> Delete</button>
          </span>
        </div>
      </div>
    </div>
    <div class="center">
      <p><button class="btn btn-primary">Load Older
Messages</button>
    </div>
  </div>
</div>
<!-- right side //-->
<div class="col-lg-3">
  <div class="sidebar-right">
    <%- partial("partial/_sidebar-right") %>
  </div>
</div>
</div>
</div>
```

Coding the friends section

Time to start the final template of this project and the book! The last page that we'll cover is a friends page for our social networking website. It will include a list of all our friends, their bios or descriptions, and a way to delete them:

Like the previous templates, the left and right sidebars won't be changed for this one. We'll only need to edit the middle column, so open up `friends.ejs` and insert this `page-header` code at the top of the column:

```
<h1 class="page-header">
  Friends
  <span class="pull-right"><small>134 Friends</small></span>
</h1>
```

I'm using the same pattern here as that of the other page headers. But within the `<span>` tag on this `<h1>` tag, we are going to use the `<small>` tag to indicate the number of friends the user has. A `<small>` tag with a `header` tag in Bootstrap provides some built-in styles you can take advantage of.

Adding a friend entry

As in the previous templates, let's dissect a single friend entry and figure out how it's built. Insert the following code below the `page-header` in the center column:

```
<!-- friend //-->
<div class="well">
  <div class="row">
    <div class="col-lg-2">
      <img src="img/avatar1.jpg" width="70" height="70"
class="avatar">
    </div>
    <div class="col-lg-10">
      <h3>
        <a href="#">Mike Michaels</a>
        <span class="pull-right">
          <button class="btn btn-danger btn-xs"><i class="fa fa-
trash"></i></button>
        </span>
      </h3>
      Pellentesque habitant morbi tristique senectus et netus et
malesuada fames ac turpis egestas. Vestibulum tortor quam, feugiat
vitae, ultricies eget, tempor sit amet, ante. Donec eu libero sit
amet quam egestas semper. Aenean ultricies mi vitae est. Mauris
placerat eleifend leo.
    </div>
  </div>
</div>
```

Let's take a closer look at how a friend entry is built:

- We're back to using our regular Bootstrap grid column classes again. No need to use the `media` component here!

- The entire entry is wrapped in a `well` component.

- At the top of the right-hand-side column, I've inserted a `<span>` with the `pull-right` class again. This time, it includes a button with a Font Awesome trash icon. The idea here is that clicking on this button would delete the friend from your list.

- The remaining content in the right-hand-side column is the friend's name, with a link to their profile and the description that appears on their profile.

This template should be really easy to understand and code. Before we finish this, let's take a look at the code for the entire page:

```
<div class="container-fluid">
  <div class="row">
    <!-- left side //-->
    <div class="col-lg-3">
      <div class="sidebar-left">
        <%- partial("partial/_sidebar-left") %>
      </div>
    </div>
    <!-- content //-->
    <div class="col-lg-6">
      <div class="content-feed">
        <h1 class="page-header">
          Friends
          <span class="pull-right"><small>134
Friends</small></span>
        </h1>
        <!-- friend //-->
        <div class="well">
          <div class="row">
            <div class="col-lg-2">
              <img src="img/avatar1.jpg" width="70" height="70"
class="avatar">
            </div>
            <div class="col-lg-10">
              <h3>
                <a href="#">Mike Michaels</a>
                <span class="pull-right">
```

```
                <button class="btn btn-danger btn-xs"><i
class="fa fa-trash"></i></button>
            </span>
        </h3>
            Pellentesque habitant morbi tristique senectus et
netus et malesuada fames ac turpis egestas. Vestibulum tortor
quam, feugiat vitae, ultricies eget, tempor sit amet, ante. Donec
eu libero sit amet quam egestas semper. Aenean ultricies mi vitae
est. Mauris placerat eleifend leo.
        </div>
      </div>
    </div>
    <!-- friend //-->
    <div class="well">
      <div class="row">
        <div class="col-lg-2">
            <img src="img/avatar3.jpg" width="70" height="70"
class="avatar">
        </div>
        <div class="col-lg-10">
          <h3>
            <a href="#">Chris Christopher</a>
            <span class="pull-right">
                <button class="btn btn-danger btn-xs"><i
class="fa fa-trash"></i></button>
            </span>
          </h3>
            Pellentesque habitant morbi tristique senectus et
netus et malesuada fames ac turpis egestas. Vestibulum tortor
quam, feugiat vitae, ultricies eget, tempor sit amet, ante. Donec
eu libero sit amet quam egestas semper. Aenean ultricies mi vitae
est. Mauris placerat eleifend leo.
        </div>
      </div>
    </div>
    <!-- friend //-->
    <div class="well">
      <div class="row">
        <div class="col-lg-2">
            <img src="img/avatar4.jpg" width="70" height="70"
class="avatar">
        </div>
        <div class="col-lg-10">
          <h3>
            <a href="#">Matt Matthews</a>
```

```
                    <span class="pull-right">
                        <button class="btn btn-danger btn-xs"><i
class="fa fa-trash"></i></button>
                    </span>
                </h3>
                    Pellentesque habitant morbi tristique senectus et
netus et malesuada fames ac turpis egestas. Vestibulum tortor
quam, feugiat vitae, ultricies eget, tempor sit amet, ante. Donec
eu libero sit amet quam egestas semper. Aenean ultricies mi vitae
est. Mauris placerat eleifend leo.
                </div>
            </div>
        </div>
        <!-- friend //-->
        <div class="well">
          <div class="row">
            <div class="col-lg-2">
              <img src="img/avatar5.jpg" width="70" height="70"
class="avatar">
            </div>
            <div class="col-lg-10">
              <h3>
                <a href="#">John Johnson</a>
                <span class="pull-right">
                    <button class="btn btn-danger btn-xs"><i
class="fa fa-trash"></i></button>
                </span>
              </h3>
                    Pellentesque habitant morbi tristique senectus et
netus et malesuada fames ac turpis egestas. Vestibulum tortor
quam, feugiat vitae, ultricies eget, tempor sit amet, ante. Donec
eu libero sit amet quam egestas semper. Aenean ultricies mi vitae
est. Mauris placerat eleifend leo.
                </div>
            </div>
        </div>
        <div class="center">
            <p><button class="btn btn-primary">Load More
Friends</button>
        </div>
      </div>
    </div>
    <!-- right side //-->
```

```
    <div class="col-lg-3">
      <div class="sidebar-right">
        <%- partial("partial/_sidebar-right") %>
      </div>
    </div>
  </div>
</div>
```

Summary

That brings the seventh and final chapter to a close. Thanks for reading this book! We just covered how to design and code your own social network site using Bootstrap. Let's review what you learned: how to code a social network using Bootstrap; how to customize the Bootstrap `well` component, `navbar` component, and `alert` and `button` components; and how to create a highly modular design for easy reuse of code and components.

Index

Thank you for buying
Bootstrap Site Blueprints Volume II

About Packt Publishing

Packt, pronounced 'packed', published its first book, *Mastering phpMyAdmin for Effective MySQL Management*, in April 2004, and subsequently continued to specialize in publishing highly focused books on specific technologies and solutions.

Our books and publications share the experiences of your fellow IT professionals in adapting and customizing today's systems, applications, and frameworks. Our solution-based books give you the knowledge and power to customize the software and technologies you're using to get the job done. Packt books are more specific and less general than the IT books you have seen in the past. Our unique business model allows us to bring you more focused information, giving you more of what you need to know, and less of what you don't.

Packt is a modern yet unique publishing company that focuses on producing quality, cutting-edge books for communities of developers, administrators, and newbies alike. For more information, please visit our website at www.packtpub.com.

About Packt Open Source

In 2010, Packt launched two new brands, Packt Open Source and Packt Enterprise, in order to continue its focus on specialization. This book is part of the Packt Open Source brand, home to books published on software built around open source licenses, and offering information to anybody from advanced developers to budding web designers. The Open Source brand also runs Packt's Open Source Royalty Scheme, by which Packt gives a royalty to each open source project about whose software a book is sold.

Writing for Packt

We welcome all inquiries from people who are interested in authoring. Book proposals should be sent to author@packtpub.com. If your book idea is still at an early stage and you would like to discuss it first before writing a formal book proposal, then please contact us; one of our commissioning editors will get in touch with you.

We're not just looking for published authors; if you have strong technical skills but no writing experience, our experienced editors can help you develop a writing career, or simply get some additional reward for your expertise.

Bootstrap Site Blueprints

ISBN: 978-1-78216-452-4   Paperback: 304 pages

Design mobile-first responsive websites with Bootstrap 3

1. Learn the inner workings of Bootstrap 3 and create web applications with ease.

2. Quickly customize your designs working directly with Bootstrap's LESS files.

3. Leverage Bootstrap's excellent JavaScript plugins.

Extending Bootstrap

ISBN: 978-1-78216-841-6   Paperback: 88 pages

Understand Bootstrap and unlock its secrets to build a truly customized project!

1. Learn to use themes to improve your user experience.

2. Improve your workflow with LESS and Grunt.js.

3. Get to know the most useful third- party Bootstrap plugins.

Please check **www.PacktPub.com** for information on our titles

Mobile First Bootstrap

ISBN: 978-1-78328-579-2   Paperback: 92 pages

Develop advanced websites optimized for mobile devices using the Mobile First feature of Bootstrap

1. Get to grips with the essentials of mobile-first development with Bootstrap.

2. Understand the entire process of building a mobile-first website with Bootstrap from scratch.

3. Packed with screenshots that help guide you through how to build an appealing website from a mobile-first perspective with the help of a real-world example.

Bootstrap for ASP.NET MVC

ISBN: 978-1-78398-728-3   Paperback: 198 pages

Incorporate Bootstrap into your ASP.NET MVC projects and make your websites more user friendly and dynamic.

1. Grasp the intricacies of Bootstrap and how to use it with ASP.NET MVC.

2. Build your own tools and helpers to assist you in creating ASP.NET MVC Bootstrap sites in an easy and fast way.

3. Master the use of Bootstrap components and plugins with ASP.NET MVC.

Please check **www.PacktPub.com** for information on our titles